ERICH von DÄNIKEN, internationally
bestselling author of

CHARIOTS OF THE GODS?
GOLD OF THE GODS
RETURN TO THE STARS
IN SEARCH OF ANCIENT GODS
MIRACLES OF THE GODS
and now ACCORDING TO THE
EVIDENCE

ERICH von DÄNIKEN—'the arch-enemy
of the closed mind . . .'

Also by Erich von Däniken

CHARIOTS OF THE GODS?
GOLD OF THE GODS
RETURN TO THE STARS
IN SEARCH OF ANCIENT GODS
MIRACLES OF THE GODS

and published by Corgi Books

According to the Evidence

Erich von Daniken

CORGI BOOKS
A DIVISION OF TRANSWORLD PUBLISHERS LTD

ACCORDING TO THE EVIDENCE

A CORGI BOOK 0 552 10870 7

Originally published in Great Britain by Souvenir Press.

PRINTING HISTORY

Souvenir Press edition published 1977
Corgi edition published 1978
Copyright © 1977 by Econ-Verlag Gmbh
Translation copyright © 1977 by Michael Heron and Souvenir Press

This book is set in Monotype Baskerville

Corgi Books are published by Transworld Publishers Ltd.,
Century House, 61–63 Uxbridge Road, Ealing, London, W5 5SA

Made and printed in Great Britain by
Richard Clay (The Chaucer Press), Ltd., Bungay, Suffolk.

My Theory

In prehistoric and early historic times the Earth was visited by unknown beings from the Cosmos.

These unknown beings created human intelligence by a deliberate genetic mutation.

The extra-terrestrials ennobled hominids 'in their own image'. That is why we resemble them—not they us.

These visits to Earth by alien beings from the Cosmos were recorded and handed down in religions, mythologies and popular legends. In some places the extra-terrestrials also deposited physical signs of their presence on Earth.

I am most grateful for encouragement, help and criticism to Professor Javier Cabrier, Ica, Peru; Professor F. M. Hassnain, Srinagar, India; Professor Edgar Lüscher, Munich; Professor Luis Navia, New York; Professor Harry O. Ruppe, Munich; Professor Pasqual S. Schievella, New York; Professor Wilder-Smith, Einigen/Thun, Switzerland.

Bonstetten, near Zurich

im Januar 1977

B. v. Minken

Photographic Credits

Contents

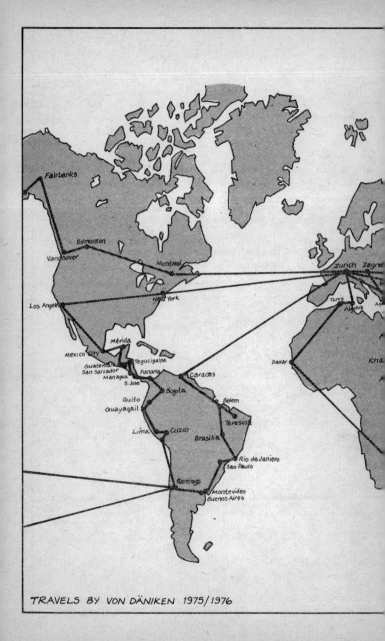

TRAVELS BY VON DÄNIKEN 1975/1976

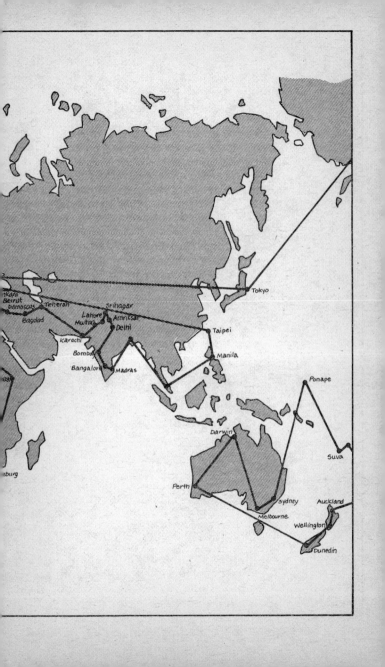

1: *Per Aspera ad Astra*

At the beginning of the seventies an event took place in a small town in Missouri that deserved banner headlines, but didn't get them.

One morning a ten-year-old boy burst excitedly into school and told everyone breathlessly that a cat with two tails had run across the road in front of him. His classmates laughed at him and said he had made a mistake. When he insisted that it had really happened, they told him he was crazy.

The rumpus had not died down when the teacher came into the classroom and asked what it was all about. The rest of the class told him and he called the lad to his desk. Then he tried to make him admit publicly that he had lied. The boy stubbornly refused and repeated: 'I saw a cat with two tails!' Amid the other boys' laughter the teacher put the boy across his knee, grabbed a cane and tanned his backside. From then on the boy had the reputation of being a congenital liar; he was tormented and even sent to Coventry. Soon he became a bad pupil, too, for he stopped listening to this lessons and did not do any homework. As soon as the bell rang, he rushed through the streets, in the woods, down by the river. He was looking for 'his' cat, the living proof that she existed and that he had not lied.

This went on for several weeks until one evening he did not come home. His parents, who had often scolded him for his crazy behaviour, alerted the sheriff, who in turn told the neighbours and they all set out to look for the missing boy by torchlight.

They found his body hanging from the bough of a tree. A lot of people, including his classmates, attended the funeral and they all had twinges of conscience. During the burial service everyone saw a cat with two tails jumping over the graves.

I reflected that it would be an unprecedented thing to supply proofs, when one knows the cat all right, but cannot get it by the tail.

When they start their arguments, i.e. when they have not yet caught the cat by the tail, scientists put forward hypotheses, and experiment until the desired results emerge either from a series of experiments which can be repeated, or until so many deviations from the desired result occur that they have to abandon the hypotheses.

Legal proofs – and that is what we think of when talking about proofs – have different qualities. Unlike scientific proofs, they vary considerably depending on the country in which they have to be produced. But generally speaking it is true that each party must prove the facts on which they base their claims.

Before the High Court one party makes claims to which the other party can make objections. That is good law. The party bringing suit has to back up its claims with facts; the other party likewise has to justify its objections with facts. But, as we shall see, facts are not always the same 'facts'.

Looking through the literature of international legal terminology, I find the following commentary significant:

'Apparent proof can be used to show causality. Thus with the help of apparent proof it is possible to come to a decision on the basis of results, but vice-versa by working back from results, to come to a conclusion about a specific event as cause'.

Jurisprudence says that objects, documents and experts produced in evidence, should be valued at the same level as *auxiliary facts*. Their value depends on: the identity and undamaged state of an object produced in evidence, the authenticity and contents of a document, and an expert's technical knowledge.

As I have already consulted Dame Justitia, dubious symbol of justice with her eyes blindfolded, I now know that in her view indirect, circumstantial evidence is equally important.

Circumstantial evidence is evidence that tends to prove a fact at issue by proving circumstances which afford a basis for a reasonable inference of its occurrence. However, one must be able to convince Justitia of the truth of the circumstantial evidence if it is to form the foundation of one's proof.

JUSTITIA CANNOT FORESEE THE FUTURE

I can tell my esteemed critics that agreements between

litigants are inadmissible if they lay down *how* a specific conclusion based on proof is to be valued or if they limit the free demonstration of proof.

In addition to the objects and documents produced, I naturally use experts to supply circumstantial evidence. Experts supply empirical principles or opinions based on research. Unfortunately one is always learning that experts can make mistakes. So perhaps 'my' experts will make mistakes, but the other side too, is only human and not exempt from error.

A 'factual court' – if there were such a thing – should deliver the verdict. But who holds the copyright of absolute truth? My critics – in legal terms, the opposing party – act as if they were the guardians of ultimate truth. Surely they are often only the perpetuaters of alleged 'truths' that they take over from their ancestors and continue to carry? Truths, perceptions, knowledge and 'facts' are dependent on time. They are often overtaken by time and time shows that they are errors. Time is constantly consigning yesterday's knowledge to the rubbish heap of scientific aberrations. The passage of time (=progress) daily forces us to say goodbye to 'facts' which yesterday were indisputably considered as the last word in wisdom.

A factual court which had the courage and intelligence to decide *today* on the truth or falsehood of my theories, i.e. the conclusiveness of the circumstantial evidence in their favour, would have to be equipped with the knowledge and information available in the future. He who judges in the present judges with his eyes blindfolded. He cannot see the future.

If only a single wise man were (or could be) in possession of absolute truth, I would be the first to urge a trial of opinion and 'facts'. Time and time again scientific spokesmen have erred, and often they have been quite blind. So for me they cannot have the status of a factual court that pronounces the last decisive judgment.

Mistakes are nothing to be ashamed of if we draw a useful lesson from them and are cautious about judging and condemning. I find this moderation conspicuous by its absence.

Because it happened in the past and has been repeated until very recently, I can even produce factual proof of grandiose errors. It is the easiest thing in the world to give endless examples of the blindness of scientific popes, but not so easy to select from them, otherwise they would fill an encyclopaedia as big as the Old Testament.

I am chary of dipping into the storehouse of intellectual and scientific developments. Nevertheless I offer some turning-points in epoch-making thoughts. If I mention Nikolaus Copernicus (1473–1543), who shattered the world-picture

Fig. 2. Nikolaus Copernicus

Fig. 3. Johannes Kepler

Fig. 4. Giordano Bruno.

Fig. 5. Galileo Galilei.

when he postulated the sun as the centre of the circular orbits of the planets . . . If I speak of Johannes Kepler (1571–1630), who proved the accuracy of the heliocentric world-picture . . .

If I adduce Giordano Bruno (1548–1600), who was bold enough to assert that there were many worlds . . . If I quote Galileo Galilei (1564–1642), who finally dislodged the world from the central point of the universe . . .

The 'opposition party' will claim that these great men were persecuted by the curia only on religious grounds, although scholars have known for a long time that the vast majority of contemporary scientists too rejected the revolutionary new ideas.

That's all well and good. For a long time now there has been no inquisition, no stake and no excommunication for the champions of daring new ideas. If the church once defended the bastions of its dogma, science, now free from fear, can open the door to the propagation of new theories and hypotheses, i.e. open the way to revolutionary ideas.

I am not thinking of those cranks who year after year discover the secret of perpetual motion. I am thinking of the men who can back up their theories with sound circumstantial evidence, indeed with factual proof.

But leading scientists still get their backs up if something new threatens their fabricated structures. That is why arguments are often more rancorous today than in the past when the stake put a rapid and unpleasant end to anyone who bothered the Establishment. Many of these worthy academics, well nourished at the inexhaustible bosom of their *alma mater*, launch themselves against awkward opponents like flabby tanks. They are not so dumb among themselves, but to the outside world – "always together" is their motto – they erect a stubborn facade around a precinct which they irrationally consider 'sacred'.

Their methods vary from the subtle to the aggressive. The most troublesome new items of knowledge are squashed like flies with killer phrases, as the Americans call them.

I could understand all this, even the artificially fostered vanity of these elders, if this cherished vanity did not hinder progress so much. You have only to imagine the measure of self-renunciation required of a scholar who is expected to surrender the fortress he built by the sweat of his (studious) brow.

There are plenty of superficial critical tricks. Until they are seen through they can completely blind the naive. Here are some examples:

This theory has definitely not got a classical enough foundation – a phrase that is very imposing and often has a positive effect.

This theory is too radical; it ruins the basis of scientific knowledge – a killer phrase that has no equal as a deterrent.

The universities will not go along with that – an argument that is impressive in its simplicity and astonishing in its effect.

Nonsense! Others have tried that already – it remains the secret of the man who utters the phrase whether it was tried successfully, or, if unsuccessfully, why?

We can't make any sense of it – effective, because their own professional blindness is successfully ignored.

The opposite was proved long ago – possibly, but perhaps with antiquated knowledge?

Religion forbids us to accept that – incomprehensible, but this 'argument' still lives on.

That has not yet been proved – a learned reference to the phrase *quod erat demonstrandum* (that which was to be proved) which was used by Euclid, the Alexandrian, *circa* 300 B.C.

Scientific guardians of the 'Grail' command a respect handed down from generation to generation...and a fabulous, automatic public relations system.

Wide awake journalists, who are always on the alert when it comes to politics, willingly accept the total anaesthetic of this publications system and so become blind and deaf to genuine progress. In this kind of public relations I see one of the biggest and most admirable achievements of the inhabitants of the ivory tower.

Back to the demonstration of scientific mistakes?

AN IRREFUTABLE CASE

Until far into the seventeenth century the scientific concept of *horror vacui* (horror of empty space) was dominant. Nature abhors a vacuum, the scholar said, because it uses all its powers to fill it, according to God's will.

If an outsider tried to upset such a firmly anchored dogma, he was immediately rebuked for being a crazy visionary. That was the fate of the statesman and physicist Otto von Guericke (1602-1686) who was alderman in his home town, Hamburg, and later Mayor of Magdeburg.

Von Guericke was not scared off by the religious warning about nature's *horror vacui*...and invented the air pump. He created a vacuum. In 1654 he demonstrated in the Regensburg Parliament that a bell struck in a vacuum cannot be heard and that burning candles and other open flames are extinguished immediately. His 'Magdeburg hemispheres' became famous. He constructed a sphere, with a diameter of four metres, of two exactly fitting copper hemispheres, and pumped the air out of it. Afterwards eight strong horses could not pull the two halves apart.

Then the Mayor opened a valve in the sphere through which the air could flow into the vacuum. The hemispheres separated easily.

What next? Scientific teaching of the time insisted that a vacuum could not exist, and now Mayor von Guericke had demonstrated that a vacuum certainly did exist and also that the air itself exerted an enormous pressure. The scholars played the age-old, but ever new game, to make mincemeat of him. What he had demonstrated was only the product of chance, they said.

Von Guericke refused to be shaken. With 'his' vacuum he refuted the scientific view that light could not be diffused in a space empty of air, and he proved that noise too was swallowed up in a vacuum.

Fig. 6.
Otto von Guericke.

Fig. 7.
Johann Philipp Reis.

Fig. 8.
Robert Mayer.

Not until the really striking facts of his discovery could no longer be denied, did his high-minded opponents become the foremost champions of this revolution in physics. Clever theses were written in the universities, but the copyright 'Otto von Guericke' was forgotten.

On 26 October 1861, the merchant and later private teacher Johann Philipp Reis (1834-1874) introduced the first telephone at a session of the Physikalische Verein in Leipzig, and in 1864 at the Congress of Natural Scientists at Frankfurt. He could not yet transmit coherent sentences but he could show clear proof of the possibilities of his invention. He was ignored. Reis found no understanding among scientists.

When Karl Kramarsch published the *History of Technology* in Munich in 1872, it contained neither Reis's name nor the word 'telephone' which he had coined. He and his invention had been so completely forgotten that they were not even mentioned. Perhaps the name of Reis would never again have figured in the book of great inventors if Alexander Graham Bell (1847-1922) had not produced an improved version of the Reisian apparatus in 1872, and claimed the idea of the telephone as his own. No one at the time remembered the self-taught man from the village in Hesse, and two years later Reis died destitute. His invention had been of no use to him. Yet with a royalty of only a couple of pence on each telephone he might have become one of the richest men of all ages.

The fact that the 'law of the conservation of energy' (the first law of thermodynamics) was undisputably proved in 1845 by the little ship's doctor Robert Mayer (1814–1878), sent the scientific world crazy. How did this outsider, legitimised neither by education nor academic chair, come to lay down a principle of eternal validity over the heads of scholars, and in Batavia of all places?

While Doctor Mayer was treating members of the crew by blood letting as was usual in those days, he noticed that the difference in colour between the venous (dark blue) and arterial (bright red) blood of Europeans recently arrived in the Tropics was less than when they were in temperate European waters. Mayer was not satisfied with this observation. He asked himself why it was so. And he recognised the equivalence of heat and work. In the tropics the body needs a smaller production of personal heat, combustion is slowed down, and less oxygen, which maintains the blood's bright red colour, is used. How is it, asked Mayer, that work increases heat? If it can, work must be convertible into heat, and vice-versa. After lengthy experiments which he made in the back room of his father's chemist's shop in Heilbronn, the scientific discovery of the millennium was complete.

If there was any justice in the world, we should have to assume that Mayer's law of energy was accepted enthusiastically. Don't you believe it! I cannot recount the ship's doctor's calvary here, but simply put on record that scientists – down to Justice von Liebig, who printed a contribution of Mayer's in his *Annals of Chemistry,* although it had no effect on the scientific world – attacked and mocked Mayer so persistently that he got encephalitis and later, owing to *intrigues,* was shut up in a lunatic asylum as a megalomaniac. The goal was reached. Mayer's law of energy could be dismissed as the product of a madman's fancy.

After this 'triumph' by German scientists when Mayer's work was hushed up for nearly ten years and he was even reported dead in the lunatic asylum, it is unlikely that his basic scientific discovery would have remained linked with his name if the English physicist John Tyndall (1820–1893) had not won for the outsider both recognition and the birthright to the law of energy by his unconditional intercession on Mayer's behalf at a meeting of the Royal Society in 1852. Honourable men of science such as Hermann von Helmholtz (1821–1894), Rudolf Clausius (1822–1888) and other celebrities disputed the priority of Mayer's discovery and helped to ruin his private practice in Heilbronn. After all, who wants to be treated by a lunatic?

Often not even the 'murder weapon' in the hand of the wrong-doer seems to be sufficient proof!

The augustinian monk Gregor Johann Mendel (1822–1884) had proved the inheritance of simple characteristics in his small botanical garden behind the augustinian monastery at Brno and published the results. He had done this by years of experiments in the hybridization of peas and beans.

Contemporary scholars, completely befogged by the Darwinian belief in the mutability of everything living, made fun of the provincial augustinian, who had first demonstrated the continuance of the species. Mendel took radical measures, and as he was convinced of the results of his experiments, sent

Fig. 9. Gregor Johann Mendel.

reports to all the authorities in Europe, including the most eminent contemporary botanist Professor Karl Wilhelm von Nageli (1817–1891) in Munich. Mendel emphasised that he ought to be in possession of all the facts for understanding his series of experiments. Von Nageli mocked the augustinian's naivety, like the rest of his colleagues.

After all, they had just accepted Darwin wholeheartedly. Surely this was a dog baying the moon? After Mendel was appointed Abbot, he had hardly any time to pursue his hobby of research. The academicians, finding the field free, took the opportunity to denigrate him.

Not until 1900 were the 'Mendelian laws', tempered in an inferno of criticism, scorn and suppression, generally and definitively recognised as being right. The augustinian never knew about his late-flowering fame, at least not in this world, but he had the firm base of his faith, otherwise he would not have been able to say with such calm conviction that his time would come.

Even such a successful and recognised inventor as Thomas Alva Edison (1847–1931) in whose name 2,500 patents were registered all over the world, had an experience with scientists that is worth telling.

On 11 March 1878, Edison arranged for the physicist du Moucel to present his first phonograph, playing the Stanniol waltz, to the great men of the Academie des Sciences in Paris.

When the first sounds of a human voice were heard, Bouillaud, a member of the august Academie, stood up and shouted at du Moucel: 'Cheat! Do you think we're going to be made fools of by a ventriloquist?' After a thorough investigation, the academician declared on 30 September 1878, that he

Fig. 10. Thomas Alva Edison.

was convinced that the presentation was a particularly sophisticated case of ventriloquism, for it was impossible to admit that base metal could reproduce the noble sound of the human voice. Monsieur Bouillaud did not know that Edison's phonograph had been granted a US patent on 19 February 1878.

Often even the cleverest people are not up to date with the latest state of knowledge, quite apart from the dubious quality of the evidence. 'Belief' in an inherited and therefore preconceived opinion, that what you have learnt and can read in black and white stays true for all eternity, has no power as proof. That is really ventriloquism.

On closer examination it becomes clear that even world famous members of elitist associations are capable of quite astonishing mistakes. Unfortunately, for all their learning, they do not possess absolute truth as we ordinary citizens are only too willing to assume they do.

Antoine Laurent Lavoisier (1743-1794) who died on the

Fig. 11. Antoine Laurent Lavoisier.

guillotine is a classical example of the fact that no one is immune from scientific error.

Lavoisier was director and treasurer of the Academy of Sciences, deputy of the National Assembly and a bank manager, but he was also the founder of modern chemistry, one of the great revolutionaries of science. He separated air into its component parts and had the audacity to assert that water was a compound substance. The dogma was that air and water are elements. The idea that this dogma could be thrown overboard by Lavoisier incited the speaker of the Academy, Antoine Baume, inventor of the hydrometer, to hold forth. At a plenary session he declared:

> The elements or basic components of bodies have been recognised and determined by physicists of every century and every nation. It is inadmissible that the elements recognised for 2000 years should now be included in the category of compound substances. They have served as the basis for discoveries and theories...We should deprive these theories of all credibility if fire, water, air and earth were no longer to count as elements.

Scientists show no mercy when they are in the wrong. They even clash vehemently with awkward colleagues, although they prefer outsiders.

In 1814 the English engineer George Stephenson (1781-

1848) built the first steam driven locomotive. Although it had already been used successfully in the Killingworth coalmines, Stephenson received warnings from academicians, and even politicians took seven years to grasp the possibilities of his invention. When Stephenson put before Parliament a plan to build railway lines, they laughed him to scorn, and shouted him down in the good old parliamentary way. He had to listen to objections which sound ridiculous to us today. The locomotive would set houses on fire; the noise would drive people crazy; property alongside the lines would lose its value. However, the politicians recognised the possibilities of the

Fig. 12. George Stephenson.

new technological advance quicker than scientists usually do and what is more they corrected their mistake. In 1821 they passed the law authorising the building of the first Liverpool-Manchester railway line by thirty-six votes to thirty-five. Its opponents stuck to their opinion that the age of disaster was about to dawn.

To mention yet another means of locomotion, if the automobile manufacturers had listened to Wilhelm Launhardt (1832-1918), the European expert on road and bridge building and Director of the Hanover Polytechnische Hochschule, it is possible that we would still not be able to drive about in our favourite plaything. This scientist urgently advised the manufacturers to give up their pointless experiments.

It would be comforting if one could say that professional academic blindness was a thing of the past. One man who had to survive bitter struggles and bear all kinds of calumny is still alive. He is Herman Oberth (b. 1894) – now the undisputed 'father of space travel'. In 1917 Oberth designed a rocket 25 metres long and 5 metres in diameter, with a payload of ten tons. He envisaged alcohol and oxygen as fuels. His critics thundered in his ear that the thing would never be able to fly.

Fig. 13. Hermann Oberth.

When Oberth published his realistic yet prophetic book *Rockets to Planetary Space* in 1923 and amplified it in 1929 with *Ways to Spaceship Travel,* the books were not worth serious appraisal in the view of his critics. In 1924 the world-famous scientific periodical *Nature* commented on Professor Oberth's book, saying that the project of a space rocket would probably only be realised shortly before the extinction of mankind. Oberth was not disconcerted; he insisted on supporting his plans against all the scientific sceptics.

Herman Oberth, that much ridiculed man, was proved right all along the line. Rockets have long been a familiar sight to us. Mankind has not died out and we have heard nothing more of the critics who were so venomous in their day.

It is nice that Herman Oberth has lived to see the realisation of his audacious plans for the future.

Yet in 1953 a German scholar could still pontificate that 'Astronautics is on the same level as astrology.' And Sir Harold Spencer Jones (1890-1960), Director of Greenwich Observatory, declared in 1957: 'Man will never set foot on the moon or on Mars!' Twelve years later, on 20 July 1969, Apollo 11 landed on the moon.

I don't want anyone to tell me that in the non-stop series of scientific mistakes (someone should write a fat book about them some day) it is always a case of justifiable academic reservations in the face of unprovable new theories. Going much further than reservations and genuinely forgivable mistakes, it is often a question of definite defamation. Otherwise what reason had the members of the 29th International Congress of Americanists for deciding not to mention Thor Heyerdahl's Kon Tiki voyage? The influential Professor Raphael Carstens described the Kon Tiki expedition to the press as a 'swindle'!

There we have it, the label with which cheap headlines can be made. About 35,000 articles that have been published all over the world about me and my theories are simmering in my files. The snowball system can easily be proved. A ball with the word 'swindle' on it is thrown into play. Surely enough there is someone there to catch it. Next two brave lads are playing swindle ping-pong. Soon the ball rolls into the hands of a full team who at lightning speed – there are no communication barriers – are playing an international match with another team.

It is easy to prove a second equally unfair rule of the game. Someone somewhere makes a statement about details of my theory. A reporter asks me for my comments. If our conversation takes place within handy reach of my files, I can lay concrete proof of my attitude to the statement in question on the table. But in spite of the documents, treatises, etc. produced, my comment is either not printed, or garbled, or cut.

The third rule of thoroughgoing cheating is really deplorable. An interview is taped. Clear questions, unambiguous answers. This time, I think, still believing in fair play, although I ought to know better, nothing can go wrong. Weeks later the interview appears in print. Here I am answering questions that were never asked – there my answers

have been meaninglessly torn out of context. I can't believe
my eyes. I try to remember that even a tape does not protect
one from deliberate distortion of the facts and that New York
is not the only home of inquisitive *con-men*. There is nothing
subtle about the means employed when that hardy perennial
von Däniken has to be made into a headline again.

My supporters tell me I could protect myself. That would
be possible if I could read such articles *immediately,* but I am
travelling for 300 days of the year. I do not see them in print
until I happen to be home again. Then it is too late for a reply;
the news has spread. Ping-pong. The opportunity to reply has
gone past. Even if I ask for it, no newspaper can print a
correction to a month-old article. And there is a snag about
corrections. For the readers' sake I am forced to summarise
briefly what I am charged with, otherwise they will not
understand my reply. So inevitably a 'letter to the Editor'
becomes a small article and then the editor regrets there is no
room to print it.

As I no longer want to breathe in a suffocating mist of lies,
distortions, half-truths and defamations, I have worked out
my own rules for interviews. I ask in advance for a written
agreement about the text to be published. The American
maxim that it doesn't matter what's printed so long as it is
printed may be all right for film stars and boxers. But not for
me, because it's a serious matter. That is my new ju-jitsu, my
gentle art of self-defence.

As I am already doing the spring-cleaning, and have
developed a nose for my assailants, I am going to intercept a
blunt arrow that someone will surely try to shoot into the
centre of my proofs. People will say that I am selective,
making a choice that suits my purpose from the extensive
material available. And that, they will say, is inadmissible.

Well, what about it? Is not the scientific world selective?
Every scientific book in my library is the product of choice. I
know several hundred museums and each one can only exhibit
a selection. Plautus (*circa* 250 BC), the Roman writer of
comedies, had experience of this: *Duo quum idem faciunt non est
idem* – when two people do the same thing, it is not the same. I
am going to take the minor liberty of operating as the
approved academic school does. Given the abundance of
material, there is no other method for either them or me. In

the process I can, Zeus be my witness, pluck so many arrows from my quiver that they will seem like a mist before the eyes of my notorious adversaries, even though I am only presenting a selection.

In 1950 Immanuel Velikowsky published his book *Worlds in Collision*. At the time he was a little known doctor and psychoanalyst in America. Today he is known because he has become the target for persistent attacks. This outsider made the following claim:

Space is not a vacuum; it is torn by magnetic fields and charged particles rush through it. The planet Venus is younger than the other planets. Venus originated during a violent outburst from Jupiter.

In very early times the earth was frequently convulsed by near collisions with other celestial bodies. These caused a series of catastrophes which are recorded in myths and legends.

In the fifteenth century BC the earth in its orbit round the sun entered the outer zones of the dust and gas belts of the protoplanet. The continents and the oceans were dyed red by the red dust in the air.

The gases in the tail of the new planet Venus combined with the oxygen in the earth's atmosphere and partially burnt up, so that 'the sky glowed red'. Another part rained down on the earth as a sticky mass, similar to crude oil.

The earth's crust rose up. Quakes convulsed our planet. Islands sank. Oceans flooded the continents. The earth's axis tipped over. The majority of the earth's population was destroyed. Chaos was complete.

What was the official echo, as it were? A lot of nonsense! Professor Harlow Shapley, well known astronomer and then Director of the Harvard Observatory, said after reading the manuscript: 'If this Doctor Velikowsky is right, the rest of us are idiots!' He threatened to break off relations with the New York publishers, MacMillan, who wanted to publish *Worlds in Collision*. By no means bashful, other colleagues followed suit. They did not want to see their own books on the list of a firm that published Velikowsky. Macmillan brought the book out and since 1950 Velikowsky, in spite of all the facts that speak in his favour, has been crudely attacked, not just discussed – which would have been legitimate. Even in 1974 the celebrated public relations conscious astronomer Carl Sagan began a fifty-seven page satirical essay with the phrase: 'Where Velikowsky is original, he is most probably wrong. Where he is right, his ideas come from others.' (Echoed from a famous retort of Sir Winston Churchill's in the house of Commons: 'The noble lord's speech was good and it was new. Where it was good, it wasn't new and where it was new, it wasn't good.') Quite recently the geologist Stephen Jay Gould wrote in *Natural History* that he would 'continue to oppose the heretical ideas of non-academics.' Unfortunately I cannot believe for a moment that Velikowsky will be among the victors in this most difficult of all games.

No one who puts forward a new theory has any claim to be embraced, kissed and congratulated, but the very least he can reasonably expect is that his theory will be seriously examined and discussed. There should be some sporting fair play. How do the suppositions Velikowsky made in 1950 look today?

Velikowsky asserted that there were electro-magnetic waves in space and that the universe was not a vacuum. Today everyone knows that radio signals on different band widths are received from outer space. This knowledge has become so commonplace that the new, unknown signals from space that are received by radio telescopes only rate two or three lines in newspapers.

Velikowsky claimed that Venus became white hot when it broke off from Jupiter . . . and that it must still be very hot. The latest Soviet space probes measured the surface temperature of Venus at about 400°C.

Velikowsky said that Venus must have a dense atmosphere. American and Soviet probes confirm this. Venus's atmosphere is 95 times as heavy as the earth's.

Velikowsky said that Venus's atmosphere must contain carbon, hydrogen and oxygen. In February 1974 Mariner 10 radioed the presence of these three elements to earth from Venus's upper atmosphere.

Velikowsky claimed that when Venus, in its white hot state, flew past the earth at comparatively close range, it must have left traces on the moon. In 1969, when the first man set foot on the moon, the *New York Times* published an essay by Velikowsky:

I assert that less than 3000 years ago the surface of the

moon was frequently molten and bubbled (craters!). The lunar rocks and lava remains could be rich in residual magnetism. I should not be surprised if bitumen, carbide and carbonates were found in the composition of the stones. I claim that very high radio-activity will be found in scattered places. I also claim that moonquakes are very frequent.

Nearly all Velikowsky's claims have already turned out to be right. 145 teams with more than 500 scientists have examined fragments of lunar rocks in the biggest communal research project of all time. Velikowsky made his diagnoses with the flair of a good doctor who often knows more than he can tell by palpation or from X-rays. Specialised research work would probably show that his few remaining published claims were also correctly diagnosed.

Where do they get the courage from?

It is simply a question of *examining* new theories. This obviously requires a kind of courage that is quite rare. For example I would not have the courage to swear as openly as Professor Carl Sagan did that UFOs do not exist. Unfortunately I have not seen any flying saucers, but it would not occur to me to give the lie to the numerous people who are positive that they have observed such objects. Even professors should show a little of the tolerance they themselves expect as a matter of course. I still stand by that wise remark of Thomas Mann: 'The positive thing about the sceptic is that he considers everything possible!'

And I ask myself: how will a scientist like Sagan come down from his pedestal – everything is possible! – if a UFO is actually located or lands? He will not be able to, because he has so adamantly excluded a possibility that against all expectation has become reality.

I have noticed, and I am speaking from personal experience, that my radical opponents from the fields of physics, astrophysics, astronomy, botany, biophysics and archaeology have so stubbornly adopted a negation of the possible that they can hardly take the slightest step out of their splendid isolation. It would require such a degree of self-conquest that it would be inhuman to hope for or expect it. I place my hopes in the younger scientists, those who are not yet on the chain and tamed. I am thinking of people like Professor Luis Navia of the Institute of Technology, New York. Navia writes:

I am convinced that the fact that we do not use the postulate that there were visitors from other regions of the universe in antiquity itself transgresses the strictest principles of scientific methodology.

In my opinion the theory of a visit from space in the distant past is a completely meaningful hypothesis.

Anyone who calls this theory childish, pernicious, absurd or pseudo-scientific should find another field of activity in which to exercise his failing creative power, his stagnated mentality and his ignorance of scientific methodology (1).

In this sense I am setting out to support my theory with *proofs*. I shall supply circumstantial evidence. I shall refute the Darwinian theory of evolution, at least in so far as it deals with the birth of man's intelligence. I shall present *proofs* from the storehouse which the strangers left behind.

Once again I am going to put my head in the wasps' nest. Fortunately an article from the internationally known *Frankfurter Allgemeine Zeitung* (29.12.71) on a study by the American molecular biologist Gunter S. Stent sums up the fallibility of scientific assessments for me:

By and large progress in science consists in vanquishing dogmas. Almost every fundamental new discovery is rejected at first before it is generally accepted – often only decades later. Ecclesiastical and Aristotelian dogmas, still the 'received doctrines', have resisted scientific developments well into modern times. And they may even now prove a decisive obstacle to acceptance of a new idea if its discovery is 'premature'. The American molecular biologist Gunter S. Stent of Berkeley University, born in 1924, explains the circumstances and causes of this phenomenon . . .

The deeper cause of conformity in rejecting new discoveries is to be understood from a social-cum-psychological point of view, namely from man's need – corresponding to his nature as a *zoon politikon* (political animal) – to live in harmony with the general convictions of his group. According to Stent's explanation, scientific judgments going as far as the negation of experimental facts become more understandable, but not pardonable . . . Is there another criterion of the prematurity of a discovery besides that of remaining completely ineffective? Yes, there is such a criterion. A discovery is premature when its effects cannot be connected with contemporary valid canonical knowledge by a series of simple logical steps . . .

Is the absence of recognition of premature discoveries attributable solely to the intellectual inadequacy of scientists who, provided they were more receptive, would immediately give recognition to a new, well verified scientific idea?

The 'good scientist' is considered to be an unprejudiced man with an open mind who is ready to accept any new idea that is supported by facts. As the history of science shows, scientists obviously do not act in accordance with this popular view.

These are harsh words. If I were to permit myself to use them, I should immediately be accused of being hostile to science. This accusation does not concern the *Frankfurter Allgemeine Zeitung,* but cannot touch me either because I constantly seek the understanding and co-operation of scientists, when I point to the unsolved puzzles of our past. Consequently, when putting forward well founded circumstantial evidence I hope to find some of those good scientists, as they exist in the popular view: unprejudiced, open-minded, ready to accept a new idea.

I wish my readers an interesting discussion, one that will brighten up our drab days.

Per aspera ad astra!

Over rough paths to the stars!

2: Cosmic Dimensions

'It is virtually certain that radio messages from extraterrestrial civilisations are reaching the earth at this minute.'

That was said in February 1976, by someone who ought to know, Professor Frank Drake, Director of the biggest observation station for ionosphere* research in the world at Arecibo on the north coast of Puerto Rico.

The Government of the United States commissioned a group of top scientists, 'to study methods and submit proposals for making contact with extra-terrestrial beings during the next fifteen years'.

What is up with the American Government? Did a group of crazy scientists put a flea in its ear that sucked money instead of blood at the right moment? Money for a rather 'other worldly' undertaking?

I am convinced that this is one of the cleverest capital investments that has ever been made.

Dr John Billingham, Head of the Biotechnical Department at the Ames Research Centre of the US Atomic Energy Commission in Iowa, says:

> We believe that there are distant planets that are a billion years older than the earth. This implies that their civilisations, too, will be billions of years ahead of ours. It is a daunting thought, but I am sure that there are extra-terrestrial civilisations that are as far ahead of us as we are in comparison with Stone Age man. (1)

---

* Ionosphere: part of the atmosphere in which electrons and ions are present in such numbers that the diffusion of radio waves is influenced. Other planets, too, have ionospheres, in so far as they have atmospheres. It has already been shown that Mars and Venus have ionospheres.

Dr Ichtiaque Rasool is head of space research at the Washington Headquarters of NASA. He says proudly: 'Ours is the first official government research group which is making practical preparation to discover extra-terrestrial life.'

Working on a budget of little more than £¼ million, the Research Group is due to submit a report to the President in 1977 that will show the best and most effective way of making contact with intelligent extra-terrestrial beings. In their present state of knowledge and using the technology available the scientists are aiming at making their first contact with extra-terrestrial civilisations some time during the next fifteen years. In the course of only two decades an enormous change of attitudes has taken place.

For it is barely twenty years since most scientists thought that intelligent life in the part of the cosmos accessible to us was impossible. Only a few forward-looking scholars did not exclude the *statistical and philosophical possibility* of intelligent life in the universe, but by and large they all doubted that they would be able to discover intelligent, technically advanced forms of life within a radius of 50 light years.* What is the reason for this change of attitude?

Meteorites examined in laboratories showed that the building materials for life must be present on other celestial bodies. The American biochemist, Cyril Ponnaperuma, of the NASA Ames Research Center discovered 17 amino acids, 17 building materials for life, in the Murchison meteorite.

But how can it be proved that they really came from the cosmos?

I know that it is not in my province to create suspense with the tricks used by detective-story writers. However at this point I can only draw your attention to one critical event without giving the game away altogether! In this way it may lurk in the back of your minds as you read on.

All the amino acids used in building life on earth have left-hand spirals. Yet of the 17 amino acids in the Murchison

---

* Light year: The unit used to measure astronomical distances – the distance covered by light in a year, i.e. 9,461 milliard Km.

meteorite only five have the left-hand spirals that are prerequisites for the building of life on earth. The following five can
be used for the construction of terrestrial life: glycine,
glutamine, alanine, valine and proline. (2) All the other amino
acids exhibited right-hand spirals, a characteristic they do not
have on earth. That gives the game away. The meteorite must
be of extra-terrestrial cosmic origin. Waltzers can turn to the
left or to the right. That *is* possible. Terrestrial amino acids
spiralling to the right do not exist. We shall go on dancing the
'waltz of origins' together – as soon as the music for it strikes
up. I beg you to be patient a little longer.

All molecules have specific radiation values that have been
clearly established in laboratory tests. Measurements in the
various frequencies permit exact conclusions about the material emitting its own specific radiations. Since the existence of
neutral hydrogen was observed on the 21.105 cm line in 1944,
even complicated *organic* relations could be proved. These
linear radiations are of great importance to astronomy, as the
presence of the building materials for life in space can be
proved by the comparison of radio-astronomical measurements with the wave lengths of the various molecules known
from laboratory measurements.

In the course of this important and difficult radio-
astronomical work, it has been possible to demonstrate many
kinds of building materials for life in space – down to organic
molecules. Today science knows that the universe is teeming
with the ingredients for forming life. This knowledge has been
largely responsible for changes in attitudes.

The existence of a planet to support it is a prerequisite for
the development of life. In the past, statisticians were unable
to give reliable data showing whether other suns (fixed stars)
in our galaxy were also circled by planets.

Today we know for sure that Barnard's Star – discovered in
1916 by the American astonomer, E. Emerson Barnard (1857-
1923) in the constellation Ophiucus – 'only' six light years
away, is accompanied by at least two planets. We are
indebted for this discovery to observers at the Sproull
Observatory in Swarthmore, Pennsylvania, U.S.A.

Not long ago astronomical statistics were working on a
figure of 100 milliard fixed stars in our galaxy. Today we are
quite sure that there are at least 200 milliard fixed stars in our

Milky Way alone. Yet these milliards of our cosmic neighbours are but a handful of dust in the turbulent universe. The latest results of research talk of ten billion (10^{13}) galaxies in the cosmos. We can file away all previous statistics while we turn over a brand new page. With the progress of astronomical technology even the latest figures will probably have to be erased.

As the basis for my theory, I am quite satisfied with the calculations of the two leading American astronomers, Professor Frank Drake and Professor Carl Sagan, who assume that there are about *one million highly developed civilisations* in our galactic system alone. (3)

I make only modest claims: one million highly developed civilisations in our stellar neighbourhood? Greetings, dear colleagues, on the other planets.

CONTACT WITH EXTRA-TERRESTRIALS

What use is the most beautiful garden to me if others are walking in it?

What do the best astronomical calculations matter if no contact can be established with the vast numbers of highly developed civilisations?

Making contact is the most important thing. I can envisage three possibilities:

1. Direct contact by interstellar travel.

In the present state of our technology this possibility still lies in the distant future. We do not even know where we could get the amounts of energy needed for powering interstellar spaceships. Nevertheless, space travel experts are busy – not only in their dreams – with serious technical and scientific projects for future interstellar travel.

2. Sending unmanned probes into interstellar space.

The unmanned probe Pioneer F* has been on such an exploratory mission since March 1972. Without motive power it will roam through interstellar space for millions of years. No one knows whether it will ever be captured by unknown interstellar intelligences.

In fact I consider that this way of making contact with alien

*The Gold of the Gods, pp. 185 et seq.

civilisations is very doubtful, but I think that even these experiments with only vague chances of success have their place among the projects that could lead us out of our terrestrial isolation. I have read of less useful investments in our glorious days.

3. Interstellar radio contact.

Our high frequency technology is in a position to bridge

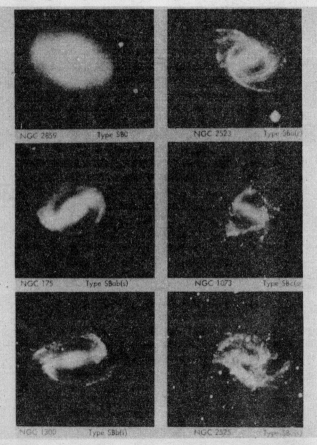

Fig. 14 : A sample of six galaxies from a collection of ten billion galaxies.

gigantic interstellar distances. The huge parabolic aerial at Arecibo, Puerto Rico, can send faultless signals into space, signals that could be captured anywhere in our Milky Way. The radio telescope under construction at the Caucasus could likewise send signals into the galaxy. There are no longer any technical obstacles from that side.

What signs or numerals should be transmitted? What news? What messages? What statements?

Years ago anxious people with shrill critical voices warned against sending radio-telescope signals to extra-terrestrials. We could reveal, 'betray', our position and we would not know whether the extra-terrestrials were favourably disposed towards us, whether they would approach us with friendly ideas or whether they might not invade us one fine day. Perhaps they would even put us on their menus as exotic titbits; or put us on show in cages in their zoos as the botched products of an exceptional race. (Incidentally no one has ever explained whether or not monkeys look on *us* as the ones who are locked up! It all depends from which side of the bars one looks at the world.)

There were actually such crackbrained objections to extra-terrestrial radio signals. Excuse my laughter! These crazy objections mouldered in the dustbin of the past. For a long time, *deliberately aimed* radio signals have been sent into space from many points on the globe. But even without these aimed radio signals we must long ago have made the position of our earth known. Intelligences with an advanced technology could pick up our daily radio or television transmissions.

Here is a long-lasting sedative to dispense to the fearful. There is really no danger of our ending up on the menus of extra-terrestrials, because we are too expensive. The mere expenditure of costly energy for transport to another solar system is too great, for energy can never be got for nothing. If extra-terrestrials felt their mouths watering at the idea of eating earth men, they would not preserve us in cans in our own countries. The would rear us at home as delicacies. That would be simpler and cheaper, because they would only have to put a pair of intact human cells in the fridge.

We ourselves no longer pick mushrooms in the woods and fields; they are grown on farms. Lobsters are rarely caught in the open sea any more; we fish them out of special breeding beds. But don't worry, highly developed intelligences are certainly not cannibals.

An 'invasion' by alien beings would be pointless anyway because they would have nothing to gain from us. This is only logical. Any beings who are in a position to visit the earth with an armada of spaceships would be a) enormously technically advanced; and b) able to dispose of incomparably greater resources than we. Clearly conscious of their superiority, they could have no desire to take back a lot of junk from a clearance sale on the blue planet.

There could be only one motive, namely the one that has driven all the peoples on this earth to invade and colonise: territorial expansion. But this reason for an expedition by extra-territorials too has no real validity, for there is no shortage of room in our galaxy. Just think of all the uninhabited planets!

The postulate of the existence of an almost inconceivably large number of highly developed extra-terrestrial civilisations is undisputed.

We transmit radio signals to them using the impulses, signs and numbers familiar to us. How and what are the 'others' transmitting? For mutual understanding we should correspond in an intercosmic language. Is such a language conceivable?

In 1960, Hans Freudenthal, a mathematician at the University of Utrecht, Holland, presented a mathematical language worked out to the last detail. (4) It is transmitted on radio impulses, but unlike many previous brainwaves could not possibly be misunderstood by any technically informed living being.

Freudenthal's starting point is quite simple. Whatever the aliens may look like, as highly advanced intelligences they will be able to build radio-telescopes, because they, like ourselves, want interstellar communication. Anyone who has the knowledge necessary to build a radio-telescope, will be familiar with electronics and that is not conceivable without a mastery of the rules and formulae of mathematics. In other words mathematics is the multiplication table of an intercosmic language.

We use the decimal system. It is not unreasonable to assume that our ten fingers supplied a natural calculating machine for it. We imported this system about 600 B.C. from India where it had developed from the Brahman method of writing numerals. Egyptian hieroglyphs stood for 1, 10, 100, 1000 etc. but we should not be so arrogant as to take it for granted that counting is done on ten fingers all over the cosmos. Who knows whether other 'lords of creation' may not have eleven or twelve or eight fingers and yet be highly intelligent?

Any living being would have at least two fingers. So we can guarantee that the binary system is practicable. It works with the basic figure 2. The advantage of the binary system is that every number can be formed from the product of the numbers 0 and 1:

1	for one
10	for two
11	for three
100	for four
101	for five
110	for six
111	for seven
1000	for eight
1001	for nine
1010	for ten
1011	for eleven
1100	for twelve
1101	for thirteen
1110	for fourteen
1111	for fifteen
10000	for sixteen
10001	for seventeen

and so on.

```
1111110111111
111101011111
11110111011111
111101011111
1111110111111
1111110111111
111000011111
110000000111
110100000101111
101100000110 1
111000001111
111000001111
111001100111
111001100111
11001100111
11001100111
```

The binary system became the language for all computers, which can claim to be faultless because there are never more than two possibilities: 1 or 0, good or not good, right or not right, yes or no.

There is not a mathematician in the world who still denies that it is easier to count with the binary system than with the decimal system. Using this simple system of counting, Professor Freudenthal was able to formulate whole messages and even philosophical texts for extra-terrestrials. He demonstrated that it was possible to communicate *everything* using this method. Even pictures could be formed and transmitted.

I can demonstrate this on my typewriter. I take a page from my daughter Cornelia's exercise book and number the squares sideways starting from above. Typing with one finger I begin to 'transmit' in the binary codes:

1st Line: one one one one one one zero one one one one one one

2nd Line: one one one one one zero one zero one one one one one

I go on transmitting like this until the outline of a man is clearly visible.

As you can see, it's child's play to imagine communications of all kinds with the binary system. Mathematics *can* be the basis for an intercosmic language. It is a practical way by which we could make ourselves noticed in space. And how does news from the cosmos reach us? Are the communications audible or convertible into signs and numbers?

Presumably the aliens use the simplest method of counting, the binary code. Technically speaking it is much the same when the Mars probe transmits pictures to earth from its landing site on Utopia. T.V. cameras break the pictures down into dots. These dots are transmitted to the receiving stations by radio impulses, not simultaneously, but at minimal intervals of time. On earth the dots assemble on the screens provided for them and form astonishingly clear pictures. My typewritten man followed this example of pictures made of dots...

So far, so good, so bad.

Fig. 16. Radio photograph of the surface of Mars.

There is still a snag. We know the wavelengths on which our probes transmit from the Moon or Mars or elsewhere. But we haven't the faintest idea which frequencies extra-terrestrials use for their transmissions.

For years now we have been aiming radio-telescopes at thousands of stars from many sites all over the world and hoped with each attempt that we would capture radio signals from alien intelligences.

Unsuccessfully.

We do not know their transmission frequencies.

There is no point in my writing the universal four letter word said by many astronomers when they have to give up yet another experiment. Its echo lingers in the domes of all the great observatories. And we can understand why.

In 1960, project OZMA was begun in a most optimistic mood. It was carried out by a team of scientists at the Greenbank Observatory in West Virginia. They used the 21 cm wavelength that corresponds to neutral hydrogen. Because hydrogen exists throughout the universe, it was thought that other extra-terrestrial intelligences might be on this, so to speak, international wavelength. 'No reply from this number. Subscriber has moved – address unknown.'

Since then scientists have realised that the 21 cm wavelength is tremendously susceptible to interference. Some radiospectral lines of hydrogen are significantly stronger than the wavelengths used. The affair was made even more annoying and hopeless because loud cosmic noises spoilt reception via the 'trunk line'. .

At present most experiments are being made on the 3 to 8 cm wavelengths. Professor Frank Drake, of the Radio Institute of Arecibo says:

Two facts about the wavelengths we have chosen are encouraging. Firstly they are wavelengths that penetrate the earth's atmosphere. Thus they can be controlled from earth with comparatively cheap telescopes. Secondly, and most important, if we take only the radio-telescopes we already have for work on these wavelengths, we find that signals of intelligent origin can already be received from distances of the order of magnitude of 1000 light years (5).

In spite of all the efforts and the impassioned research that has been carried out, no radio messages from alien intelligences have as yet been received. We are using the wrong wavebands. When I discussed this problem with American astronomers, I asked why they did not operate with a similar technique to that used in car radios. Stations have their wavelengths programmed on the band. You press the button for the station you want, and the station sought automatically comes through with startling clarity. I was told that this was technically possible in principle but that there was simply not enough time for such continuous automatic experimental transmissions to space. The giant telescopes would have to be trained on *one* star with a fantastic degree of accuracy and even then months would pass before all conceivable band-widths for this one object had been tried.

Nor is it enough to tap the thousands of possible frequencies for a few seconds. If an impulse is recorded, it is necessary to check whether it is an 'intelligent signal' or simply a source of interstellar interference. Observers often cling all day to one wavelength from which a hotchpotch of sounds can be heard. Cosmic noises, hisses, pulsations, whistling etc. must be filtered out before arriving at a possible 'core' of genuinely 'intelligent signals'. With more than 200 milliard stars in our Milk Way alone the attempt to make interstellar radio contact is a necessary, but in my view, on grounds of time alone, unprofitable endeavour. Simply because we do not know the wavelengths on which extra-terrestrials are trying to reach us! Because we are searching in the void without the faintest inkling of the frequencies in use!

A CONSTRUCTIVE PROPOSAL FOR INTERSTELLAR COMMUNICATION

Why do we limit ourselves to chemistry when considering possible wavelengths for communication with extra-terrestrial intelligences?

Hydrogen is universal, so we clamber on to its 21cm wavelength, yet it is only one of countless possibilities.

But is chemistry what we are looking for in the cosmos?

In interstellar space there are about 0.1 to 1000 atoms inside one cubic centimetre. Atoms have to combine to form molecules, the larger unit. They do this when they are struck by light from a star, or by a 'solar wind'. The formation of molecules creates a higher level of energy, which radiates a quite specific wavelength. Every molecule that originates in this or any other way has its own specific wavelength that can be measured and transmitted on with our highly sensitive radio-telescopes. We owe our knowledge of the 'quality' of the most varied kind of molecules in the universe to their consistency and measurability by radio-telescopes.

Here are some examples of molecules and their wavelengths:

Chemical symbol	Molecule	Wavelength
OH	Hydroxyl	18.0cm
NH_3	Ammonia	1.3cm
H_2O	Water	1.4cm
H_2CO	Formaldehyde	6.2cm
HCOOH	Formic Acid	18.0cm
H_3C-CHO	Acetalhyde	28.0cm

The search for life in the Universe has one clear aim.

Every *living being* consists of complicated chains of molecules, whether on earth or on a planet 30,000 light years away.

The following questions suggest themselves:
What kinds of chain of molecules have all living beings got in common? Once this common basis for life is established, have we not also found the interstellar wavelength that will make cosmic communication possible?

Every living thing on earth, whether man, animal or plant, is based on the DNA (Deoxyribosenucleic acid) molecule. DNA itself does not live; it is not a cell but a chain of molecules. Like other molecules or chains of molecules, DNA has a specific radiation.

So wouldn't it be logical to set our radio-telescopes on the DNA wavelength in order to find forms of life in the universe? After all we are not looking for hydrogen or carbon monoxide or formic acid. We are looking for life. As DNA is the basic of all life, *that* is the wavelength that should be ascertained and used, in my humble opinion.

I have assured myself of a kind of registered trade mark for this idea by writing the following letter to several leading institutes and scientists.

Dear Professor XY,

    The common denominator of all forms of life is DNA. So would it not be logical for intelligent life to communicate on the wavelength that gives it its common basis?

Interstellar transmitting stations, manned by *living beings*, have been functioning for millions of years. We only need the right wavelength to join them. DNA is the common denominator.

On 28 September 1976, Professor Frank Drake, Director of the National Astronomy and Ionosphere Centre at Ithaca, New York, wrote to me:

Dear Erich,

The radio frequencies of DNA have not yet been measured in a laboratory and theoretically cannot be calculated because of the complex structure of the DNA molecule. Nevertheless, there is a frequency for Adenin, an important component of DNA. We have already used it in searching the radio spectrum, but without success.

With kind regards,
Frank Drake.

As yet we are at the dawn of the search for living beings in interstellar space. Perhaps our laboratories will discover a method of establishing the wavelength of DNA before evening falls.

Commissioned by the NASA Ames Research Center, American scientists under the leadership of the physicist, Bernard M. Oliver embarked on a study of new ways of making radio contact with extra-terrestrial civilisations. The reason for this study was the realisation that although we can *transmit* beamed signals into the galaxies using present day radio-telescopes, we cannot *receive* the weakest signals on various band-widths unless they are *deliberately aimed* at the earth.

Project Cyclops proposes a gigantic park of directional aerials. Each one would have a diameter of 100m*. If 1500 of these mammoth aerials were arranged in an enormous circle and integrated with a complex computer system, this, the biggest 'ear' of all time could receive from the cosmos even

---

* That is the size of the one aerial which the Max Planck Institute has at Effelsberg.

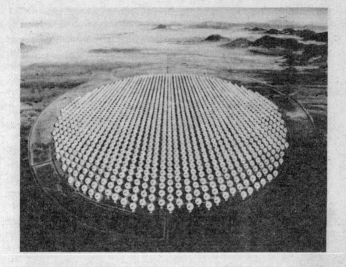

Figs. 17, 18, 19. 1500 antennae in one enormous 'parking place' could record radio transmissions from solar systems that were as much as 1000 lightyears away. Beginning with an overall view, the antennae are shown in increasing detail.

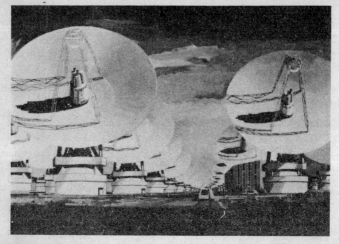

quite simple radio transmissions by extra-terrestrial communities. This forest of aerials would be able to 'register two individual photons* per second and million square metres, so that even the weakest planetary communications of another world as much as 50 or 100 light years away could be located' (6).

The scientists engaged on the study prognosticate that through Project Cyclops we would make effective contact with extra-terrestrial civilisations in this century.

With Project Cyclops we could almost eavesdrop on the whispered conversations of our neighbours in the universe. As we could obviously also transmit with our forest of giant aerials, one of our fleas coughing could be made audible on another star.

In spite of all the technically feasible possibilities, any kind of communication over the vast cosmic distances is a difficult undertaking. Whether we send or receive, electro-magnetic waves are inexorably bound to the speed of light. If we were to receive a message from a solar system 100 light years away, from the moment these lines are being read and answered on the spot with a thank you message, our transmission would take 200 years to reach its addressee. Even a question directed

* Photon: an elementary particle without mass

at the nearest fixed star, Alpha Centauri, only 4.3 light years away, would not get an answer for 8.6 years. No one can think of a dialogue in such postal conditions. It is more likely to assume that intelligences with advanced technologies are transmitting into space continuous progress reports of their cultural situation. If that is so, any civilisation with adequate technical means can listen in to these nonstop transmissions. If ever both partners land on the same wavelength, situation reports could be exchanged. Although it is obvious, I should like to mention in passing that we are certainly not the only ones trying to make interstellar contacts.

I should find it by no means uninteresting if radio connections should turn out only to travel one way, if we could only receive them. Uninteresting? Not at all. We must realise once and for all that all historical knowledge from the past reached us on a one way street. Precious information from the Egyptians, Greeks, Romans, Incas and Mayas flowed to add to our store of legal, philosophical and technical knowledge. We cannot reproduce an echo in the past; we cannot ask a single question. Nevertheless, we profit by the transport of knowledge on this one way information street. A one way street into the cosmos would be a present from heaven, for we should come across future knowledge on it. Simply listen would be the word. Dialogue would not be necessary.

I am upset by the constant objection in technical radio-astronomical publications that only a minimal part of the potentialities of a radio-telescope would be used in the search for radio messages. There are more important things to be done, they say.

Is it more important to hunt for new combinations of molecules in the universe? Is it more important to aim signals at and to measure extremely remote galaxies that do not concern us? Undoubtedly, these and other kinds of astro-physical knowledge obtained through radio-astronomical in-struments are tremendously important. Every new detail fills one of the gaps in the leaky concept of the origin of the universe in which we live. But I am shocked by the low priority given to the most important task: the search for contact with extra-terrestrial civilisations. I consider this search to be a more profitable expenditure of time and money. Once we made contact we could ask our more knowledgeable neighbours in space, en bloc, about what we so laboriously, accidentally and imperfectly put into the saving box of our knowledge. For all our highly commendable efforts and heavy investment, we have not yet been able to put any solid capital (of knowledge) to our credit.

In the situation in which the inhabitants of the earth find themselves today, there should be a popular uprising with the following slogan: SEEK CONTACT WITH INTELLI-GENT EXTRA-TERRESTRIAL CIVILISATIONS! WE NEED THEIR KNOWLEDGE!

TIME DILATION IS A LAW

In the long run we should like to hold the sought after bride in our arms, not just telephone her. With this metaphor I should like to go straight to the rough path that could lead us to the star.

One phenomenon is not sufficiently taken into account by opponents of my theory. It is an eternally valid physical law. I did not invent it – on my honour!

When spaceships reach very high speeds between stars, a phenomenon occurs that is called time dilation. This piece of knowledge, brand-new for our century, runs through ancient mythologies and religions like the celebrated red thread. This fact, which in effect is not new, is difficult to grasp, but it is such an important link in my chain of proof that I must introduce it with an outstanding specialist in the field.

This is a record of the questions I asked Professor Lüscher, a physicist at the Munich Technical University.

Is it possible to make time dilation on interstellar flights intelligible to an ordinary man?

I assume that to begin with there is a general agreement about what time actually is. It would take us too far afield to interpolate a definition of time at this point.

In physics it is extraordinarily important *how* and *where* we measure time. For the result of the measurement depends on the state of motion of the system in which the measurement is carried out. The result of measurement in a system in motion will be different from measurement in a comparatively static system. Here is an example: Think of twins. One of them sets

Fig. 20. Conversation with Professor Edgar Lüscher.

out in a spaceship, the others stays behind on earth. Before the launching of the spaceship both of them set their watches which, we shall assume, also show calendar dates and years. Then one of them sets forth in his ship, for which we postulate a very high velocity. After a clearly fixed period of time, the space traveller returns. Provided he finds his brother, both will observe on comparing their watches that the space traveller's has gone much slower than that of his twin who stayed on earth'.

Why? Nobody can understand that!

The twin brother in the spaceship completed a different process of motion from his brother on earth. The change in the measurement of time is caused by velocity, for all physical processes unfold in different systems at different speeds.

Clever people from faculties other than physics are always claiming that this time dilation theory cannot be right. They say Einstein went wrong on that point.

Einstein did not go wrong. There is no conjecturing in physics; the highest judge is always the experiment. Einstein's forecast, which is contained in the general theory of relativity, has been checked countless times up to the present day, with ever greater accuracy.

Can that be illustrated by an example too?

As you know, we have extremely accurate methods of measuring time at our disposal. We can even demonstrate inaccuracy in the course of the stars. In 1971, a group of physicists from the University of Washington and the U.S. Naval Laboratory loaded such a precision time measuring instrument on a Boeing 707. The Boeing set off round the world once in a clockwise direction and again in the opposite direction. When it landed a difference in the measurement of time was actually observed. The apparatus that had gone on the flight showed a minimally slower time than the apparatus on earth, actually of 59 and 273 ± 7 nano seconds.*

And this difference in time was produced at a speed of 900 km an hour over a relatively short distance.

Why does time dilation become more pronounced the greater the speed is?

It is connected with the law that lies behind it, the so-called Lorenz transformation. This is an equation which links a comparatively static system with a system in motion. In order to be able to compare both systems we need a kind of 'translation'. The Lorenz transformation forms a bridge from one system to the other, as it were.

$$\text{Formula:} \quad t = Y \left[t^1 + \frac{VX^1}{C_2} \right]$$

What kind of figures do we get from this equation?

Here is a time dilation table. From it you can read off how much time passes on the earth and how much in the moving spaceship.

* The milliardth part of a second.

Duration of outward and inward flight for the crew of the space capsule	Total duration of flight for the inhabitants of earth left behind	Distance of the point of return
1 year	1 year	0.018 parsecs
2 years	2.1 years	0.075 ,,
5 years	6.5 years	0.52 ,,
10 years	24.0 years	3.0 ,,
15 years	80.0 years	11.4 ,,
20 years	270.0 years	42.0 ,,
25 years	910.0 years	140.00 ,,
30 years	3100.0 years	480.0 ,,
35 years	10600.0 years	1600.0 ,,
40 years	36000.0 years	5400.0 ,,
45 years	121000.0 years	18400.0 ,,
50 years	420000.0 years	64000.0 ,,

Speed: 9.81 m/sec^2

1 parsec equals 3.262 light years equals 19.2 trillion miles.

I am concerned that people without training in physics and mathematics simply will not be able to grasp this incredible process. Can it be explained to a layman in a simple way?

Let us assume that we have a small cart standing in front of us, with a small sphere on the loading surface. If I gave the sphere a gentle push it would move on the loading surface. But when I accelerate the cart itself, the sphere on the loading surface will be influenced by the speed of the cart. That is a physical process. The speed of a rocket would influence physical processes in exactly the same way.

Here is something people don't understand: why should these physical events unfolding differently in different systems also have an effect on the biological age of the participants?

In order to understand that we must take a step further into the complicated system of chemistry. Basically chemical processes are nothing more than physical processes, for they too 'obey' physical laws. I can define mineral salts and phosphates chemically. But as that is a case of combinations of matter they are in the last resort physical . . . and therefore subject to physical laws. Let us take a short leap forward: biological processes again are nothing more than the end result of complicated chemical processes. So the unfolding of biological processes also takes place in accordance with the state of motion of the system. From this it results that a man's age does also.

So biological processes and subjective experience will be the same for the twin brother in the spaceship as for his brother on the earth. Both of them will have the impression that one hour is passing perfectly normally and also the feeling that they are growing older in the normal way.

Naturally. Not until their watches are compared after return from a spaceflight will they notice that the two times have passed at quite different rates.

What possiblities has the man in the spaceship of checking how his age is changing compared with that of his brother back on earth?

The astronaut twin would have to compare watches with the earth from time to time. As long as the spaceship is still in radio communications range, that could be done by radio.

It is constantly being claimed that time dilation would only work in one direction and that as soon as the Spaceship turned round it would be compensated for by the effect of the return!

Anyone who says that has not understood the theory of relativity. Anyone who uses that argument is probably referring to the special relativity theory that depends on systems that are *not* speeded up. The special theory of relativity deals with systems which move towards each other at a uniform constant speed. With time dilation, however, we must go beyond the special theory of relativity, for the two systems are no longer equivalent. The idea that the aging processes would be compensated for on the return journey is quite wrong.

Professor, have you ever had to explain to an intelligent biologist how time dilation works in practice?

No, because he or she would have absorbed the process long ago. A modern biologist has to know an enormous amount of physics. Molecular biology is simply not intelligible without physics.

I hope that after this explanation of time dilation from the lips of such a competent scientist as Professor Lüscher my critics will allow me once and for all to use this physical law in demonstrating the truth of my theory. It is valid for all ages. If, for example, comrades from other stars spent only 40 years on board, 36,000 years would have passed on our earth! Who knows when and how many spaceships have set off on expeditions somewhere in the Universe? At any rate, it would not surprise me if one day a cheerful crew clambered out of their ship in front of our door.

I FOLLOW A PIECE OF
ADVICE FROM JULES VERNE

An hour ago a leading medium succeeded in putting me in telephonic communication with Jules Verne, the forerunner of the science-fiction novelist, who died in 1905. I was anxious to ask the old gentleman for advice, because I was afraid my imagination might run away with me.

I reproduce the spirit-telephone conversation literally: *Von Däniken here. Honoured master, I have just come back from America.*
How do you do, Mr von Däniken. You did it in five and a half hours, I know. My crazy idea of a journey round the world in eighty days has long been obsolete. I would give a lot to live in your day.

All the same you were ahead of your time once. But that's not what I want to talk to you about.
If you are making forecasts about the future, I can give you one good piece of advice. From now on proceed from realistic assumptions.

It was precisely about that point I wanted to ask your opinion. I am proposing to claim in my new book that by around the year 2000 there could be a city in space with 10,000 inhabitants living, working, researching, producing, raising children and feeding themselves, and that they will even supply people on earth with energy. What do you think of that idea? Is it unreasonable?

I got no answer. There was a rushing noise in the air. When it died down, I asked again:

Do you think I ought to put this idea before my readers?

Excuse me Mr von Däniken, I had to laugh and some of the eminent men floating about near me are bursting their sides with laughter too. Perhaps you heard them. How do you get such absurd ideas? I must warn you against writing anything like that. No one will publish a word of it. A space station with 10,000 people. No, keep your imagination on the ground and stick to what is technically feasible.

All right. Following the advice of the ancestor of science fiction, I *am* sticking to what is technically feasible.

In front of me I have four sources, which have this to say about the technical possibilities of the project:

Der Spiegel, No. 36, 1 September 1975

National Enquirer, Lantana, USA, November 1975

Die Weltwoche, Zurich, No. 4, 28 January, 1976

Bild Der Wissenschaft, Stuttgart, May, 1976

I quote first from *Der Spiegel:*

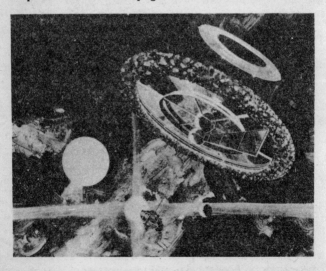

Fig. 21. This is the model of the first space city, which can house 10,000 people. A communal project by NASA and Stanford University, it could be built in this century. It is only a question of money...

The idea of a space station for 10,000 people is within the bounds of technology and is already technically possible. A group of 28 professors and technicians who were commissioned by Stanford University and NASA to examine the problem came to this conclusion. The space station, which would be about equidistant (384,000 km) from the earth and the moon and would cost about 100 milliard dollars could be finished by the end of the century. It would be built in a two-stage programme. First an earth orbiting 2000 man space station and a smaller moon station would have to be constructed. From there all the building materials, made from lunar minerals, would be transported and assembled in space. Only carbon, hydrogen and nitrogen would have to be supplied from earth. The

Fig. 22. Partial view of the construction of the first space city. It show an agricultural zone.

finished space station, which would revolve once a minute to produce artificial gravity, would have all the vital necessities on board: fields and meadows would stretch for 800 m before the eyes of its inhabitants, the drinking water would be constantly regenerated, the air would be cleaner than it is over our terrestrial cities.

Before I fill out this bare report with details, I should like to be allowed to make a brief personal remark.

When I sent my publishers the manuscript of *Return to the Stars* in 1968, they soon wrote asking whether it would not be better to leave out the chapter entitled, 'The Sphere – The Ideal Shape for Cosmic Spaceships', as technicians who had been consulted considered my proposition as the unproveable and highly improbable speculation of a science-fiction writer. Moreover, my idea of producing artificial gravity in such a spaceship by rotation was not much more than a fanciful hypothesis. So perhaps I would like to omit these passages in the book for the sake of credibility of my theses.

I did not omit them*. And to my publishers' credit, I must say at this point that they have always had the courage to print my most hazardous and debatable assumptions unchanged. Incidentally I know that the Econ Verlag, like

Fig. 23. According to the plans, the inhabitants of the first space colony could build a second incomparably bigger station. It would be able to house between 200,000 and 3,000,000 people. The 'living' cylinders are 32 km long and 6,400 m in diameter.

**Return to the Stars*, pp. 71 *et seq.*

MacMillan's in New York with Velikowsky, have had a lot of trouble with their other authors who were worried that having a crackpot on the list might harm their reputations.

The very people who objected to my assertion that space-ships of the future would be spherical are now convinced by the shape of the technically feasible giant space station that I was not so far wide of the mark after all. As regards the creation of artificial gravity, it forms an essential feature of all projects for the future.

The cosmic city would be stationed at what is known as the libration point, (L=5), where the gravities of the earth moon and sun combine and so guarantee a stable flight path. The moon's gravity is only $1/20$ of the earth's. So the expenditure of energy on transporting material from the moon to the space city would only be $1/20$ of that used in moving it from the earth.

The scientists and technologists based their planning *exclusively* on the technology that we have at our disposal *today*. First of all an advance commando of 2,000 mining engineers would be taken to point $L = 5$. The commandos would live in prefabricated quarters and workshops. The Boeing Company could have the transport system for these heavy loads ready for take-off by the beginning of the 1980s!

Thanks to the lunar rocks probe made by Apollo we know for certain that iron, aluminium, titanium and magnesium exist on the moon. Iron-works personnel would treat these ores and raw materials metallurgically and use them to build the first settlement. There is energy to spare for this process: solar energy! Simultaneously with the work of this advance troop a station would be set up on the moon, the weight of its total equipment being estimated at from 15,000 to 50,000 tons. The construction of a launching pad for space transports has been planned. It is estimated that building the first stage would only take two years.

The material dug up on the moon would be 'shot' to point $L = 5$ where technologists of all disciplines would await it. The lunar material would be assembled into gigantic cylinders, 100 m thick, 1 km long. The casing of the cylinders would be divided into six long strips, each 1 km long, in this order: metal/glass, metal/glass. Moveable mirrors which would reflect the sun's light into the interior of the cylinder

Fig. 24. The landscape inside the cylinder is just like home. Every 114 seconds the cylinder revolves once on its own axis in order to create an artificial gravity similar to that of the earth.

would be mounted on this casing.

The whole station would rotate once a minute on its longitudinal axis. The centrifugal forces so generated would provide the colonisers with the conditions of life they were used to at home. No one would float about as we know our astronauts did in their weightless state. People would move about just as they do on the old familiar earth. Everything in the station would have its normal weight.

The second detachment with 2000 men and women would enlarge the terrain for the total settlement of 10,000 inhabitants.

The planners have not confined themselves to the sphere of technology; they have also thought of providing pleasant living conditions. Trees and plants would grow; there would be rivers and lakes. Livestock farms would provide meat; goats would ensure the milk supply. Male goats would not be taken up to the station. If there were any problems about rearing further generations of goats, sperm ampules would be used for artificial insemination.

Dr Thomas Heppenheim, space travel engineer at the California Institute of Technology, said to *The National Enquirer:*

Life in the planned space city would not only be pleasanter than on earth, but people up there would also have everything necessary for maximum growth. No crop

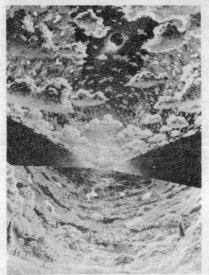

Fig. 25. This view from the end of the cylinder shows the onset of night. At the sides long manoeuvrable rectangular mirrors let the sunlight into the interior. They regulate the seasons and control the cycle of night and day. The atmosphere inside the cylinder is the same as it would be on earth.

would fail. The first 10,000 people would live in terraced apartments with the most up-to-date home comforts. Through their windows they would see vaulted fields full of crops and have a view of green parks. Life would be pleasant and sunny. People would be able to work in their shirt sleeves.

Professor Gerrard O'Neill of Princeton University, a physicist with an international reputation, and a leading member of the research and planning group, thinks that a second space station, to be erected by the settlers of the first station, could be 30 km long and provide space for 200,000 inhabitants. Professor O'Neill has no doubt that in a hundred years time 90 per cent of the world's population could be living in such space colonies. His actual words were:

The settlement of space is no longer a science-fiction story. We already have the technology we need. The first colony could be functioning before the end of the millennium.

Professor O'Neill supplied *Bild der Wissenschaft* with tables of the projects worked out by the research group. Two of them will give the reader some idea of what is technically feasible:

Model no.	Length (km)	Radius (m)	Rotation (secs)	Settlers	Year when operational
1	1.0	100	21	10000	1988
2	3.2	320	36	150000	1996
3	10.0	1000	63	1000000	2002
4	32.0	13200	114	10000000	2008

Material for model No.1	Lunar Material (tons)	Terrestrial Material (tons)
Aluminium	20,000	—
Glass	10,000	—
Generating station	—	1,000
Initial structures	—	1,000
Other special apparatus	—	1,000
Machinery	—	800
Earth, rocks	420,000	—
Liquid hydrogen	—	5,400
2000 settlers (building team)	—	200
Dehydrated food stuffs	—	600
about	500,000	10,000

Dr. Richard Johnson, the NASA Head of Planning and Research on extra-terrestrial life says:

All that is technically possible. All we need is money! Money, that expensive commodity! It is estimated that the project of a space city that is technically feasible in the immediate future would cost 100 milliard dollars. A utopian sum? By no means. It is an amount we can contemplate without fear and astonishment, perhaps even with pleasure. For the Pentagon has been allocated a defence budget of 104 milliard dollars for 1977! If technicians estimate the costs of the three stages before the functioning space city is achieved at a 'mere' 100 milliard dollars, a 'mere' four milliard dollars a year would be due until completion in the year 2000 – a twenty-fifth of the defence budget for a single year! Invested in a project that would rapidly produce a high rate of interest.

During my next telephone call to the aged Jules Verne, I shall tell him that I have kept my feet on the ground of what is technically possible. He won't laugh this time.

Fig. 26. In order to give an idea of the comparative size of the space city, the Golden Gate Bridge (2.15 km long) at San Francisco has been drawn in. The manoeuvrable rectangular mirrors that reflect the sunlight are visible in the upper half of the picture. Night has already fallen on one part of the space colony, the other part is still lit up by the sun. All the illustrations of the space city were drawn by Don Davis from NASA and Stanford University plans, and kindly made available to me by NASA headquarters at Washington.

It remains only for me to ask my stock question. Why should not older intelligent beings, far superior to us in every respect, have been able to use our *existing* technological achievements in *their* space undertakings?

WHO KNOWS WHERE RESEARCH STANDS AT THIS MOMENT?

I was very pleased to read about proving that it is technically possible to construct a cosmic city, because I am convinced that extra-terrestrials founded strategically placed colonies from which they operated in space and which enabled them to use the life produced there even to manipulate the law of time dilation.

The space city anchored at point $L = 5$ would run on solar energy. So this project could only be settled within range of the sun's light. I postulate that a spaceship the size of a large town is also possible and that it could even operate independently of solar energy. The fast breeders, fusion reactors, (which we are now developing) could replace solar energy by atomic energy. Uranium, available in very limited quantities on earth, would also exist on other planets. I am not going to speculate here about how this spaceship city would be propelled. High speeds would not be necessary; it could cruise along at a snail's pace. In a few thousand years it would drift into the Alpha Centauri system, if that was its goal. Perhaps the happy landing would not be celebrated until the fiftieth generation of space travellers had been born. What would it matter? An interstellar journey would have succeeded.

Only those who are directly engaged in research projects, and they generally work under top secret conditions, know what is being invented, developed, constructed and got ready for production on our planet at this moment. We ordinary mortals have not the faintest idea of what is going on. Somewhere, at some time, there is a brief report that research that will change the future has been successfully carried out. Then all is silence, although further work on its technical realisation goes doggedly on.

The distance between the imagination and reality, between idea and realisation, gets shorter and shorter. Anyone who does not want to look a fool to his children should be very,

very careful before the over-swift banishment to the realm of
fable of an 'inconceivable' idea. We are experiencing what
kind of seven-league boots our research workers wear and the
goals – inconceivable only 'yesterday' – to which they have
pushed on in one generation. We must realise that the
progress that reveals itself before our eyes is already old hat to
the research workers who took part in it. They have long since
been aiming at new 'inconceivable' targets.

If you ask me how I have the nerve to think that hardly
anything is now technically *impossible,* I can only reply:
because my archives teach me that *everything* is possible. Just
take these topical examples!

ESPIONAGE PHOTOS FROM SPACE

Cosmic reconnaissance with spy satellites has reached a
technical perfection that borders on the unimaginable.
American celestial spies can determine with a radiometric
fingerprint whether Brezhnev's dacha is lived in or not, or
whether President Carter's swimming pool is heated. Or
the Russians can check whether there is a visitor in one of
the 18 subterranean fortresses with intercontinental missiles in the Arizona desert. (8)

A TANK WITH DEATH RAYS

The first US Laser Tank, an improbable mixture of tank
and submarine, from the manoeuvrable tower of which a
deadly laser beam can be fired, is being produced at the
Radstone Arsenal in Huntsville. The Laser beam – several
hundred kilowatts strong per pulsation – is reputed to be
strong enough to penetrate human beings, aircraft fusel-
ages and even thin steel plate. 'The thing goes through
anything without trouble,' was the comment of the arms
expert of the US Army on this weapon of the future. (9)

DEATH RAYS – ENGLAND'S SECRET WEAPON

The British Government's most secret project, in which
several million pounds has already been invested, to
promote the development of death rays to destroy aircraft,
rockets and tanks, was revealed last night. The rays, which

turn science-fiction into reality, are so strong that they can perforate thick sheets of metal. The spokesman for the Ministry of Defence said, 'I can confirm that work on the use of Lasers as destructive weapons for the Navy, Royal Airforce and Army is under way.' (10)

RAYS THAT ATTACK THE BRAIN

The London engineer Charles Bovill describes his new invention as a genuinely humane weapon. It sheds no blood, is easily portable and works mainly by the panic it causes. The weapon consists of supersonic and infra-red projectors which disturb certain electric currents (alpha waves) in the human brain. People are seized with panic and run away. An ideal way of dissolving demonstrations without bloodshed. (11)

SEVEN TERRIBLE WEAPONS

They can raise people's blood pressure and high blood pressure rapidly leads to death. A super radiation bomb liberates Röntgen and gamma rays of great intensity. It kills by electromagnetic radiation and leaves no radioactivity. (12)

THE WEATHER AS A WEAPON

Hail, rain, and snowstorms as weapons in future wars – in the view of the International Institute for Strategic Studies in London that idea has long since ceased to be a theme for novels about the future. Since the introduction of plant poisons of the most varied kinds with which crops can be destroyed and whole forests defoliated, we now have the threat of military 'weather makers' influencing our environment. Wars could be waged in this way without the world noticing that a war was going on. Artficially stimulated bad harvests would not be distinguishable from those caused by nature and a country could be brought to its knees without war ever having been declared. (13, 14)

It seems as if I hear a reader standing behind my desk and whispering in my ear: 'But what have these reports of apocalyptic weapons of destruction to do with your theory?'

Quite a lot!

I am trying to take the bearings of the approximate position of our modern technology, making use of the reports and announcements available to me. It has become clear to me in the process that my estimate of the position will always be hopelessly out of date. When technical achievements are publicised they have already been overtaken. The *future* horrors that technologists may have in store for us are already in the *past*. They are old hat.

It is a fact that the weapons involved are not new. We are far from au fait with the weapon technology of our early ancestors. Mythologies tell realistic stories of horror weapons, of weapons of the ancient gods such as the primitive brains of our forefathers could never have imagined. As neither the keepers of sacred scriptures not the tellers of myths can have had any idea of our present and future weapon systems, they must have tapped an accessible and contemporary source for their accounts. Observation and experience in the arena.

Consequently, in an inventory of present-day and future technology I refer to weapon systems that have already exercised their destructive *power in the past*.

Being familiar with old mythologies and holy scriptures, I cling to the refreshing idea that extra terrestrial visitors had fully mastered and still master everything that we invent today and develop tomorrow. Technical possibilities from our past and future can serve us as divining rods with which we can find ore in the past.

DOES THE ENERGY FACTOR PRECLUDE INTERSTELLAR SPACE TRAVEL?

It is continually being claimed that the energy factor alone makes interstellar space travel an impossibility. More energy would be necessary for an interstellar spaceship with a launching weight of 200,000 tons than is produced by the total present day composition of fossil energy. Does the well-being and future of mankind lie buried in fossil energy?

In September 1975 at the 26th Congress of the International-al Astronautical Federation in Lisbon, the construction of a satellite solar power station was urgently recommended. Research groups, who have tackled this project in the meantime, plan to have a satellite circling the earth in a stationary orbit at a height of 36,000 km.

The satellite, 'consists of a 4-km-wide and 12-km-long solar cell collecting area with a disc-shaped microwave relay installation 1-km in diameter. The electricity, of the order of 8,000 megawatts, produced by such a photo-voltaic solar power station will be relayed to stationary flat antennae on the earth in the form of microwave radiation. After deducting losses due to relaying, 5,000 megawatts will still be available for use.' (15)

Technically speaking there are no longer any problems to prevent the realisation of such a project. We are capable of putting satellites in orbit and making them radiate solar energy to earth. Unfortunately these relays of energy could also be used as weapons. Pencil rays from space could burn up crops, reduce whole cities and countrysides to embers and ashes, melt the ice at the Poles and deliberately provoke another Flood. The 'divine lightning' from the cosmos of which the myths speak is not a fairy story. It wasn't in the past and it still isn't.

The over-hasty would like to put an end to the debate on the possibilities of interstellar space travel by stating categorically that it would inevitably come to grief on the problem of energy.

The reports of the Club of Rome (16), and the revolt of the oil-producing countries have caused world opinion to wallow in the pessimistic idea that sees the end of all progress in the lack of sources of energy. Everything that runs on wheels – with the possible exception of electrified trams, which are driven by 'fluid current' – is supplied with energy from the limited supply of fossil fuels: coal, petroleum, natural gas, shale. And the energy obtained from the radioactive element, uranium, will also have its natural limits. The average uranium content of the earth's crust is 2 gr per ton and these 2 gr have to be extracted by expensive techniques from ores that are very poor in uranium. Atomic power stations of the kind that have sprung up in every country as sheet-anchors of the economy are based on uranium. Some very intelligent and farseeing sceptics think that in the years to come when all the atomic power stations planned are in production, there will no longer be enough uranium (on the earth) to run them.

Fossil sources of energy cannot be regenerated. Once burnt up, they vanish from the globe–leaving behind the evidence of a highly industrialised technology resulting from that energy. But this legacy contributes nothing to our general well-being, because it is worthless and unusable without energy.

Nevertheless, I cannot share this pessimism about energy. Sources of energy that are running out must be replaced by new ones. Even now technical developments could put a stop to the wasteful expenditure of precious stocks of energy and raw materials. For example, engines of all kinds can be converted to run on liquid hydrogen (LH_2). Successful attempts to use LH_2 as a source of energy have been going on for years at firms such as General Electric and Pratt and Whitney. There is still one technical problem to be solved before it can be used in vehicles. Engines driven by LH_2 need much larger fuel tanks.

The *Neue Zürcher Zeitung* summed up the advantages of a future hydrogen industry:

Hydrogen is a completely synthetic product that can be obtained from an inexhaustible and practically omnipresent basic substance, namely, water.

Hydrogen is by far the cleanest fuel, since after combustion with oxygen only harmless water is left. The production of pollutants like CO_2, CO, SO_2 and soot, as occurs with the combustion of fossil fuels, is avoided.

Hydrogen, like its 'ash', water, is completely non-poisonous and so is *recyclable* via the biosphere in association with the normal cycle of water.

Hydrogen can be stored in liquid and solid forms, or as a gas.

It is easily transported and can be distributed by pipeline.

Hydrogen is *universally useful,* and already forms the basic substance of highly technological and chemical processes. (17)

No, interstellar space travel will not founder on the problem of energy. We shall simply have to say goodbye to the old forms of energy.

THE MODERN 'GODS' ARE EVERYWHERE

8,529 objects were orbiting the earth in space on 1 October 1976. Among them were 794 satellites, 54 of them probes. And the rest? Space rubbish: Fragments of rockets and satellites. A glove that the astronaut, Edward White, lost on a walk in space.

Fig. 27. The outer walls of the Relay satellite consist of eight alveolar aluminium layers with 8215 solar cells. The satellite's main function is the relaying of TV and radio programmes and the transmission of transcontinental telephone conversations.

What did people do before the invention of the zip fastener? What would we stare at in the evening, if there was no television screen? Can we imagine the present without the telephone, the fridge, the car and Coca Cola? They are a few inventions which we use as naturally as the doorhandle, which was invented in Mesopotamia about 600 B.C. Satellites are not in our field of vision but we could not maintain our lifestyle for long without them. Their 'divine eyes' are omnipresent.

Satellites transmit radio and television programmes, telephone conversations and schools programmes. They provide navigational aids for ships and aircraft; they send astrophysical data to earth and are in constant use in the espionage game between East and West. Satellites discover plagues of locusts, warn of forest fires, hurricanes and enemy invaders. They sound the depths of the sea and transmit maps of new subterranean supplies of raw materials.

Satellites can be used for more than mere short-term

weather forecasting. In mid October 1975, NASA launched the first operational weather satellite into a geo-stationary earth orbit at a height of 36,200 km above the Equator. At 30 minute intervals it can transmit photographs of the earth and clouds covering 25% of the earth's surface.

That is a lot, but insignificant in comparison with the plans that can be put into practise by 1985. Then a network of satellites, each consisting of 4 to 6 large satellites in synchronised geo-stationary solar orbit, will deliver and evaluate their data, all co-ordinated by another satellite. The target is to achieve a one year regional weather forecast and ten-year forecast for each hemisphere by the year 2000. (18)

The modern 'Gods' are omnipresent. The eye of Horus keeps watch.

So far it is the satellites' function to observe and report. But the hour is not far away when they will be able to intervene in events on earth, either by radio commands from earth . . . or independently. Mini-computerisation makes it possible.

It is estimated that more than 500 scientists are working on

Fig. 28. This satellite studies the atmosphere. It finds out how much ultraviolet radiation there is in the earth's atmosphere and checks chemical processes in the ionosphere. Its orbit can be changed from earth by a nautical-type steering system.

the realisation of an intelligent computer at the present time. They do not like it if you say that the end product of their research will be an intelligent robot. Nevertheless, that is their target! They constantly protest that intelligence is reserved for mankind and that a computer – read robot – will never be able

Fig. 29. This telescope satellite was built for measuring gamma rays in space.

to think. That is a cock-and-bull story and also a sedative for those who are afraid of futuristic technology.

The branch of computer technology that aims at creating intelligent robots is called Artificial Intelligence (A.I.). The centres of A.I. research are the Massachusetts Institute of Technology and Stanford University in California. I find it appropriate always to keep robots (artificial men) in mind when people talk of future computers.

Computers and robots are of the same race. Computer programmes can be drummed into a robot's brain. In the case of the technological freak that plays chess with men, where is the border between robot and computer? Computers are gifted 'beings'. They solve the most difficult mathematical problems quicker than man, who compiles them; they regulate complicated technical processes better and with fewer mistakes than their constructor, man; they read and write quicker than their teacher, man; they have an imcomparably more reliable memory than their archivist, man; they can check their activities as quick as winking and more accurately than their instructor, man; they can learn and think things out like man.

Today, in large diagnostic clinics, computers are fed with medical data: age, race, height, weight, previous illnesses, operations, medicines taken, current troubles and their symptoms, etc. The computer registers the information conscientiously . . . and spits out the diagnosis in fractions of a second. The patient knows where and why it hurts him. People say, (and it's true), that this is not genuine knowledge. But knowledge originates in the human brain in the same way, namely through the adaptation of information via impressions, which are fed in through sensory organs, such as the eyes, nose, ears, skin and tongue and by education and the formation of words and ideas, etc. Like the computer, the brain is programmed binarily. The brain draws conclusions from the sum of stored information. What else does a computer do? It thinks things out by summoning up, comparing and combining the information fed into it. Equipped with *its* knowledge, it draws independent conclusions. It acts. The fact that it cannot buy its clothes in Saville Row yet is a bit odd, but that may come too and anyway this is not the place to bother about externals. The Mona Lisa isn't 'beautiful' either, but it is of the greatest interest.

Japan's car industry works on a more favourable cost basis than the rest of the world's automobile industries. Like all its competitors it has rationalised, but it is also using robots on an increasing scale: (19)

Robots undertake such difficult jobs as arc-welding heavy steel sheets or the pressing of parts. Nissan uses a robot for welding panelling, which speeds up body assembly considerably. This robot is also planned for future export!

Space travel planners have long since shaken hands with their colleague, the robot! They know that through minimodule techniques he can become the most important 'man aboard', because he weighs less than most astronauts, who with their partial knowledge could assemble only a minute part of the knowledge that the robot has ready and evaluates in fractions of a second, while the lords of creation are still racking their brains over the right method. This reliable technical companion is not liable to fall ill; if he does not feel up to the mark in some section, he can switch to independent healthy circuits in nano-seconds. He does not eat or excrete. What living creature can enter the space travel business with the same advantages? Ten years ago* I suggested a supercomputer which would be linked with other computers in

* *Chariots of the Gods?* p.162

critical centres throughout the world. (15) In this way the whole world's treasury of knowledge would (a) be stored in one place, (b) always be on call and (c) could be kept up to date by a programmed learning process. It would be infinitely superior to all the libraries with their milliards of books. In the spring of 1975 I read that the Federal Republic of Germany has set aside 440 million Deutschmarks (up to 1977) in order to store all the published knowledge in the world in 16 super-brains. (20)

In the peripheral field of the justification of my theory it is important to value this aspect of technological developments highly enough. Although it may be futurology at the moment, a robot will be ready for space flight one fine day in the not too distant future – a robot who can read and be in control in space without human assistance. He will 'know' when and if 'his' spaceship is approaching a hostile satellite. He will destroy it with heat rays. He will recognise the ballistic trajectories of high-flying death-dealing rockets and explode them. I see a future in which robots behaving just like humans will act as 'thinking' expert household helps; in the absence of human domestic staff. Advertisements like 'Baby-sitter urgently needed by the hour' will no longer exist. People will have their robot to play with the children, talk to them and look after them.

Robot research is more advanced than we would imagine. The intelligent computer/robot is already outside the door. He will open it himself.

That is only one path taken by research, at the end of which man will gradually be dethroned. But incomparably more receptive than the computer and taking up the minimum of room is a brain, with its many milliards of cells. The living brain has one advantage over computers. It is immune to jamming by electro-magnetic radiation. Small wonder then that the intensive work is going on in the USA and USSR to transplant solo-brains in guided missiles as a substitute for computers. Here is a report from the *Neue Zürcher Zeitung*.

It must be admitted that guided missiles steered by animals could be very cheap and effective, and in addition be completely immune to electronic interference . . . The ultimate goal of such studies is then to get the animal brain, i.e. that very compact and efficient biological data processing system, to produce the desired reaction on an impulse caused by an image of the target territory. (21)

We do not have to overcome cosmic dimensions solely for the sake of interstellar spaceflight. Even the most inveterate opponents of space travel will admit that in view of the rapidly dwindling supplies of raw materials on our planet every effort must be made to produce substitutes.

'Mining in space is possible,' declared Thomas B. McCord, an astrophysicist at the Massachusetts Institute of Technology. 'Iron, nickel and other metals could be mined on asteroids* and shipped to earth. There are no insoluble technicals problems in this field.' (22)

It was reckoned that metals worth 140 milliard dollars could be extracted annually from asteroids. Through telescopic and spectral analysis we have known for a long time that some asteroids in the asteroid belt between Mars and

Fig. 30. America's Space Shuttle, the space ferry that can be used over and over again.

* Asteroids: small planets revolving round the sun in elliptical orbits.

Jupiter consist preponderantly of iron and metal.

Miners would have to be stationed on suitable asteroids. Using solar energy, the metals would be smelted, cast into bars and fetched in space ferries. One single cubic kilometre of asteroid material could meet world requirements for iron for 15 years, and of nickel for 1250 years. A fantastic journey to Never-Never Land? I do not think so. Industry is not in the habit of producing beyond its needs. Spacesuits are mass produced, off-the-peg tailoring, so that space pioneers can be suitably clad. The age of ready-to-wear clothing for Mr X, the astronaut, is already here. Even the fantastic TV spaceship *Enterprise* is no longer mere science-fiction. President Gerald Ford decided to give the name *Enterprise* to the space shuttle, the re-usable American space ferry, which will shoot back and forth between satellite stations and the earth in the eighties.

INTERSTELLAR PROJECTS

We mentioned interplanetary projects as in part already realised and in part in an advanced state of development. What is the actual position regarding interstellar space travel?

Various projects that really smack of science-fiction have emerged from the stage of basic research. This included medical and biological research aimed at prolonging the life of man or putting him into a kind of hibernation for an accurately determinable period of time. At the end of February 1974 Dr Albert R. Dawe of the Office of Naval Research in Chicago, reported that he had succeeded in extracting from the blood of hibernating squirrels a serum that clearly caused the long energy-saving period of sleep.

We know that squirrels, hedgehogs, certain species of bears and mice hibernate. A hormone regulates their supply of energy; their circulation is maintained by the smallest possible pilot-light so to speak. If it becomes possible to use the Dawe serum on man, the lengthy travel periods of interstellar flights can be bridged for the human organism. Then space travellers might be able to reach their goal fresh as paint even after 200 years! The effect of the serum is obviously not confined to squirrels, for Dr. Dawe made hedgehogs hibernate in the middle of summer by injecting them. As if obeying nature, all the organic functions continued as if in a genuine state of hibernation.

This biological and medical research aimed at prolonging life can advance interstellar space travel considerably. Interstellar journeys will be possible with *slower* spaceships, measured in terms of human life.

Is research also making the construction of faster spaceships its target?

Professor Joseph Weber works at the University of Maryland. He has the reputation of being the foremost expert on gravity waves. What do we understand by gravity waves?

More than ten years ago Professor Weber had the first gravity wave antennae built and measured the gravitation signals that Albert Einstein had postulated in his general theory of relativity.

Every day many stars in our Milky Way disintegrate. Novae, new stars, is the name of this class of alterable stars which increase their light a 100 thousand fold in a spontaneous outburst of brightness. The interior is compressed under inconceivable pressure, a fundamental atomic process. In a very short time gigantic energies are radiated – gravity waves.

Professor Weber can seek out and measure these gravity waves with his latest antennae. Expenditure on this project is vast, but can be worthwhile. The biggest antenna is a massive aluminium cylinder weighing 3.6 tons, nearly 4 metres long and 65 centimetres thick. Protected from all environmental influences, the gravity wave antenna is suspended in a vacuum pressure chamber.

In this field science is concerned with basic research. Nevertheless there is a suspicion that gravity waves may become the ideal medium for propelling interstellar spaceships.

Professor Eric Laithwaite of London has already built an apparatus that functions on anti-gravity and so neutralises gravity waves. In the presence of journalists Professor Laithwaite put a chest weighing ten kilograms on a kitchen trolley. Two clearly visible fly-wheels were turning inside the chest. Driven by electricity, they were rotating very rapidly in opposite directions. When the flywheels were revolving, the chest weighed only 7.5 kg. Gravity had been partially removed. Laithwaite thinks that one day we shall fit space-ships with antigravity motors. Such interstellar vehicles would have to be transported outside the field of terrestrial gravity. From then on this motor could be driven by nuclear energy and possibly also by the gravity waves that are liberated during supernova outbursts.

Professor Laithwaite is not just any Tom Dick or Harry. He is the inventor of the electrical linear motor (23).

As surely as the sun rises, I am constantly confronted with this complex theme in discussions and readers' letters: 'That's all very well, Mr von Daniken, but how are the vast interstellar distances ever to be overcome? Our present space travel technology just enables us to make up for the compara-tively nearby planets, Moon, Mars, Venus and Jupiter.'

I accept and understand their scepticism. I am not a scientist. I am a keenly interested layman. A team made a film about me and my travels and entitled it: *Tramp between the Sciences.* I find the title appropriate. If I, without vanity, can attribute even a modest value to my work, it is because by passing the frontiers between the sciences I have been able to make them a little more flexible and penetrable – and because I induced divergent faculties to make communal attacks on me and so join in exchanges of opinion. However, I do not possess academic titles in any of the fields relevant to my interests, but I do have a capacity for thinking based on sound human reason that is not necessarily conferred by passing exams. So I am one with the sound human reason of all my contemporaries and I am nourished by the scientific solutions I admire and which entail practical progress. I cannot supply immaculate scientific knowledge; I have to acquire it from its leading representatives. But when I use experts to demon-strate my theories, you can be sure that I go to the top men, not the second raters. The snag about such enquiries is often that pure science finds it hard to make itself intelligible to the general public. Science has a habit of serving black bread with hard crusts and if you don't tackle them carefully, you can lose your eye-teeth.

THE BLACK BREAD OF SCIENCE

In order to tackle the most important subject, namely whether we shall ever be able to overcome interstellar distances, I went into the lion's den – in fact, to see Professor Harry O. Ruppe, who holds the chair for space travel technology at Munich Technical University. Ruppe is not only a scientists of high international repute, but also a practical man, who worked at NASA for a long time,

Fig. 31. Professor Dr Harry O. Ruppe.

eventually as Director of the Office for Planning Future Space Travel Projects. The decisive aspect of this, rocket propulsion technology, is the strong point of his research work. I asked Professor Ruppe about the future possibilities of interstellar space travel. Unlike T.V. reporters I let my partner do the talking.

It is said that Albert Einstein had only two colleagues who could understand him, but that no one has ever found them. Just as everyone has heard of his relativity theory, today the whole world is familiar with the idea of stress without knowing that Professor Hans Selye coined it for his theory of adaptation.

Selye, who was called the 'Einstein of medicine' for this discovery, wanted to inform his colleagues and laymen about it in a book. While writing, he noticed that he had to go so deeply into medicine for the sake of his fellow doctors that laymen would no longer be able to follow him. So he recommended readers to skip the unintelligible bits, because the rest was enough for the understanding of his theory. As I don't want any of my readers to suffer from stress, I recommend that they select only the easily intelligible parts of the interview. Unfortunately, it was not possible to make it any simpler!

Within two decades we have experienced an astonishing development in space travel. Starting from modest beginnings with small unmanned earth satellites at a height of only a few kilometers, man has landed on the moon and we have reached the majority of the planets and even approached the sun. We have got used to achievements following in rapid succession. Will things go on at this tempo?

'It is not surprising that people assume on the basis of what they have already experienced that the stars and even the remotest objects in the cosmos could soon come into the category of the technologically reachable. But let a few figures show that that is not necessarily the case.

A low earth-satellite orbit is reached in a matter of minutes; that needs a speed of 10 Km/s. With one and a half times that speed, the space to the moon and the planets* was opened up.

It took a few days to travel to the moon and a few years in the case of interplanetary traffic, but there the earth's motion in its annual orbit helped us a great deal.

If we were to undertake interstellar flights at interplanetary speeds, i.e. several 10 km/s, which is perfectly possible, the space probe Pioneer X is already doing it – we have flying times of 10^4 times the distance of the target, or if we express this in light years, i.e. 4×10^4 years for the nearest object ($\ddagger$ 4 light years) and 10^{14} years for the further object

---

*Planets are stars that revolve round the sun in elliptical, almost circular orbits. In ascending order of distance from the sun, they are: Mercury, Venus, Earth, Mars, Jupiter, Saturn, Uranus, Neptune, Pluto.

($\ddagger$ 10^{10} light years). The age of the universe is assumed to be 'only' 10^{10} years, but even the 'near' objects are too far away, if we compare 40,000 years with the span of a human life or the age of a typical terrestrial civilisation.

So does a specialist like you see any possibility at all of interstellar space travel?

Of course. Here are some sample ideas.

Unmanned flights: machines (robots) carry out the expeditions and radio their conclusions back to earth.

Generation journeys: a whole settlement of people would be sent out. With its own source of energy (a mini-sun). With a closed, economically self-sufficient life cycle etc. the group that reaches the target is no longer necessarily the one that started the journey.

Slowing down life: the astronauts' life processes are so slowed down (hibernation) that they change very little during the long flight.

Preservation of life: incubators, semen and ovary cells in appropriate storerooms etc. are taken on the journey. Human life is not produced until the spaceship is the right period of time away from the target.

Prolonging life: the life of the crew is prolonged to such an extent that even long journeys only require a fraction of the expectation of life. In this hypothesis Cyborg (abbreviation for cybernetic organism*), a combination of man and machine, plays a part.

Don't the previous considerations force us to examine the existing frontiers of our propulsion technology?'

Perhaps things are not so difficult after all?

Of the fully intelligible rocket systems today the most efficient is ion propulsion**, which gets its energy from a fixed nuclear reactor (fission type).

The highest speed is several 100 km/s. Consequently it

*Return to the Stars, pp. 19-20.

**Ion motors accelerate ionisable colloid particles loaded with molecules/atoms by means of electric fields.

is unusable for interstellar flights. As a visual explanation
for your technically interested readers I supply you with a

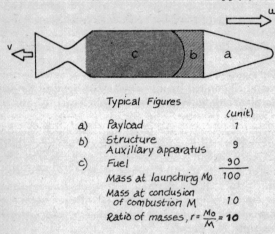

Fig. 32   *Typical rocket (Fig.1)*

Typical Figures

		(unit)
a)	Payload	1
b)	Structure Auxiliary apparatus	9
c)	Fuel	90
	Mass at launching M_0	100
	Mass at conclusion of combustion M	10
	Ratio of masses, $r = \frac{M_0}{M} = \mathbf{10}$	

drawing of a typical rocket. To define a rocket clearly: it is
an apparatus with the impulse-bearer wholly on board. No
details are given about sources of energy. Frequently
impulse bearer and energy bearer are identical.

Let us talk about the most efficient of the systems that are
not highly speculative! The fraction a of the mass of fuel m
is transformed into energy – for fusion a optimistically $= 3 \times 10^{-3}$.
This energy reappears as the motive energy of the exhaust
emission with the mass m $(1-a)$ which with. . . .

But my dear Professor, I don't understand a word!

You don't? But they're simple formulas.

*No doubt. But I don't understand them. I am far from being a rocket
expert and my readers are only laymen interested in my theories. They
won't understand your scientific secret language either!*

The system I'm trying to explain more or less has to be

expressed in formulas. We're frequently going to be faced with that block in the course of our conversation!

Can I make a suggestion? Let's take all the formulas unintelligible to the layman, which are certainly a titbit for the expert, in the appendix to this interview. Let's make that explanation No 1 for experts.

All right – Project Daedalus, which was carefully worked out and elaborated by my friend Alan Bond of the British Interplanetary Society, is the one which can make interstellar journeys possible. The nuclear pulse propulsion for it was first suggested in the fifties by S. Ulam, of the USA. In this concept comparatively conventional atom bombs (nuclear fission) would be exploded behind a spacecraft which is connected at its stern by means of shock absorbers with a 'baffle-plate'. Closer examination of this principle showed that larger versions could also use hydrogen bombs. Here again special technical details would be necessary. How would you like them?.

Explanation No 2 for experts.

All right. Used sensibly the pulsation system could open up the whole solar system. Nevertheless further improvements are needed for interstellar traffic. In this decade it became likely that small thermonuclear* explosions could be set off by lasers or relativistic electronic rays. In this way we could limit explosions to the equivalent of a few tons of TNT**, instead of the megatons*** which result from detonating fission bombs. Here explanation No 3 for experts is due.

O.K. Can we be a bit clearer, please?

I'm providing you with a sketch of Daedalus and a view of the course of a flight driven by this system.

---

*Nuclear reactions caused by heat.
**TNT Abbreviation for trinitrotoluol, an explosive with high explosive power and insensibility to shock and heating. It is made to explode by initial detonation. The explosive effect of atomic weapons is expressed in the equivalent explosive effect of tons and megatons of TNT.
***One million tons.

The mission:

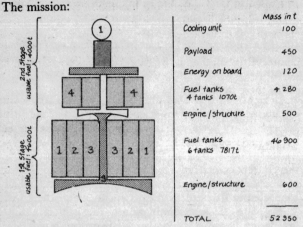

	Mass in t
Cooling unit	100
Payload	450
Energy on board	120
Fuel tanks 4 tanks 1070t	4 280
Engine / structure	500
Fuel tanks 6 tanks 7817t	46 900
Engine / structure	600
TOTAL	52 950

(The numbers give the sequence of ejection)

Diagram of Daedalus

Fig 33.

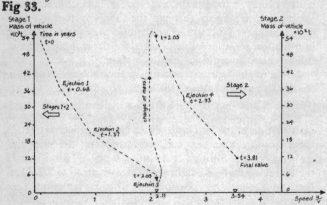

Daedalus, propelled flight, mass and time against speed

Fig 34.

An unmanned flying machine, flying out of our solar system, has to reach Barnard's star, which is 5.91 light years away. To keep flying time as short as possible only a fly-past is planned. Small thermonuclear explosions (helium 3, deuterium) set off by lasers or relativistic electron rays drive the craft. Radiation speed (v) is 10^7 m/s.

Things would go something like this. Flying out of the parking orbit the first stage operates. Whenever a fuel tank gets empty, it is discarded. After 2.05 years the first stage is exhausted. The second stage separates itself and starts to operate. After another 1.76 years it too has used up all its fuel.

Now these figures apply:

Time   3.81 years after the start.
Distance from the sun   0.2 light years.
Speed   min. 0.1 max. 1.0 average 0.3 m/s^2.

Another 48.5 years bring the craft to its goal, Barnard's star.

Naturally the situation must be regulated – possibly by spin* and observation of the stellar background in order to maintain radio contact with the earth. Small corrections to the flight path would have to be made, and inaccuracies put right.

About five or ten years before arrival, several, perhaps ten or twenty, subordinate craft would be discharged from the master ship to fly through the target system together like small shot. That would be the only way to get plenty of information about possible planets, for the stopping time in the neighbourhood of the target is short.

To the flight time of 52 years we should have to add six years for the news to reach the earth. 58 years after the start the results would be available.

If we assume that it might take 15 years from the construction of the first craft of this type to its launching, 73 years would elapse between commissioning the ship and the first results. Supposing we substitute 100 for 73 years the target would be 8.8 light years away instead of 5.9. I feel that with that the possibilities of this technique are exhausted, if not exceeded. If this craft looks comparatively simple, that is naturally owing to our superficial description. Hence explanation No 4 for experts!

I shall type out everything you say, even if I don't understand a word of it. I promise!

Detonating nuclear explosions obviously only makes modest interstel-

*Spin: the craft's own rotation.

lar flights possible. Do they exhaust the possibilities? Are there more powerful sources of energy?

The answer is an unequivocal yes. Before I answer your question in detail, I would remark in passing that throughout the years spent developing Project Daedalus, new scientific advances not available at the beginning might indicate better ways of carrying it out.

In answer to your question about more powerful sources of energy, only 0.3 per cent of the mass is transformed into energy during atomic fusion. But what would happen if we transformed the whole mass into energy? Then it would be possible at least in theory, to approach the speed of light.

Such processes are well known on a small scale. For example a positron* and an electron** can be wholly transformed into energy when they combine.

Speaking generally we have only to bring matter and anti-matter*** together and reciprocal disintegration takes place. Whereas nuclear fusion seems to be a normal source of energy in the cosmos with the necessary very extravagant 'oven', the stars, total destruction of matter on a large scale does not apparently take place in nature. Therefore many observers conclude that this process is impossible. I don't find the inference at all convincing. For it makes it a premise that every realisable process also happens in nature. And that is an article of faith rather than a scientific law.

We have discussed the question of propulsion and the connected problem of flying time. They must be clarified before other problems are tackled. Further discussion of such specialist questions lies outside the scope of this book. So let's talk about generally intelligible interesting aspects of further space travel technology.

I appreciate your concern, but when a professor starts to talk about his own subject, he often assumes that his

---

*Positron: positively charged elementary particle, the mass of which is equal to the mass of the electron.

**Electron: negative electrical elementary particle.

***Anti-matter: form of matter consisting of atoms made up wholly of antiparticles: anti-protons, anti-neutrons, positrons.

audience knows more than it does, because everything is so familiar to him.

Anyway, basically before planning such a difficult enterprise as an interstellar flight, we should have at least minimal data about the existence of planets and broad ideas of the environmental condition, possibilities of life etc. The rapid interstellar ship experiences strange effects when observing the environment from inside the craft, a fact to be taken into account in the astro-navigation.

Knowledge of interstellar co-ordinates and their changes is not so accurate as our knowledge of similar details in the solar system. Steering and control would have to watch that.

Interstellar space is virtually empty, but this vacuum is a prerequisite for reaching really high speeds, because otherwise gas resistance would be too great. Previous assessments show that this resistance is only slight at relativistic speeds, but naturally even that would have to be taken into account for long flight times.

But engineering solutions would have to be found for other things besides overcoming resistance. They would have to be found for heating, against erosion, we well as for the radiation arising from bombardment by particles. The great duration of the mission would make heavy demands on the reliability of the technical systems.

That goes for unmanned and even more so for manned ships.

Undoubtedly significant changes in our general attitude would have to take place before the finance for an undertaking such as interstellar space flight would be provided. The 'returns' are only vaguely forseeable. Probably they would consist 'solely' of scientific data and they would not be available for many decades after the investment of capital. So it is a question of having the courage to provide finance for a very distant future. So far the sociological problems of the crew making a 'journey into the future' have scarcely been thought about, while the problems of those left behind on earth would also have to be included in the overall planning. Today the problem of propulsion may be basic, but when it is solved, there are still many questions to be answered.

*In view of the many incredible earth-changing discoveries made down
our own day, can this process be considered as finished?*

Almost certainly not! You've only got to think of the
discovery of neutron stars* or the discussion about black
holes** or present day models of elementary particles. The
future may also reveal possibilities for interstellar flights
that are inconceivable today or seem to contradict existing
knowledge. It is impossible to make rational prophecies in
this field – as a spur to thought I shall merely suggest a few
fantastic ideas that come from technical novels of the future
at the moment.

I think it is common knowledge by now that spacecraft
flying past a heavenly body in motion may experience a
change of speed. This effect was made use of by the space
probes Pioneer X and XI with the help of the planet
Jupiter.

It can be shown that such changes in speed can be very
great when the fly past concerns a star whose rotational
speed is very high and which itself is moving very fast
around another star. We might think of a neutron star
revolving round a black hole. During such a manoeuvre the
speeding up can be almost as great as you like because the
main forces work equally on every atom. But in any case
there are forces here that can be used.

I've already said that space is not completely empty.
Perhaps a still unknown phenomenon can be used there.
Radiation pressure, electric or magnetic fields, do exist, but
they seem to be much too weak for the main sources of
propulsion. However they might be strong enough to effect
changes of direction. But if ever research into the nature of
gravitation is allowed to transform gravitation at will into a
thrust off – the consequences would be enormous. Of course
even then energy would have to be taken along, otherwise
the ship would be in perpetual motion up from and down
into the earth's field of gravity like a yo-yo. Nevertheless a
discovery of this kind would be a very significant aid. Using
anti-gravity (or other fields) our craft could thrust itself off

*A star originating after the loss of 'normal' energy by collapse. It has the mass
of the sun with a radius of 10 km.
**Like *, but the star is so rich in mass when collapsing that it cannot attain a
state of equilibrium again and dwindles to a point.

from heavenly bodies, indeed from the whole universe. The problem of the rocket carrying its own impulse would be solved.

Perhaps one day we may be able to set in motion the sun and the whole solar system – in such a way that interstellar distances can be bridged.

It is usually said that Einstein's theory of relativity precludes faster than light movements for all particles, or quanta*.

But strictly speaking the theory of relativity is not so limiting. Its conclusions are merely that material particles below the speed of light can at most achieve the speed of light, and that faster-than-light particles can never move slower than light. Faster than light particles are called tachyons** and their existence is speculative. I find it unlikely that they could be of any importance for interstellar space travel. But who knows? Perhaps an improved relativity theory would, under certain realisable conditions permit the 'forbidden' transition into the sacred precinct of speeds faster than light?

It would also be a great help if our starship could take suitable materials aboard while on its journey. The problems mentioned earlier would still remain, but the 'impossibility' of the flight would be reduced. When matter falls into a dark hole, a substantial fraction of about 10 per cent is transformed into energy. If mini black holes exist and if they produce and stabilise matter they could conceivably act as sources of motive power.

From the standpoint of present-day physics the gateway to the stars in the film *2001* seems unintelligible to me. Time and distance cannot be suspended in this mystic way. Equally in the realm of fable are the hyperspaces of *Spaceship Enterprise* in the TV series *Star Trek*.

But: Isaac Newton, the important English seventeenth-century physicist and mathematician, would certainly have described present-day television technology as 'unintelligible'.

If so-called occult phenomena do exist in any form, they

---

*The smallest indivisible quantities: elementary particles.
***Return to the Stars*, pp. 23-24

will ultimately be incorporated into the rational world picture. Perhaps brand new ideas will then be possible.

However, enough of speculation. Perhaps I have managed to show, in spite of the virtual impossibility of interstellar space travel today, that there is a tiny glimmer of hope. For even this virtual impossibility is relative, dependent on our earth and our present-day knowledge.

'A tiny glimmer of hope!'

Professor Ruppe's concluding remark has made it worthwhile biting the 'scientific black bread', as we have his three observations that unusual, as yet unforeseen knowledge could turn rational planning topsy-turvy. Naturally science must carry on systematic research – but luck and coincidence also play their part in scientific discoveries.

I was once told the fabulous story of how the brilliant chemist Adolf von Bayer (1835–1917), who won the Nobel Prize for Chemistry in 1905, is supposed to have discovered artificial indigo. In the laboratory all kinds of mixtures that Bayer and his colleagues had concocted were bubbling away in glass flasks over Bunsen burners. When the professor went to lunch with his colleagues, the laboratory assistant was supposed to turn off the gas, but he forgot. When Bayer returned, all the glass receptacles had burst. Their contents shimmered on the laboratory tables in a bewildering variety of shades. The laboratory assistant and Bayer's colleagues were in a hurry to sweep up the shattered fragments, but the brilliant Bayer said: 'first we'll analyse what's lying on the tables.' In one of the stains he is supposed to have discovered the chemical synthesis of the precious dyestuff which until then had had to be obtained from indigo-forming creatures by a complicated and expensive process. That was in 1880. As early as 1897 artificial indigo in the purest form was on sale commercially. What did Giordano Bruno say? 'Se non è vero, è molto ben trovato!' 'If it isn't true, it's a very good story!'

Professor Ferdinand Porsche (1875–1951) related in an interview that he had drawn countless feasible shapes for the Volkswagen on the drawing-board, before he spent a whole day of his holidays watching a colony of beetles and suddenly realised that the insect's shape was ideal for his Volkswagen. Science should take out a subscription to luck and coincidence.

I should only like to point out that neither is calculable. Starting from my theory, I would like to state that extra-terrestrials with a culture and civilisation thousands of years older than ours were probably faced with the same hurdles that seem insurmountable to us today. And that they conquered them by planned research and/or luck and/or coincidence and/or spontaneous brilliant ideas.

No one can reproach me for talking about the miracle of a speedy realisation of mankind's wish. I only claimed that the fact that *we* have not yet mastered interstellar space flight technology does not mean that extra-terrestrials have not long since had it at their fingertips. The pointers to their former stays on the blue planet are too impressive.

A few weeks after my conversation with Professor Ruppe the post brought me the August 1976 number of *Ancient Skies*, a periodical published in Chicago. In it I read an article of Ruppe's and I should like to quote its conclusion.

I was interviewed by von Däniken for his new book. Much to my surprise I had to revise my fixed former position that interstellar travel was impossible. Now I declare that limited interstellar journeys to targets that are not more than ten light years away seem feasible.

3: Myths are Eye-witness Accounts

On 16 May 1792, Henri Guellemin went to dinner with his friend Charles Sanson who lived in the Faubourg Saint Germain. Guellemin stayed the night, because Robespierre had again imposed a nine o'clock curfew all over Paris.

Sanson (1740-1793) was an executioner. Like many of his colleagues, he worked the machine invented by Dr Guillotin that enabled Robspierre to have 15000 people 'painlessly' decapitated in the capital alone. Sanson had the honour of sending King Louis XVI and Marie Antionette to the other world.

When Guellemin left Sanson's house in the early morning of 17 May, he was arrested before he had gone a few yards. He was charged with having distributed subversive pamphlets on the Ile de la Cité the night before, and with having stabbed a Jacobin in a brawl.

When the honourable and indispensable Charles Sanson heard about the arrest hours later, he went to the Revolutionary Tribunal and put on record that Guellemin must have been wrongly convicted of the crime he was accused of, as he had never left Sanson's house from the evening of 16 May to the morning of 17 May.

They did not believe the executioner, for Guellemin, admittedly under torture, had described a number of details which could only have been known to someone who had witnessed the previous night's affray: the fact that the penultimate line of the pamphlet was upside down, that two women had taken part in the brawl, that a Jacobin had pulled their caps off their heads, that the fatal dagger had a damascene blade.

Sanson could not understand how his friend could have known all this. By making his statement Guellemin had delivered himself up to the guillotine.

On 29 May Henri Guellemin was led to the guillotine in the Place Grève. His friend let the blade hiss down.

No one has ever been able to explain where Guellemin got his knowledge, but it was expensive knowledge because he paid for it with his head.

The equally uncanny knowledge which the Dogon of West Africa possess, but theoretically could not possibly possess, can on the other hand be explained – by means of a first-hand account. I am speaking of the mystery-enshrouded knowledge

Fig. 35. Dogon dance at the Sigui feast near Sangha in Mali. According to Marcel Griaule the cross is the symbol of equilibrium between heaven and earth, an emblem of the heavenly order. The Sigui celebrations can be traced back to the twelfth century, but they are estimated to be 1000 years older.

of the Dogon, who live – 225,000 of them – on the Bandiagara plateau and in the Hombori Mountains of the West African Republic of Mali.

At the end of 1975 I read in a newspaper that a British astronomer Robert Temple had written a book which confirmed my theories. He had shown that specific details of the system of Sirius were handed down in the age-old mythology of the Dogon tribe, exhibiting knowledge they could not possibly have had according to their level of culture. Temple, it said in the report, had proved that from the earliest times the Dogon had the position, gravitation and orbit of Sirius's invisible satellite.

I was electrified by this report.

Who were the Dogon tribe? I had never heard of them. And who was Mr. Temple?

I wrote some letters to my 'Fifth Column' in England, asking who this Robert Temple was and what he had published about the Dogon and their mysterious knowledge. At the same time I bought a lot of books about the Dogon. Among them was *The Sirius Mystery* (1) by Robert K. G. Temple. A fascinating book. I wrote to him and congratulated him on his discovery. A few months later we met in London.

Contrary to the report, Temple turned out to be an American linguist, not a British astronomer. Born in 1945, he is an exceptionally quiet, correct man who as yet has no idea of the malice and odium that lies in store for him when his book becomes the success which it deserves and I wish for him with all my heart. The fact that Temple is a Member of the Royal Astronomical Society proves his scientific qualifications.

For the extract about the Dogon's extraordinary knowledge of the Sirius system I am chiefly indebted to my conversation with Robert Temple, for it was through him that I first came across the literature on the Dogon.

In 1931 the French anthropologist, Dr Marcel Griaule, visited the Dogon people when on a scientific expedition in what was then the colonial territory of Soudan, in French West Africa. It was an encounter that bewildered and fascinated Griaule. He heard about a mythology that was complicated and difficult and seemed to be impenetrably bound up with the stars. Among the tribes there were ceremonies that were only repeated, and even today can only be repeated, once every fifty years. Each generation has to prepare new masks for these ceremonies, and for centuries the Dogon have stored them away as a kind of village archive to give future generations information about the past.

In 1946 Griaule visited the Dogon again. This time he was accompanied by the ethnologist Dr Germaine Dieterlen, who is now General Secretary of the Societé des Africanistes at the Museé de l'Homme in Paris.

In 1951 the two scholars published the results of four years' research under the title *A Sudanese Sirius System* (2). But the ethnological account of the myths of an African tribe was read seriously only by a small circle of experts. A delayed time-fuse was smouldering away in that account which exploded twenty-five years later.

What is it that is so astonishing about the myths of the Dogon? Dreams, religious superstitions, phantasmagoria or accurate knowledge?

Griaule and Dieterlen found out that the knowledge of the Sirius system was held by four Sudanese groups: the Dogon of Bandiagara, the Bambara and Bozo of Segu, and the Minianka of Kutiala.

The authors begin with a statement that the reader must bear constantly in mind, if he wants to understand the objectivity of their information. They write:

> For our part the documents assembled have not given rise to any hypotheses or research into their origin. They were simply arranged in such a way that the testimony of the four most important tribes could be combined in a single book. There was never any question of finding out how people, who possess no instruments at all, can chart the course and special characteristics of practically invisible stars.

Every fifty years the Dogon celebrate their Sigui Feast. The point of this ceremony is the desire to renew the world. *Po Tolo*, the star of Sigui, determines the date of the feast. *Po* is the smallest grain of corn known to the Dogon. The botanical name for *Po* or *Fonio* (as it is known in West Africa) is *Digitaria Exilis* and the little *Po* has gone into the literature on the subject under the heading *Digitaria*.

Digitaria, so Dogon mythology tells us, revolves around brightly shining Sirius once every fifty years and this satellite is *invisible*. Moreover, the Dogon go on, Digitaria is the *heaviest star*, and determines the position of Sirius, *in that it revolves round it on its course.*

Fig. 36. Every fifty years, for every Sigui feast, the Dogon make masks which are carefully filed away. They trace the continuity of this festival back to an as yet undated past.

Dogon mythology dates back to the dim mists of time. Where does it get this information about Sirius and Sirius B that was not known to us until the last century?

In astronomy Sirius is also known as the Dog Star. In other words it comes from the time when Sirius rose during the dog days, i.e. during the fairly regularly hot periods occurring at the end of July and August. It has long been known that a retrograde movement of the point of intersection (equinoctial point) between the celestial equator and the ecliptic (path of the earth) takes place owing to the spinning motion of the earth's axis, i.e. the co-ordinates of the constellations change. Because of this change observations of a star have to be replaced by observations of another star.

Sirius is a star of the first magnitude in the constellation Canis Major in the southern sky. It is the brightest star of the hemisphere, white in colour and 8.5 light years (one light year = 9.5 billion km) away. Sirius also has a permanent white satellite of the ninth magnitude. It was discovered in 1844 by the Königsberg astronomer Friedrich Wilhelm Bessel (1784-1846) and *seen* for the first time in 1862 by the American optician and mechanic Alvan Clarke (1804-1887). Whereas

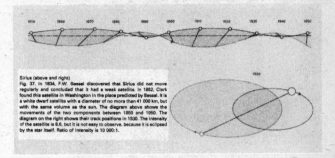

Sirius (above and right)
Fig. 37. In 1834, F.W. Bessel discovered that Sirius did not move regularly and concluded that it had a weak satellite. In 1862, Clark found this satellite in Washington in the place predicted by Bessel. It is a white dwarf satellite with a diameter of no more than 41 000 km, but with the same volume as the sun. The diagram above shows the movements of the two components between 1850 and 1950. The diagram on the right shows their track positions in 1930. The intensity of the satellite is 8.6, but it is not easy to observe, because it is eclipsed by the star itself. Ratio of intensity is 10 000:1.

Sirius is a normal star, its companion Sirius B belongs to the class of white dwarfs with a very great density.

The following story can be found in any good reference book:

In 1834 Bessel first discovered that the motions of Sirius were irregular, that it did not move in a straight line but rather like a kind of wave. For 12 years he had his assistants plot the positions of Sirius at regular intervals. For he found his suspicion confirmed that *something* influenced Sirius's orbit. The astronomer called the invisible *something* Sirius B. It was impossible to see Sirius B even with the best telescopes of his day, the first third of last century. Astronomers assumed that it was a star giving off no light. That is what they *assumed*.

But in 1862 the American Clarke, who had already made a name as a constructor of many large telescopes, used a telescope with a lense 47 cm in diameter and found the hitherto invisible Sirius B in the position postulated by Bessel! It had not been possible to make out the brightness of the newly discovered satellite owing to the minimal distance from the ultra bright Sirius. Sirius B was not in the shadow, but in the excessively bright light of its big brother.

Meanwhile Sirius B was registered as a white dwarf. White

dwarfs have very great density but a luminosity of only about 0.0003 per cent. In relation to Sirius A the density of Sirius B = 0.42 : 27000! Sirius B has a diameter of 41000 km but has the same mass as the sun. Because of this incredible mass, Sirius B is able to influence the orbit of the brighter Sirius A in a rhythm of 50.04 ± 0.09 years by directing it along a repeating wave-like line.

In tabular form it looks like this:

Absolute brightness			In solar units	
		Mass	Radius	Density
Sirius A	1.3	2.4	1.8	0.42
Sirius B	11.2	0.96	0.034	27000

Present-day knowledge	Dogon knowledge
Sirius B as the guider of Sirus A was first discovered and sighted in the middle of the last century.	Sirius is not the basis of the system. It is one of the central points in the orbit of a tiny star called Digitaria. The Dogon have never seen Digitaria.
Sirius B was not visible. It took the most modern powerful telescopes and intensive research before its orbit could be observed.	The spiritual and material components of the sacrifice were sent to Digitaria whose existence was *known* but which remained *invisible*.
Sirius B is a tiny star, a white dwarf.	Digitaria is *infinitely small*. During its development, it gave everything that existed.
Sirius B's orbit lasts 50.04±0.09 years.	Digitaria's orbit lasts *about 50 years* and corresponds to the first seven periods of government, each of seven years.

| Sirius B is a white dwarf of exceptional density. | Digitaria is the *heaviest star*. It specifically determines the position of Sirius, in that it circles it with its orbit. |

The American linguist Robert Temple drew diagrams of the orbit of Sirius B according to information in Dogon myths and according to data supplied by the latest astronomic research. In his commentary he states:

The similarity is so striking that even the most inexperienced eye will see at once that the identicalness of the two sketches is achieved down to the smallest detail. There is no need for the perfectionist to bring out his millimeter ruler. The fact is demonstratêd and what it says is that the Dogon tribe has a thorough knowledge of the most incredible and subtle principles of Sirius B and its orbit round Sirius A.

In other words modern knowledge and the wisdom of ancient myths coincide completely!

When the Dogon tradition relates that Digitaria *revolves round itself in less than a year* we do not know whether they are talking about a terrestrial or a Digitarian year, but I find it amazing enough that a primitive African tribe should know anything about a heavenly body's own rotation. After all, the knowledge that our earth rotates on its own axis is not so very old. Yet the Dogon have known since very ancient times that a *whirlwind motion is the basic movement of the world!* Today everyone knows that the galaxies rotate with a spiral motion.

Presumably our astronomers will discover one day what the Dogon have long since – how long since? – known, that Sirius B is by no means the only satellite of the radiant Sirius. Dogon myths tell of the star Emme Ya, female Sorgho, bigger than Digitaria, but four times lighter in weight, which is also supposed to have a *larger orbit* in the *same direction* as Sirius B once in 50 years. After a heartening verification of the Sirius system of the Dogon, our astronomers should take the lessons of the myths seriously. They tell us that Emme Ya is *accompanied by a satellite,* which is called the 'star of women'. They also know about a third companion of Sirius to which they give the name *Shoemaker*. The Shoemaker is supposed to be further away from Sirius than all the óther planets and to revolve in the *opposite direction*.

It is not yet possible to check the details about Emme Ya and the Shoemaker. We lack the astronomical apparatus to locate the satellites of a star 8.5 light years away. So until they have been scientifically verified I do not number Emme Ya and the Shoemaker among those visible objects which clearly prove that the Dogon had at their disposal knowledge they *could not have had* according to their general state of knowledge.

I see my critics looking desperately for a back door behind which they could lock the Dogon story up. After all, I hear them ask, can we really 'believe' the investigations by the two French scholars. I say! Who's babbling about 'believing'. Griaule and Dieterlen worked more seriously than those who instantly want to call on 'belief', when in fact accurate knowledge is involved. When the two French scholars published their report in 1951, a landing on the moon still seemed to be pure fantasy and my books came out nearly twenty years later, so I cannot have infected them with my imagination. Why, by all the Dogon gods, should two reputable scholars invent such a story? No, they brought factual material out of the African bush.

It is worth considering whether an African explorer could not have introduced the extraordinary knowledge of the Sirius system into the Black Continent, someone who knew about the astronomical discoveries of the middle of the nineteenth century. This explorer would have had to be a high-ranking astronomer . . . and would have to have been half crazy. Who else would have had the absurd ambition to supply primitive peoples with information about the invisible Sirius satellite?

I shall have to bitterly disappoint all the sceptics who cling to the straw that some great unknown must have given the Dogon their information at some time, because one must admit in all fairness that their knowledge is simply inexplicable. For this Mr X must have given his astronomical extension course in Mali, the home of the Dogon, centuries ago, at a time when we knew absolutely nothing about Sirius B! The wooden Sigui masks form a collection filed away in uninterrupted sequence which scholars have dated to the beginning of the fifteenth century. I invite anyone who can show me knowledge of the Sirius B system in the storehouse of verified western knowledge of that time to make an immediate journey to Mali.

The Dogon also observe rituals connected with their family beer receptacles which enable us to draw inferences about very very old Sigui celebrations.

From time immemorial every Hogon (village chief) had to weave a container from the fibres of a special tree. It was a watertight woven vessel into which the first ritual beer was poured. This beer was served to every family in small portions and they mixed it with their own brew. During the Sigui ceremony the family 'beer barrels' have to be brought into contact with the Hogon's receptacle. After the festival all receptacles are hung on the main beam of the Hogon's house in clearly arranged and permanent series. The patriarch Ongnonlu Dolo, one of the oldest Dogon in the district, relates that his great-grandfather had had eight more, much older vessels, in addition to the ones hanging in his house. Apart from the evidence of the masks, the first Sigui celebration can be traced back to the twelfth century by the beer containers. But ethnologists are by no means sure that the first celebration should be dated to this period. They attribute another 1000 years to the Sigui celebrations, because as far as is known the Dogon have not always lived in the same geographical territory. It is assumed that they immigrated to Mali from regions as yet unknown. Regardless of when they may have begun, Sigui ceremonies would not have been possible without knowledge of Sirius B.

If I postulate that the Dogon *must* have got their knowledge from extra-terrestrials, the bright boys will object that Sirius B is not a planet and consequently no extra-terrestrial beings could have come from it. I would never claim that they did. Nor do we find this in the Dogon myths. They mention *satellites*.

There has been a good deal of discussion on whether a double-star system could have planets and whether a planet could exist at all inside the vital zones of two suns. In general, science rejects the idea of planets with suitable conditions for life revolving round double stars, because the planets, conditioned by the complicated gravitational relations between the two suns would have to trace an 'impossible orbit' around their two central bodies.

Those are current opinions. They cannot be proved. We cannot make out planets in other solar systems with the telescopes available today. But whether or not the Sirius system has planets does not alter the fact that the Dogon have known Sirius B from the earliest times. Without mirrors and double-bottomed boxes and without telescopes of any kind.

When nothing else will help, people nowadays have recourse to acupuncture . . . or the boundless possibilities of parapsychology. Acupuncture is painless. Parapsychology hurts when it tries to explain the rational by the irrational. Some smart readers are probably saying: 'It's quite simple! Somehow, somewhere, at some time, a Dogon brain developed mediumistic powers. His spirit floated up to Sirius and came back omniscient!' Please, gentlemen, things cannot be explained as easily as that.

In 1970 Mme Geniève Calame-Griaule published the book *Black Genesis*, (3) based on material belonging to her dead father. It contains answers to the question: where did the Dogon get their knowledge from?

Amma was the original and only god.

Amma created the stars out of clouds of earth which he hurled into space.

This old tradition is very reminiscent of the Big Bang Theory currently accepted by science as the most probable explanation of the origin of the universe. The Belgian physicist and mathematician Georges Lemaître introduced it. It postulates that milliards of years ago all matter was concentrated in one primordial atom, a heavy mass of matter in the universe, which constantly pressed inwards on its core. The forces multiplied so powerfully that the lump of matter exploded and shattered into billions and billions of parts. During a long, long period of consolidation the parts assembled into an infinite number of galaxies.

Is the name of the God Amma a substitute for this Big Bang process?

The Dogon priest Ogotemmeli put this on record:

The vital force of the earth is water. . . This force exists even in stone, for moisture is everywhere. . . Nommo descended to earth and brought grains from plants, which already grew in heavenly fields. . . After creating the earth, plants and animals, Nommo created the first pair of humans, from whom later eight human ancestors issued. These ancestors lived to an incredible age.

If you are at all familiar with the mythologies of all five continents, you will find it natural that Nommo returned 'to heaven' when his work was done. But the statement that 'water exists even in stone' is new and staggering. A daring idea of the myth-teller, when you think that he saw masses of unexploitable and useless stones lying around in the Savanna and the Sahara.

Water does exist in stone, but that is a brand new item of knowledge. When all possibilities for the survival of men in manned space-stations on the moon were being examined, scientists carried out experiments with stones. They discovered an admittedly expensive technique for extracting hydrogen and oxygen molecules and linking them up.

We are indebted to Ogotemmeli for traditions which seem to be quite mysterious. He put on record that the very first human ancestors had tried to seek out their creator Nommo in heaven, but although they were *all like one another in their being*, they had always had to live apart and they were not allowed to visit each other. One of them, who later became the first smith on earth, disregarded the ban and visited another woman. Ogotemmeli says:

Since that had made them unclean, they had to separate from each other. And so that they could live, they went down to earth. . .for there they purified themselves.

I at once think of quarantine!

We assume that Nommo, as an extra-terrestrial, did not grow up on our planet for he had no terrestrial forbears. So Nommo, who lived in the cosmos, altered existing, but in his view underdeveloped, life 'in his own image' by deliberate artificial mutation. This 'ennobled' form of life then continued to grow under the conditions on the planet earth. Out of and against this environment it developed defences against terrestrial bacteria that endangered life. The mutated life immunised itself within its living space. In order not to risk his own life, Nommo could not meet his own creations even in 'heaven'. They were forced to return to their own kind on earth where they 'purified' themselves.

Fourteen years after their first account Griaule and Dieterlen published more material on the Dogon's knowledge of the Sirius system in their book *The Pale Fox (Le renard pâle)*. Their reports showed that the Dogon's astronomical knowledge went far beyond the system they had already investigated. They also handed down information about our solar system, Jupiter and Venus. The Dogon were not only familiar with the Sirius calendar, they also possessed a solar calendar and had a special agricultural agenda.

It would take us too far afield to go into all that.

My task is to present the Dogon's scientifically documented knowledge of the Sirius system. *Strictly speaking* – who can deny it – they could not have had that knowledge.

The knowledge is centuries old. At no time did the Dogon have any optical or astronomical aids; nor did they know how to use algebra . . . nevertheless they have been familiar with items of knowledge which have only been available to us for a hundred years.

The Sirius mystery has been discussed in the famous scientific periodical *Nature*.[4] Professor Michael Ovenden, Professor of Astronomy at the University of Vancouver, Canada, tried to find explanations for the inexplicable:

In order to understand the survival of ancient traditions among the Dogon, we have only to remember that a leading Moslem university was flourishing at Timbuctu in Mali during the sixteenth century. The traditions of the Greeks, Egyptians and Sumerians flowed through Timbuctu.

So what? What difference does that make? Whether the Dogon were the first to know the most accurate details about Sirius B or whether the knowledge was even older and already familiar to the Greeks, Egyptians and Sumerians, does not alter the fact at all. For up to now there is *no other* accurate tradition about the Sirius B system, except the Dogon one!

I even accept Professor Ovenden's 'explanation' if that is what it is supposed to be. It leads back into an even more distant past.

MYTHS ARE HISTORICAL MEMORIES

For me the Dogon myth is a perfect example of the fact that all myths contain, as the ancient Greeks would say, the concepts 'word', 'talk' and 'story'. Their timeless traditions, therefore contain a claim to truth we should take note of.

Once, in their origins, they were eye-witness accounts of real events. The first tellers of myths knew what they were talking about.

Get hold of a very old potsherd from some archaeological site or other, bury it under two metres of sand or stone in a different place, and then take an archaelogist with a spade to the spot. He will weave you a fantastic story about this find, telling you who settled there, and when and why.

Hand an etymologist, theologian or philosopher the text of a myth hitherto unknown to him. You will be amazed when you hear everything that the ancients must have *thought* and *believed* in and all the nebulous and fantastic ideas they were trying to express in the myth.

You get the impression that the scholars must once have played marbles with the authors, so accurately but also differently (according to their faculty) do they interpret the ancient myths. We understand why the great philosopher Karl Jaspers (1883-1969) mistrusted the 'superstition of

Fig. 38. Mythology in stone. A winged deity, photographed in the Museum of Colima, Mexico.

science'. For him myths always contained symbols and cyphers that needed clarification. If we take the core of the myth's content as the beginning of historical consciousness, the door to our early history lies open.

In my opinion it cannot be a question of understanding word after word, sentence by sentence. At best we can find the highest common factor in the information and still not know how shaky the ground it stands on is. Mythological research itself shows this. What was considered absolutely certain yesterday, often becomes a rubbish heap over which a few bright boys still stumble and others are glad to sweep under the carpet.

It is more profitable to seek the heart of the myth and dispose of the obfuscations with which time has covered it. The grotesque thing is that the essence of the stories was not understood by the narrators themselves. For lack of suitable (e.g. technical) words it was hidden in a desert of words and abstruse images.

My curiosity is boundless. I want to know all about the mythological gods, the meaning of the circumstances under which they appeared and acted. What sort of personalities had they, what were they made of? If they were spirit, how could people see and talk to them? Why did 'gods' appear at all, why did they work and enjoy themselves on our ancient earth? What was their purpose in showing their power, their knowledge, their superior abilities? Why did they always return to their heavenly home and where was it? Why did they announce that they would return? Were all these gods in every country and on every continent real beings or simply the products of riotous imaginations?

To me the core of the messages is in the exact description of the gods' arrival and behaviour, factual references to the origin of the universe and the first life on earth, as well as the 'birth' of the first being endowed with reason and every clue to the beginning of human civilisation: the cultivation of plants, the rearing of animals, accurate travel reports of the unknown visitors. I consider reports of the original act of creation which are so accurate that they do not have to be believed, but can be accepted, as elementary news.

My fellow countryman, that great biologist, Professor Adolf Portmann (b 1897), described both science and myth simply

Fig. 39. Mythology woven into cloth. A symbolic figure depicted in a very technological way on an old Peruvian cloak – ca 200 B.C.

as 'the human spirit's attempt to classify things'. His words encourage me to consider myths from the point of view of present-day classification. I should like to classify under the heading of present-day knowledge, classify without philological hair splitting, classify in order to find the answers to the why, whither and wherefores of our existence.

Classification is a stimulating occupation for a stamp collector like myself. You begin with empty spaces and watch with pleasure how they gradually fill up. In my collection of myths the Greek spaces were almost over-richly filled, but others stayed desolate and empty. The Dogon myths inspired me to put African myths under the microscope. A fruitful attempt at classification!

ATTEMPTS AT CLASSIFICATION

Space 1 : 'Heaven'.
What were the characteristics of heaven in African myths?

I know from books interpreting mythology that our ancestors imagined heaven *qua* heaven as a nichevo, a void. In our
great-grandfathers' day that it was acceptable insurance
against surprises. At that time there was no space travel. At
that time there were no giant telescopes to allow us an
astronomical look into the 'void' through a great window. At
that time people did not know that heaven is a very real world,
in which our Milky Way alone is estimated to have 200
milliard stars.

I am not blaming earlier mythological scholars for this in
the least, but I do not understand present-day ones who still
represent heaven to man as an imaginary dream-world, in
spite of modern knowledge. Do they do it, so that myths can
go on 'floating' in the uncontrollable irrational?

Fig. 40. Mythology in stone. Man or monkey? I don't know. At
all events this being carved out of a 20-ton monolith gazes
fixedly at the heavens, an observation post that was obviously given him in the distant past. An Olmec statue from San
Lorenzo, Mexico.

At any rate heaven has always been a real and bustling world to the African peoples and tribes. Differing in colour, physique and brain capacity, with varying cultures and religions, separated from one another by social and political structures, they *all* shared the idea that heaven was inhabited and that the gods, in flesh and blood, came to them from there.

So here I give some examples* from African myths about a peopled heaven which sent its omnipotent messengers down to earth: (5)

Masai: Divine couples produced the bright heavenly people with eternal life. God sent some children to earth.

Ja-Luo: The primaeval Apodho came down from heaven with his wife and all the gifts of civilisation.

Madi-Morui: The first men lived in heaven. Until the bluebird pecked the ladder of heaven to pieces, a lively traffic to the earth existed.

Ganda: The two original women fell from heaven.

Nyoro: God sent the first human couple down from heaven when he established the world. The man had a tail and produced two maidens and a boy, who for their part bore the chameleon, the father of mankind and the moon.

Kivu pygmies: The progenitor fell from heaven.

Kuluwe: The first human couple came from heaven with seed, a rake, an axe, a pair of bellows, etc.

Bena-Lulua: God sent his four sons down to earth.

Ashanti: Seven men created by god climbed down to earth on a chain. After they had produced men there, they returned to their heavenly home.

* Further examples from African myths with a similar content can be found in the bibliography for this chapter.

There was quite a lot of activity in the uninhabited void in which the ostensibly primitive tribes believed.

The large Masai tribe in North East Africa tell in their myths of the red, blue, white and black original gods who all came down *from cloudland.*Apparently these gods had divergent conceptions of their earthly missions, for one destroyed what the other had just built up. According to Masai beliefs the 'gods' were quarrelsome heroes.

The Masai say that there were animals, too, in heaven, for the white god, who produced the sun, moon and stars, and created plants, brought *animals down from heaven,* after he had seen to it that there was food for the fauna.

Things are just as turbulent in the myths of the Ziba, a Bantu people in Tanzania. Their original god was called Rugaba. Shrewdly they do not appeal to him or make sacrifices to him, because they know that he dwells far away *in the universe,* surrounded by *ghostlike beings,* with whom he spent a long time *in the darkness.* Rugaba produced the first human being when the darkness came to an end. Indeed, since the first T.V. programmes showing the moon flights every child knows that space, =heaven, is apparently infinite darkness. Today we understand why Rugaba created the first man after he had this darkness behind him, in other words when he reached our planet.

Scholars claim that the heaven so frequently described was supposed to be the paradise of perfect happiness and eternal life for primitive peoples. This new 'myth' does not hold water, for people died in heaven, too. The Jagga, a Bantu tribe near Kilimanjaro, relate that one man who was sent back to heaven died there, as did a forgetful woman who was supposed to bring to earth her present from above. (6) No, the heaven of the myths was no Nirvana to their narrators. It was a place in which life and death existed cheek by jowl, a real world. A propos: extra-terrestrials are not immortal.

Space 2: Technical gods.

The Nandi tribe and the closely related Suk live in Kenya, between the Masai steppe and Lake Rudolf. Their highest heavenly chief is called Tororut. He lived in heaven, was like men but had wings, *whose beating produced lightning and whose flapping was thunder.*

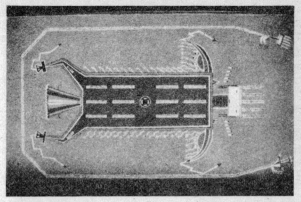

Fig. 41. Mythology in the form of a technical drawing. The Navajo Indians, USA, stylised the 'gods' they observed like technical drawings. Note the symmetry these 'natives' were capable of and the 'exhaust jets' they put between the deity's legs.

The Nandi have a god with the tongue-twisting name of Chepkeliensokol. Translated this jaw-breaker means *'the thing with the nine ray-legs'*.

Unusual?

This strange myth, (7) well worthy of attention, is handed down by the Pangwe, an important Bantu people:

The lightning lay packed in a special egg. The first mother received fire from it. The egg broke and from its two halves came all visible things. The upper half turned into a tree mushroom and rose high up into heaven. The lower half remained behind.

Naturally I am tempted to comment on this eye-witness account, but it would embarrass me, because the cypher is so obvious that we at once realise that the ancient, technological event that was experienced and handed down is identical with a modern technological event that we have all seen.

Space 3: The original state of the earth.

The Bemba are a negro tribe in Zambia. Their myths tell

that in the beginning the earth was *bare and made of mud*. The god Kabezya came – guess where from? – and created order. He controlled the water, created plants first and then brought animals from heaven, whence at the same time he also let two humans fall to earth, which they populated with their useless descendants.

The Pende tribe, in the southern Congo, relate that at the beginning of time there was *nothing*. Darkness was everywhere. There were still no rivers on earth although it rained incessantly. Only when the rain stopped did the highest god Mawese arrange the water into watercourses, then he created ignorant men, who had incomplete bodies, an *only-body*. Mawese was creator of the universe and all the stars, but also an instructor in the cultivation of millet, maize and palms, and even the loathsome snakes were his handiwork.

Mawese, weary of being alone, took Muvadila to wife, and became the father of all peoples, showing his potency. When at last the earth seemed sufficiently colonised, he returned to his heaven, taking with him some of his men whom he later sent back to earth bearing fire.

Mawese really thought of everything!

The Bushongo, a Bantu Tribe, give a chronologically perfect account of the creation in their mythology: (8)

In the beginning there was only darkness on the earth, which was covered with water. Then came Bumba, a light-skinned giant, who got a stomach-ache one day and vomited. First he vomited the stars, the sun and the moon. The water dried up with the heat of the sun and sandbanks appeared. A son of Bumba vomited a plant from which all other plants proceeded. The he vomited the living creatures of the earth, first the most important animals, then men. He also vomited medicines, meteorites and the razor. Then *the animals continued the creation*. Once the earth had been created by this universal vomiting, Bumba went to the villages of men and proclaimed the forbidden foods. He appointed a man as the first king, *as god on earth*. Then he rose into the air and disappeared into heaven.

If we disregard the unpleasant way in which Bumba got the earth going, the knowledge of the original state of the earth is staggering. Our own awareness of it dates back to 1953.

That was when Dr. Stanely Miller made his famous

experiment of demonstrating the first prerequisites for life in an artificially created primordial atmosphere, by irradiating minerals, salts, phosphates, etc. in a retort. Science christened the product of this successful experiment the 'primal soup'. Let me explain briefly. Miller was able to show that in the beginning of all organic life the water masses evaporated and rose up as thick vapour with the hot radiation from the earth. At a great height they cooled down and descended in the form of torrential rain. Science estimates some 1.2 milliard years as the period during which a medium for nourishing the first life was formed from the primal soup. A few years either way doesn't make much difference.

When and from whom did the myth-tellers get their knowledge of this elementary cycle?

For the myths give the course of events in this exact order: nothing – desert – mud – rain – solar heat – dry land – plants – animals – men – food – medicines – tools – fire.

A genesis of considerable qualities!

Space 4: The 'creator'.

If the mythological heaven were something imaginary, the end-product of longing, logically only incorporeal 'figures' could have inhabited it, i.e. spirits, whatever you understand by that.

But the gods/spirits of African myths have a firm handshake. Can you shake hands with spirits?

The pygmies were called 'Tom Thumbs' or 'dwarfs' by the Greeks because of their tiny stature. They live in the tropical rain forests on lake Kibu. They know that their god Imana is high up in heaven. But he was not idle up there, for he created men. The story goes like this:

God also created Rurema and he came in order to create the earth together with god. Although Rurema lives in heaven, he created all the things of this world and he has a body (!). The smiths (!), too, live up there; they never came to earth. Their abode is in heaven . . . The earth was a forest that came into being by itself, yet it is Rurema who created it.

The Luba (Baluba) grew from several tribes to form a Bantu people with several dialects, that lives in the southern

Congo between Lualuba, the upper reaches of the Congo and Lake Tanganyika. Although telling the story in many tongues they all have the chief god Mukulu who *lives in heaven*. First he created the stars, the sun and the moon. When he had switched on the heavenly lights, he made the earth, on which he promptly summoned up water, sowed the seeds of plants and settled animals.

After this paternal preparation he sent the chief god Kyomba, the first man, with two women down to earth. Kyomba bore – read and be amazed – valuable seeds in his hair and *the thing that kindles fire*. This multi-purpose *homo* instructed the earth-dwellers how to name things which they did not know and taught them how to use them sensibly.

The beginning of historical consciousness is the formation of names and ideas. Obviously. That this beginning was initiated by celestial visitors speaks for their superior intelligence.

As early as 1870 the famous etymologist Professor Max Müller said in a lecture to the Royal Institution of London:

> I claim that every genuine etymology supplies us with a historical fact, because the first bestowal of a name was a historical fact. And what is more a most important fact for the later development of the ideas of antiquity.

The Ja-Luo from Lake Victoria claim that their original ancestor Apodho climbed down from heaven with grain and cattle, synchronous with the Basari myth which has it that the heavenly god Unumbotte gave the people of earth seeds for sowing, yet warned them first to break *the earth, which had not been broken before*. At a time when man had not yet stripped the earth with chemicals, god gave a useful biological piece of advice.

If we follow the African myths, heaven was once a great seed firm and a luxuriant hothouse. The Tussi from Ruanda (Burundi) say that at the beginning of their existence the heavens split open and *every kind of seed fell to earth*. The heavenly prince Mugulu, progenitor of the Jagga, brought a banana, a potato, a bean, a corn-cob and a hen with him. Because he had forgotten corn for the hen, he had to go back to heaven . . . and was never seen again. There the fate of all mortals overtook him; he died. So Mugulu's heaven was no

Fig. 42. Mythology with a 'space traveller look'. A figurine of a 'god' of ancient Mexican origin, found at Tlapacoya. The accoutrements of the astronaut – face mask, belt with attached torch, and overalls – are unmistakable.

paradise of blessed immortality. Moreover the heavenly lady Unyoro suffered the same fate for the same reason. She had forgotten the seeds of eleusine (a species of grass), returned quickly to the heavenly hothouse and died. (9)

As the creators were obviously expert colonisers perhaps their organisation of things gave an answer to open questions. We have all fallen victims to the compulsory anthropological view that one thing has always developed nicely and neatly from another. There is a family tree for everything that lives . . . with negative reports, for example, as regards maize, bananas and wheat. Today new cultivated species are constantly coming on the market. On the basis of soundly based knowledge, plants, trees and animals are crossed by highly complicated processes. Who possessed such knowledge in primordial times? Who were the breeders and cultivators . . . or the importers?

The Masai myths give one something to think about. Their great white god produced Maitumbe, the first man, in heaven. After the white god had provided nourishment on the blue planet, he shipped Maitumbe to earth. There he became a kind of African Noah. He became *the progenitor of our race*. Without a female partner the highly gifted Maitumbe produced seven men: *from within himself, for he was simultaneously male and female*.

Here I pluck a kernel (a sign-post!) out of the waste of wordy reports. Even if we must sympathise with our original ancestors, we cannot ignore the fact that all the myths coincide in saying that the first earthly being was created to be both male and female at once. That is something well worth taking note of!

However primitive these simple forefathers may have been, they weren't stupid and they had eyes in their heads. Looking around them, turned into voyeurs for lack of housing, they saw how their kind coupled and devoted themselves industriously to the highly enjoyable business of reproduction.

Beings are supposed to have been male or female in one body. Was a totally unintelligible artificial act of creation indicated? That is such a remarkable kernel that I shall be glad to crack it later.

The story of Mrs Sun and Mr Moon that the Nhonga-Amo tell is also puzzling. Once the sun and moon used to take their meals together and on one occasion the moon let a piece of liver burn. That made the sun angry: 'You have erred!' she said and burnt his face. Since then the moon has had scars on it.

Only a story, but how did the Africans know that the face of the moon had 'scars' (craters) on it?

OPEN QUESTIONS

Instead of footnotes, a couple of questions:

School etymology says that these early men *must* have imagined their gods in heaven, because heaven to them was the eternal, the unattainable, in short – bliss. Where were they to seek their 'gods', except in the universe? Yet they all came down from there in very phsyical form and with the most useful things in their luggage and the wisest advice in their heads. Obviously 'heaven' was the dwelling-place of their 'gods', but it was a very animated active heaven.

If the topographies of heaven occurred only once or twice and the descriptions of divine activities were in completely different traditions, I would accept them as possible coincidences of poetic inspiration. But the themes are tuned *a capella*. Can we accept that as coincidence?

Presumably people have been creatures of habit in all ages. They have always gone through the daily routine, and still do. A beautiful sunrise is not nearly such a wonderful experience for a shepherd, who sees it often, as for a hiker who gets up early on holiday. When the return of the first astronauts from the first space flight was transmitted direct from the Pacific, the world held its breath. The viewing figures were of the order that is perhaps only reached every four years at the peak of the Olympics. As moon flights were repeated, the unprecedented became routine. Interest flagged; pictures on the news lasted only a few seconds. Once the feat could be repeated it became an everyday affair and no one spoke about it any more.

There must have been sensational events which were handed down from generation to generation. Naturally they were none of the natural processes accompanying everyday life, as we are taught. Naturally the sowing of seed in the ground, the rearing of animals and the naming of things in the world around also became part of everyday life one day. Even if that had always been so, even if no word about it had been lost, the first time was still worth communicating, because it had been accompanied by such tremendous circumstances. Gods with difficult names came out of the blue using extraordinary means of locomotion. That was news! They had to tell it to their children and their children's children.

We should read myths like these with modern spectacles, then the sensational events emerge clearly.

As far as I am concerned some of the blank spaces in the African mythology album are filled. In this collection, among all the objects of value, the Dogon myth is the 'Mauritius dark-blue'. Even at fancy prices it cannot be got rid of.

I am going to construct an example of how a myth might have originated.

A space traveller lands in the middle of Australia in 15000 B.C. The primitive aborigines withdraw fearfully to their dwellings. Gradually they become trusting, like animals who get used to the sight of a new master. They notice that the stranger does them no harm. It takes a little longer before the space traveller can make himself understood to the natives – NB *to* them, not the other way round!

The few signs they can understand are not enough to explain the essential thing: that the stranger who has landed is not a god. There is no sign or gesture for that. The stranger remains a god to the savages, for they saw and heard him arrive from heaven amid a fair old din. He must be a god.

Without some serviceable scraps of language how can the astronaut explain what is so terribly simple to him? The whole business would be settled if the natives could understand what the 'god' is desperately muttering: 'Be reasonable, my children! I am a flesh and blood being, touch me! Look up at the sky. I come from a star up there that is quite like your home. Up there, my friends, is my home! Don't be afraid of the brightness I shocked you with when I landed. It was caused by searchlights with which I was looking for a landing-place. Look, here are the cables bringing the current from the generator!'

The aborigines do not understand a word of all this and even if they did understand it they would not accept his claim that he was not a god. After they had seen him appearing from space with their own eyes. That was a really divine achievement.

What goes on in their brains, when the astronaut has long since returned to his own kind?

Their brains 'work'. Among the few words of their vernacular they search for similes which can make their incredible experience roughly communicable. God had appeared in a vessel that drew a hot, bright luminous path behind it. The sun was a great help in describing this. It was familiar to them as bright, hot and round. So they narrate that *something* came that was brighter and hotter than the sun, and revolved like a disc. The something made a tremendous noise. . like a thunderclap. The strange something came out of the clouds and moved as if it was a vehicle. But – vehicles move on the ground, and this one had flown. They had all seen it. How shall I explain it to my son? You know how birds move through the air. Yes, it was like this: a vehicle in the form of a revolving disc, enveloped in dazzling light, that was brighter and hotter than the sun, came down to the earth like a bird. The something was also very dangerous and its shape was not quite round. The giant snakes that crept on the ground were very dangerous. Yes, that's it. A vehicle, dangerous as a snake and shaped like an egg. The being who clambered out of the egg and approached us was clad in precious robes. The skins of many animals shine like that in the sun. Yes, the god wore a garment, as if it were made of skins shining like silver.

In that, or some similar way, the sensational event may have been fictionalised into a tellable story. Small wonder that the fifth generation after X day can no longer imagine what actually happened. But it *is* a wonder when philologists 15000 years later claim to know so exactly what these early men thought, indeed what they must have believed!

What does an interpretation of mythological processes by a famous etymologist (10) sound like?

The tree of heaven:

A big oak or apple tree or rosebush is often mentioned in mythological songs and there seems to me to be hardly any doubt that it is an imaginary tree on which people thought the sun grew daily in the east. The sun was called the rose and also the golden apple, and as a rose and an apple always needed a bough to grow on, people thought that an invisible tree shot up every morning, grew higher and higher until noon, and sank again or was chopped down in the evening.

Let he who will and can understand whence the experts, in so far as they themselves do not have divine inspiration, get their knowledge, from what convolutions of the brain they can be sure that our early ancestors *must* have thought ('hardly any doubt'), where they get the audacity to know what people once *believed*.

There's trickery afoot. Who ever gets a straight flush, a sequence of five cards with the same colour?

At times, I learn, the content of a myth may be history transformed into fable. If I am on the point of adapting myself to this, someone whispers: no, it's fable transformed into history. What *am* I dealing with? If history is being imparted, why does it assume the guise of a fable? If it is a fable, where is the history? Scholars should make their minds up.

Comparisons of mythological research produce results like this: people A tells the same story as people B, it used a similar etymology, was familiar with the same moral concepts, had identical deities. As a result one can draw general conclusions such as that this or that tribe had a common basis or came under the same influences at some time. But comparative mythology cannot say whether its comparisons proceed from the original *meaning* of the event described.

Naturally many myths also contain ideas and allegories the core of which is no longer intelligible to us and so can be interpreted in a variety of ways. Many communications too cannot be brought into harmony with the knowledge we know was held by ancient peoples in ancient times.

From time immemorial myths have been coveted objects of study. For centuries the religious point of view blocked access to them. It took a long time before the possibility was taken into consideration that genuine historical traditions or even relevant facts about the origin of the world expressed in popular poetry might be hidden in them. It was recognised comparatively quickly that significant data about peoples and groups of families, about the foundation of settlements and tribal patterns of behaviour were demonstrably contained in myths. Yet religious, linguistic, ethnological and materialistic interpretations constantly throw up new questions. So it seems as if we cannot get any nearer the origin of things with the dissecting knives of purely scientific disciplines.

It would ill become me to appeal to belief, when knowledge concerns me so much more. Myths can be very helpful in the search for permanent truths. Especially today! With modern technological knowledge we can sift out the hard core of truth from the traditions. This method has the advantage of leading more quickly to clear conclusions, because technology supplies the functional facts of our time. In engineering circles this is called 'working rationally'. Academic think-tanks could learn a great deal from heavily burdened technology. It takes each problem back to its simplest variant. Consequently it seeks solutions which are not superceded tomorrow, because the starting point used yesterday was wrong. Technology cannot afford the numerous unnecessary detours and wrong roads.

When it comes to mythology, the simplest variant of setting the problem has the advantage of coming closest to the possible truth. In the beginning we clearly have the poverty of language. The early narrators' vocabulary was small; their concepts were related exclusively to simple daily life and recurrent natural processes. There were words for the tribe and relations, animals and plants, the first tools and simple weapons. Fire and sun, wind and water, thunder and lightning, birth, sickness and death had their names. But should something happen that could not be directly described by their scanty store of words, the story-tellers invented paraphrases which produced parable-like but still rationally comprehensible images. Poetry.

It is a mistake to think that speech and thought are interconnected functions, that we cannot think without speech. It is also mathematics and therefore a thought process when the anonymous buyer in the back row at a Sotheby's auction raises his hand, spreads out five fingers and orders his middleman in the front row to bid £5000. If the rich man raises five fingers twice, his bid doubles to £10000. Not a word is spoken, but some intensive thinking is going on. Sign language can be communication just like pictures, songs and music. In fact it can often express things language cannot. No one knows, nor will ever know with what gestures the old narrators accompanied their stories: laughter, a tear, an inarticulate spontaneous sound may have filled out (and even initiated) complicated patterns of communication.

I remember meeting an Alpine cowherd on a mountain in the Bernina range in my home country. He told stories about a gnome who is still supposed to haunt the mountains today. When speech failed the cowherd or did not seem powerful enough, he suddenly started making all kinds of expressive gestures. I understood him. Without words.

The part played by gesture in oral tradition is completely ignored.

Language is the cherished stepchild of thought. It is always limping behind the events. It has to find and form its concepts when the new thing has already happened. Speech is not a 'thing' with a constant value; it constantly changes its conceptual content. Against the background of the current

Figs. 43, 44, 45. Mythology on cylinder seals. The Sumerians invented the cylinder seal about 3000 B.C. It was a stamp from 1 to 6 cm long, with which documents were sealed, bills receipted or tributes to the temple or the treasury acknowledged.

stage of development of those who use it, it is never free of influences. It constantly adapts to the spirit of the age. But myths go far back beyond the year zero of our era into the remotest past that has hardly been investigated. How often must the words first used have changed their meaning! In addition everyone who took over the myths as their own endowed the words with a different semantic meaning. That was one strong reason why they were so controversially interpreted from different points of view at different times. People took the poetic paraphrases literally and overlooked the *core* of the communication which had survived the passage of time, and which contained the essence of what had been experienced, and suffered. This essence has stayed recognisable in the over-rated outer wrapping.

The story of the Ascension: a Christian feast based on a biblical legend shrouded in darkness.

The story of the Ascension: A factual report in which our planet is described from a great height.

The story of the Ascension can also be read in the Babylonian Etana epic which was excavated with the clay tablet library of the Assyrian King Assurbanipal (699-626 B.C.) at Nineveh, the most important collection of Babylonian and Assyrian literature, now preserved in the British Museum, London.

We do not know when the epic originated. Parts of it are contained in the much older Epic of Gilgamesh (after 2000 B.C.) written in Ak'kadian. The myth of Etana may go back to the beginning of human history, for his image is found on a 5000-year-old cylinder seal.

I took the following extracts from the second and third parts of the Etana tradition: (11)

Etana turns to the god Samas requesting the god to procure him the herb of child-bearing (also: herb of immortality). Samas sends him to the 'eagle'. He asks Etana what his wish is. When he asks 'Give me the herb of child-bearing', Etana is carried up to the heaven of the fixed stars. During the flight, the eagle six times draws his companion's attention to the fact that the earth steadily shrinks to their gaze:

When he had born him upwards for a while the eagle spoke to him, to Etana: 'Look, my friend, how the land has changed, look at the sea, at the sides of the world-mountains.' 'The land there looks like a mountain, the sea has become like a watercourse.'

. . .

'When he had born him upwards yet a while the eagle said to him, to Etana:

'Look, my friend, how the land has changed.'

'The earth looks like a plantation of trees. (12)

The eagle soars higher and higher with the son of man and ever and anon he urges his companion to look down and tell him what he sees. Finally he can only 'see so much (of the land) as the size of a hut' and the vast sea becomes as tiny 'as a courtyard'.

This eye-witness account, which Professor Richard Henning described in the *Jahrbuch des Vereins deutscher Ingenieure* as early as 1928, as 'certainly the oldest saga of flight in the world', ends with the fascinating text:

'My friend, look how the land has changed.'

'The land has become like a kitchen and the vast sea as small as a bread basket.'

'My friend, see how the land has *disappeared.*'

'I see how the land has *disappeared* and my eyes no longer sate themselves on the vast sea!

My friend, I do not wish to climb up to heaven. *Stop, so that I can return to earth!*'

'Eagle has landed' were the words of the astronauts' report to the Space Centre at Houston, when the first manned spaceship landed on the moon.

The report of Etana's spaceflight seems to me equally sober and factual. 'Eagle has landed.'

Parts of a myth about the 'Beginning of the World' were also found in the clay tablet at Nineveh. It is hardly surprising that this very early creation story contains intimations of present-day knowledge of the origin of the world (primal soup):

Once, when the heaven above was not named,
the earth below bore no name,
when the ocean, the original beginner, the begetter,
and the noise of the waves of the sea bore everything,
when no field was cultivated, no tribe to be seen,

once, when not a single god existed,
no name was named, no fate decided,
then the gods were created,
Luhmu and Lahamu came into being,
vast vistas of time flew by. (13)

Sargon I (2334-2279), founder of the third Assyrian empire, was a progressive gentleman. He had collected valuable writings of all kinds to form a gigantic library. Scholars found stories of the Flood and a version of Genesis older than the biblical account. The biblical book of Genesis comprises thirty-one chapters. the much older Assyrian one is inscribed on both sides of seven clay tablets, with more than 1000 lines.

The American Assyriologist Fred Tamimi, President of the Assyriology Research Foundation, has been working on a new translation of Assyrian cuneiform texts for more than forty years. Tamimi, who supports my theory of visits by extra-terrestrials, wrote to me as follows:

To get the sense of the original Assyrian word 'god', the most accurate translation would be *'on the tip above the flames'*. Incidentally we ought to date the writings collected by Sargon I much further back than is usually done today.

On the tip above the flames? Take a look at Ezekiel:

And above the firmament that was over their heads was the likeness of a throne, as the appearance of a sapphire stone: and upon the likeness of the throne was the likeness as the appearance of a man above upon it.

And I saw as the colour of amber, as the appearance of fire round about it, from the appearance of his loins even upward, and from the appearance of his loins even downward, *I saw as it were the appearance of fire, and it had brightness round about.* Ezekiel 1, 26-27

Since what is written in the Bible is accepted as authentic in the Christian west, this should refer to four men on 'the tip above the flames'.

As a deep bass, we have Moses, the founder of the religion of Yaweh:

And mount Sinai was altogether on a smoke, because the Lord descended upon it in fire: and the smoke thereof

Figs. 46, 47, 48.
The scenes
on cylinder seals are
impressive evidence
of memories of
visits from the cosmos.

ascended as the smoke of a furnace, and the whole mount quaked greatly.

Exodus 19, 18

As bass-baritone David, the king:

The voice of the Lord divideth the flames or fire. The voice of the Lord shaketh the wilderness; the Lord shaketh the wilderness of Kadesh.

Psalm 29, 7-8

As passionate baritone the Psalmist:

Who layeth the beams of his chambers in the waters: who maketh the clouds his chariot: who walketh upon the wings of the wind:

Who maketh his angels spirits; his ministers a flaming fire.

Psalm 104, 3-4

As singing tenor the prophet Micah:

For, behold, the Lord cometh forth out of his place, and will come down, and tread upon the high places of the earth.

And the mountains shall be molten under him...

Micah 1, 3

Fred Tamimi says that we can recognise the callings of at least eight beings on Assyrian cylinder seals and written tablets, because their translated names give the clue. He gave me this list:

Ramani	=	the 'high ones'
Samani (Samayi)	=	the 'heavenly ones'
Khalabi	=	the 'pilots'
Sapaqi	=	the 'space travellers'
Sapari	=	the 'travelling ones'
Gabari	=	the 'giants'
Arayi	=	the 'earthbound' or the 'earthmen'
Rayi	=	the 'controllers' or the 'observers'

What would the Assyrian traditions tell us if the old ideas were given a modern translation?

World-famous etymologists claim that all mythology can be explained by knowledge of the roots of words. Undoubtedly, clarifying the meaning of words by reference to their roots is

Figs. 49, 50, 51. Space attributes like planetary systems. Figures floating weightless in space and technical-looking apparatuses are obvious subjects.

an important task for linguists. However, I see a snag there on which the most carefully worked out conclusions or research must catch. Scholars will never be able to find out the *model*, the *cause*, the *event* originating the words and concepts. What was meant originally? Since we cannot honestly answer that question, it is not possible to describe the roots whose origin in experience are unknown. But we do reach the core if we introduce suitable words from the world of modern technology into the translation. There are no tricks, but eye-witness accounts, as they were once told emerge and which we can understand again today. If only we want to. I want to use a thousand and one pieces of evidence to help this realisation to a break-through.

TENNO: EMPEROR AND GOD

Until the allied victors banned it on 15 December 1945, Shintoism was the Japanese state religion with the Tenno, the Emperor, at its head: supreme god and earthly governor in one and the same person. The allies wanted to break up the solid structure of Japanese tradition, because a head of state

Fig. 52. Mythology scratched on the rock face. A stone-age deity, flying weightlessly, on the walls of the Fogape caves in Japan.

who was worshipped as a divinity was not subject to their orders. They deposed the god. Shintoism has an ancient tradition, Koyiki, handed down in three sets of annals: the *Koyiki*, compiled in 712, contains the history of early events; the *Nihongi*, thirty books edited by Prince Toneri, is a kind of official imperial history and dates to 720; the *Kouiki* contains a history of events in primitive times. Although these works were written down in the post-Christian era there is no doubt that they are copies of much earlier originals and were adapted from a much earlier oral tradition.

May I remind you of the already mentioned Big Bang theory according to which the astrophysicists postulate the origin of the universe in the explosion of one primordial atom, before I quote the beginning of the *Nihongi*. A similarity to this very topical theory is clearly recognisable:

> Ages ago, when heaven and earth were not yet divided from one another and the male and the female were not separated (!), a chaos formed like a hen's egg and in its chaotic mass a germ was contained.
>
> The pure and bright part of it spread out thinly and became the heavens; the heavy and dull remained behind and became the earth.
>
> As regards the union of the fine, the concentration was easy, the coagulation of the heavy and dull was only fully effected with difficulty.
>
> Accordingly heaven came into being first, and only afterwards did the earth take a definite form. (15)

Professor Lemaître, who introduced the Big Bang theory, which can be verified by the Doppler Effect,* says: 'All the

---

* After the physicist Christian Doppler (1803-1853). The effect consists in an alteration of the pitch of sound when the source of sound or the observer moves. If their reciprocal distance apart increases, the tone grows deeper, if it decreases, it rises. Can be observed when a whistling train approaches or goes away from us. With light waves, if the source of light nears the observer there is a shift in the spectrum to blue, if it moves away from the observer there is a shift to red. The speed of the movement of all stars can be measure by the Doppler Effect, because it was proved that the stars in all galaxies have the same chemical consistency and very much the same physical condition as the stars in our Milky Way.

matter in the universe was united in one primordial atom as a heavy mass of matter.'

The Nihongi: '. . . *in its chaotic mass a germ was contained.*'

Today astrophysicists say that the earth cooled down in a process lasting milliards of years, forming minerals, water, metals, etc. The free floating gases were not subject to this process until they came into the sphere of attraction of a heavenly body.

The Nihongi:

As regards the union of the fine, the concentration was easy, the coagulation of the heavy and dull was only fully effected with difficulty. Accordingly . . . heaven first . . . only afterwards the earth.

The effect of the Big Bang explosion is still clearly evident in the universe. As can be proved by the red shift, the galaxies are constantly moving away from each other. And now, as in the past, various gas molecules are floating between sun, planets and Milky Way. Astrophysics can add a new verse to the old song of discovery.

The Nihongi: *The pure and bright part of it spread out thinly and became the heavens; the heavy and dull remained and became the earth.*

A little present-day geology!

Every child learns at school that the outermost skin of the earth is the earth's crust which has the thickness of an apple-skin in comparison with the volume of our planet – some 1,083,219,000,000 km³. The earth's crust rests on a granite-like layer which is lacking in many places under the oceans. The lower limit of the earth's crust lies 8-15 km below the surface of the open sea, 30-40 km below the surface of the lowlands and 50-70 km below the surface of plateaux and mountains. The earth's mantle extends to a depth of 2,900 km and the inner core begins at a depth of 5,100 km. The hot gas-drenched molten mass in the depth of the earth is called magma.

In 1912 the geophysicist Alfred Wegener (1880-1930) put forward his theory of continental drift, which has since been promoted from theory to fact by oceanological research. Wegener took as his starting point a large original continent in a large pacific sea which disintegrated in the Middle Ages of the earth's history and drifted apart – an indication of this is that for example South America and Africa, North and South America first floated away from each other during this Continental Drift. It is not so long ago since Wegener's theory was confirmed beyond a shadow of doubt.

What does the *Nihongi* have to say about this?

Then divine beings originated among them. Hence it is said that *in the beginning of the creation of the world the swimming about of the countries was comparable to the swimming of a fish playing in the water.*

Strange! Yes, it is. The Nihongi's information is accurate. What objection is there to the theory that gods, who *originated in heaven, who produced absolutely pure men,* were the informants?

Etymologists say, 'of course we can only take these divine figures symbolically. They did not exist in reality.' (16)

If we scent former realities in myths – obviously a frightful idea – then traditions, which incidentally have to suffer for all kinds of things, are 'only' myths. Only? Which family tree should we climb up, if it is merely symbolism that is hidden in the mythology of our early history? And even if it is only symbolism, aren't we allowed to ask what the symbols stand for?

Symbol comes from the Greek *sumbolus* and that means: to throw together. The lexicons explain it as follows:

The symbol assumes the figurative relationship between sign and thing designated and so makes the sense of what is meant clear as in a parable. Many kinds of signs can express one content, different contents can be connected with one sign.

All right, let's follow the instruction that myths are to be understood symbolically. Then I want to know exactly the 'sense of what is meant'; I want to learn everything about the 'figure relationship'. I want precise knowledge. Much more precise.

The sections of the *Nihongi* which tell of the origin of the Universe have this introduction.

In one scripture it says: (17)

> When heaven and earth first separated from one another, a thing with a form hard to describe was in the middle of the emptiness. Within it a divinity came into being of itself.

In another scripture it says:

> Long long ago when the land was young and the earth was young it swam around like floating oil. At this time there came into being a thing that was like a reed-sprout in form. From it, by transformation, divinities originated with the names ... There also originated in the midst of the emptiness a thing that resembled floating oil and changed itself into a divinity ...

In the middle of empty space a thing with a form hard to describe.... In the thing a divinity originated. In the interior of the land was sighted a thing that looked like a reed-sprout. Out of it came divinities....

How do I tell my child? Reed-sprouts have a streamlined tip which turns into a firmly rounded shape. People who are used to working with reeds get an idea of the 'thing', namely a space transport shuttle, from this comparison.

When it comes to finding names for the *jamais vu* we bright twentieth-century men have not advanced a step further.

Thirty years ago a man saw a 'thing' in the sky which – yes, what did it look like? – it looked a flying saucer. Since then, thousands of people, including America's Jimmy Carter, claim to have seen a 'flying saucer'. The first discoverer had no appropriate word for the unknown flying object, so he spoke of his flying saucer.

It would give me great pleasure to watch etymologists set about interpreting a twentieth-century myth in the year 4000! They would rummage in excavated newspaper archives and libraries. Everywhere they would keep on finding references to these ominous flying saucers. Long ago their archaeologist colleagues would have assembled potsherds and proved that men of that time placed artefacts of this kind underneath a drinking vessel called a cup. What was all this about these things which, if one could follow the myths, moved in the air, changed colour, described surprising zig-zags, curves, etc.

The etymologists in the year 4000 would agree that these

flying saucers must have been the implements for a universally practised kind of sport. Sometimes under the cement fragments of an arena they had excavated a bronze man who was apparently hurling a thing like these saucers into the air.

A scientific interpretation of a myth *anno* 4000 has been made.

As in the African Dogon myths, the *Nihongi* has *eight* people climbing down from heaven, a whole crew who in both cases created offensive noises and smoke when landing and taking off:

> When Susa no Wo no Mikoto first climbed down from heaven, the great sea rolled like thunder and was set in motion, and the mountains and hills groaned aloud, and all this because of the violence of the divine nature.

Now a leap sideways, a *pas de trois*, to India and into biblical territory!

In the *Mahabharata* (18), the account of Indian myths, comprising 80000 couplets, which refers far back to very ancient times, we find:

> 'Bhima flew with his Vimana on an enormous ray, which had the brilliance of the sun and whose noise was like the thunder of a storm.'

In Ezekiel 'the glory of the Lord' makes such a din when it appears that he can only compare it to 'the noise of an host' and 'the noise of great waters'. When the biblical Lord lands in the Holy Land, he startles the surroundings with smoke, vibration, noise, fire and evil smells.

Today, citizens would band together to prevent that kind of nuisance. They know in good time what is being planned. In those days, these nuisances came 'from above' without warning.

Moreover we also find metaphors, of the kind the old chroniclers used, in the stories which reporters sent all over the world at the launching of the first rocket at Cape Canaveral on the east coast of Florida. There are still no words for the unique first-time happening.

Back to Japan. In the *Koyiki*, the book of early events, the sun queen Amaterasu sends her grandson Ninigi to earth to rule the Japanese country. Ninigi lands on a mountain in the western part of the island of Kyushu and brings three requisites with him: a mysterious metal mirror, a sword and a string of jewels. These symbols of imperial majesty still exist.

Every year millions of Japanese make a pilgrimmage to the town of Ise on Honshu, the biggest of the four main islands, to worship the sacred mirror, the most important of the imperial treasures, in the Naiku, 'the inner shrine' of the temple. The sword is preserved in the Atsuta Temple near Nagoya in Central Honshu, the string of jewels in the imperial palace in Tokyo.

The original sacred mirror is supposed to be preserved in the inner shrine, wrapped in many covers, which were never opened and are not even opened today. If one cover is gnawed away by the teeth of time, zealous priests immediately wrap a new one round it. Not a living soul knows what is inside the miraculous packet.

The grandson of the heavenly Ninigi was Jimmu Tenno, Japan's first monarch. Tenno, the title of the Japanese Emperor, means heavenly monarch. The mythical dynasty can be traced back to the sun goddess Amaterasu, (we have accounts of such hierarchies from all over the world. All the Egyptian Pharaohs, for example, were descendants of the gods.)

After ascending the throne each new Tenno set forth to announce his assumption of office to the gods in the temple of Ise. There has been only one change in the ceremony since ancient times. The emperors no longer travel in closed ox-carts, but in a railway Pullman car.

Even the mythical Jimmu Tenno is still supposed to be resting in his tomb. According to tradition he ascended the

Fig. 53. Ancient Japanese imperial tomb.

throne on the first day of the first month of the lunar year 660 B.C.

When I was last in Japan in the spring of 1976 making a TV feature, I tried to get permission to visit Jimmu's mausoleum. Everyone told me it was out of the question. Entrance was forbidden to all mortals except relatives of the imperial house and only the Tenno could penetrate the inner shrine. It was a slight consolation that the Japanese television people organised a helicopter for me which circled round the fabulous grave several times. Apart from a moat which protected the mausoleum like a strong fortress, an artificially wooded hill under which the tomb is supposed to lie and a few unimpressive walls I saw nothing. Absolutely nothing.

It was a Japanese who advised me to state in this book my wish to be allowed to enter the secret place. Nowadays the imperial house was so modern that my chance of being allowed into the tomb of Jimmu Tenno might actually be enhanced by this unusual procedure! I have made greater efforts in the past in order to be able to approach the unusual, so that it was easy for me to write these brief lines as a test. Wait and see.

Mythologies teem with grandiose events which have only been intelligible since Albert Einstein's theory of relativity. Before this precious example of a 'relevant' myth, may I remind you of my conversation with Professor Lüscher in which the eternal law of time dilation was explained. This is how the story of the Island Child is described in the extremely ancient tradition Tango-Fudoki:

> In the district of Josa is a province called Heki and in this province a village called Tsutsukaha and among the inhabitants of this village was a man called the Island Child. This man was incomparably splendid and of comely appearance.

> Under the Emperor who ruled the empire in the palace at Asakura, the Island Child sailed out to sea alone in a boat to fish. As he had caught nothing, he fell asleep. Suddenly a maiden of unsurpassable beauty appeared next to him. The Island Child said to the maiden: 'The houses of men lie far away from here and there is no one on the surface of the sea. Who are you and how did you arrive here so unexpectedly?'

The maiden answered with a smile: 'I came out of the air.'

The Island Child asked again: 'From where in the air did you come?'

The maiden answered: 'I have come from heaven. Forget your doubts, I beg you, and enjoy the pleasures of being in love with me. I intend to live together with you, for as long as heaven and earth last. If you wish to obey my words, do not open your eyes for a while.'

Soon the two of them reached a strange island which was bestrewn with pearls. The Island Child's eyes had never beheld such brilliance. Out of a shimmering palace came seven boys who were called Pleiades,* and then out came eight more boys who were called Hyades.**

The Island Child made the acquaintance of the beautiful maiden's father and mother, and they explained to him the difference between the world of man and the residence of heaven. The Island Child married the maiden from heaven and their joys were ten thousand times greater than with men on earth. When three years had passed, the Island Child suddenly fell homesick. He wanted to see his parents. He grieved and lamented without cease.

Then the maiden asked: 'For some time now I have watched your face and noticed that things are not the same as they were before. Let me know your desire.'

The Island Child answered: 'Your humble servant left the home of himself and his friends and travelled far to the land of the gods. I feel overcome by homesickness. If I may so desire, I should like to go home for a while and see my parents.'

After they had said goodbye to each other, he embarked. She told him to close his eyes. Then all of a sudden he had arrived at his home in the village of Tsutsukaha.

He looked at the village. The inhabitants and the setting were quite different. He found absolutely nothing by which he could recognise his house.

---

* Pleiades, a constellation of seven stars.
** Hyades, a cluster of stars in the head of the constellation Taurus. The accurately measured movements of their members form the basis of the scale of distance in the universe.

Then the Island Child asked a villager: 'Where does the Island Child's family live now?'

The villager answered: 'Where do you come from, that you ask for such an old man? As I have heard from old people who told traditional stories, there was a man called Island Child here in olden times. He sailed out alone into the open sea and never came back. Since then three hundred years have passed. Why do you suddenly ask for him?'

Then the Island Child wandered around, sobbing.(19)

There we are biting on the hard kernel of a myth that is just to my taste. A fact, first proved in our day (according to Einstein) is hidden in a fairytale-like *love story*. Time dilation! The Island Child must have been taken up to the 'world of the gods' in a spaceship with a high velocity. The Island Child thought he had only spent three years there, but found on his return to his earthly home that three hundred years had passed there. An apparently harmless story which supplies a fact. Who can refute it?

Figs. 54, 55, 56. Mythology in stone and clay. Dogu figurines
dating to about 600 B.C. from the collection of the Suntory Art
Museum, Japan. Note the space traveller's uniform and the
large astronaut's goggles.

This valuable example, found with industry and luck, of
knowledge of the laws of time dilation in old myths is not the
only one. Even a fleeting *tour d'horizon* shows that 'only a
moment' meant a human generation to the Indian god
Vishnu, that the mythical Chinese emperors were 'heavenly
princes', who rode in heaven in fire-spitting dragons and lived
for 18,000 terrestrial years. Chinese mythology says of the first
prince P'an Ku that he travelled around in the cosmos for
2,229,000 terrestrial years. Even our familiar Old Testament
says that in the hand of God everything is a time and times
and half a time.

The Psalmist puts it more poetically:

For a thousand years in thy sight are but as yesterday when
it is past, and as a watch in the night.

Since my departure from Japan I have been sucking two
bitter-sweet bonbons. A god called Omohi-kane no kami
keeps on appearing in the old myths. I had his name
translated and found to my astonishment that it literally

meant: *divinity which unites the thinking power of many gods in himself.* This god was obviously a kind of computer. Strange.

As strange as a hint which Japanese archaelogists gave me. Archaelogy is familiar with the Japanese Dogu figurines:* figures of stone or clay, modelled like the heads of space travellers, in uniform, with enormous goggles. *This* kind of Dogu figure (there are others) first emerges about 600 B.C. And this was just the time when the gods of heaven gave Jimmu Tenno, the first emperor of Japan, his empire . . . and in 592 B.C., 20,000km away as the crow flies, the prophet Ezekiel had his encounters with spaceships.** *Coincidence* is the fine-sounding Latin-derived word for two events that tally completely. I like that word.

Diagonally around the globe, the mythology of the Eskimos gives a pointer which I feel should be included here:

The first men were much bigger then present-day men. They could fly with their magic house, and the snow shovels moved of their own accord and shovelled the snow alone. If the people of that age wanted different kind of food, they simply went into their flying houses and flew to a new place. But one day someone complained about the noise that the flying houses made when they flew through the air. As the words of the complainant were very strong, the houses lost their ability to fly, and since then men are bound to one place with their houses. . . . In those days snow could burn like fire and fire often fell from heaven. Nor was there any ice at that time. (20)

I have not included the myths of the Central and South American peoples (Mayas, Incas) and the South Sea Islanders in the globe-encircling dance of stories about the heavens. The only reason being that I dealt with their myths in my previous books and am anxious to avoid repetition as far as possible. But with all due modesty I should like to remind readers of these omissions by the 'other party', too.

Nevertheless, Latin America will be worthily represented by one uncanny tradition, not yet included in any scholarly mythological work, but deserving pride of place in one. This myth contains almost all the *essentials* one could ask for from a

---

*Return to the stars, pp. 104–106.
** Blumrich: *Then the Heavens opened — The Spaceships of Ezekiel.*

Fig. 57. Mythology sculpted in stone. Figurine of an unknown god from Colombia. Age estimated at about 3000 years. Here again the astronaut's accoutrements are unmistakable.

proper myth about the presence and activity of the 'gods'.

The historian and sociologist Karl Brugger has been living in South America for years as a journalist. Since 1974 he has been correspondent for German Radio and Television in Rio de Janeiro. Brugger is considered to be a specialist on Amerindian questions.

In 1972 he got to know the Amerindian Tatunca Nara in Manaus where the River Solimoes meets the River Negro, i.e. where the Amazon begins. Tatunca Nara is the chief of Ugha Mongulala, the Dacca and Haishai Indians.

When after taking great pains and using all his knowledge of human nature, Brugger had overcome Tatunca Nara's distrust, he heard an extraordinary story; as he says, the most extraordinary story he had ever heard. It is the story of the Mongulala tribe, 'a people chosen by the gods 15,000 years ago'. 'This story', said the chief, 'is written down, with all its events, in *The Chronicle of Akakor*'. (21)

Brugger taped a 'long narrative only interrupted by the changing of the tapes' in his hotel room. Tatunca Nara's report starts with the chosen tribe and ends in the year 12453. This means that by our calendar the chronicle begins in 10481 B.C. and ends in the present, 1972!

Finally twelve full tapes were recorded. Brugger was not sure whether he had heard a 'fantastic fairytale' or whether the report could be verified. Professionally prone to suspicion and painful rechecking, Brugger undertook some documentary research. When Tatunca Nara at a later meeting repeated his story with many additional details, 'as if he had learnt it by heart', Brugger began to believe in it, although its enormity was like a challenge to him. Brugger checked the information to see what truth there was in it, had the tapes transcribed and published the result. I got to know him and had a long talk with him.

The 'Book of the Jaguar' tells of the colonisation of the earth by the gods up to the time of the second world catastrophe. The 'Book of the Eagle' comprises the span of time between 6000 and 11000 of the Indian calendar. With the publisher's permission I quote only from the two early books, because they are intimately connected with my theme. I give literal extracts from Tatunca Nara's narrative as Karl Brugger translated, researched, edited and published it, in May 1975.

Tatunca Nara is speaking:

The Chronicle of Akakor, the written history of my people, begins with the hour zero, when the gods left us. The Ina, the first prince of Ugha Mongulala, decided to have everything that happened written down in good language and clear writing.

And so the Chronicle of Akakor gives evidence of the history of the oldest people in the world. From the beginning, the hour zero, when the earlier lords left us ... and it tell of the origins of the times when my people was the only one on the continent....

In the beginning everything was chaos.

Men lived like animals, without reason and knowledge, without laws and without tilling the earth, with nothing to wear or even to cover their nakedness. The secret of nature was unknown to them. They lived in twos, or threes, as chance had brought them together in caves or clefts in the rocks. They went about on all fours. Until the gods came. They brought them light.

We do not know when all that happened. It is only known vaguely where the strangers came from. Over the origin of our earlier lords lies a dense veil, which even the knowledge of the priests could not lift. According to the traditions of our ancestors it must have been 3000 years before the hour zero, 13000 B.C. according to the calendar of the white barbarians. Then gleaming gold ships suddenly emerged in heaven. Huge beacons illuminated the heavens. The earth quaked and thunder rolled over the hills. Men bowed down in awe before the mighty strangers who came to take possession of the earth.

The strangers called their home Shwerta, a far distant world in the depths of the universe. Their progenitors lived there. They had come from there in order to bring their knowledge to other worlds. Our priests say that it was a mighty empire consisting of many planets as numerous as

Fig. 58. Mythology in stone. An Indian drawing scratched on stone (age unknown). Discovered near Buckeye, Arizona.

particles of dust in the street. And they say further that the two worlds, that of our earlier lords and the earth, meet every six thousand years. Then the gods return. ... Who learns to understand the actions of the gods? Who learns to comprehend their deeds? For truly they were incomprehensible to normal mortals. They knew about the courses of the stars and the laws of nature. Truly, the highest law of the world was known to them. A hundred and thirty families of the progenitors came to the earth....

The Chronicle of Akakor, the written history of the Ugha Mongulala people, begins after the departure of the earlier lords in the year zero. Then Ina, the first prince of the Ugha Mongulala, ordered that all events be written down, in good language, in clear writing and with due respect for our earlier lords....

Akakor, the capital of the empire of Ugha Mongulala, was erected 14000 years ago by our forefathers under the guidance of the earlier lords. The name also comes from

Figs. 59, 60, 61. Mythology in wood. Carved out of wood, this Indian figurine of a deity from the Upper Amazon gives us plenty to puzzle over.

them. Aka means fortress, Kor the number two. Akakor is fortress two. . . .

The temple cities of the patriarchs have also remained a mystery to my people. For the gods the pyramids were not only dwelling places, but also symbols of life and death. They were a symbol of the sun, of light and life. The earlier lords taught us that there is a place between life and death, between life and the void, that is subject to a different time. To them the pyramids were the links with a second life. . . . The lords of the cosmos, the beings in heaven and on earth, created four corners of the world and four sides of the world. . . .

The gods ruled from Akakor. They ruled over men and over the earth. They had ships that went faster than a bird flies. Ships that reached their goal by day or night without sails or rudder. They had magic stones to see into the distance. They saw cities, rivers, hills, lakes. Whatever happened on earth or in heaven was mirrored in them. But most wonderful were the subterranean dwelling places. And the gods gave them to their chosen servants as their last legacy. For the earlier lords are of the same blood and have the same father. . . .

On the day the gods left the earth they summoned Ina . . . 'Ina, we are going to depart. We have given you good back to our own kind. Our work is done. Our days are accomplished. . . . We shall return when you are threatened. But now take the chosen tribe. Lead them into the underground dwelling places so that they are protected from the coming catastrophe.' And Ina watched them sail up to heaven in their ships amid fire and thunder. They disappeared over the mountains of Akakor. Only Ina saw their departure.

The gods left the earth at the hour zero, 10481 B.C. according to the calendar of the white barbarians. They gave the starting signals for a new epoch in the history of my people who faced a terrible time, after the gleaming gold ships of the earlier lords were extinguished like stars in the heavens. . . .

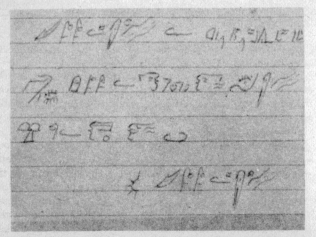

Fig. 62. I had no idea what the note said. Friends told me that Tatunca Nara was inviting me to visit him.

The chosen servants had only the images of the gods in their hearts. They looked up to heaven with burning eyes, but the gleaming gold ships did not reutrn. The heavens were empty. Not a sound. The heavens stayed empty....

The Chronicle of Akakor contains the secrets of the chosen tribe.... It describes the rise and fall of a people chosen by the gods until the end of the world, when they will return after a third great catastrophe has annihilated mankind....

So it is written. That is what the priests say. So it is recorded, in good language, in clear writing.

Tatunca Nara tells of two global catastrophes which nearly wiped out the whole of mankind. An incredible flood, connected with an extreme change in the climate, is supposed to have happened in the year 10468 B.C. Here is part of the story:

That is the news of the downfall of man. What happened on the earth? Who made them tremble with fear? Who made the stars dance? Who made the water gush out of the cliffs?... It was terribly cold and an icy wind swept over the earth. It was terribly hot and men burnt up in its breath. Men and animals fled in panic-stricken fear. They ran hither and thither in desperation. They tried to climb trees, but the trees hurled them far away. They tried to creep into caves and the caves collapsed on top of them. What was below was pushed up above. What was above sank into the depths....

When the survivors crept out of their hiding-places, the earth was transformed, but the Ugha Mongulala survived this, and also a second frightful catastrophe. And finally the gods, so long desired, returned from the universe:

Twilight still lay on the face of the earth. Sun and moon were covered over. Then ships appeared in the heavens, enormous and golden coloured. Great was the joy of the chosen servants. Their earlier lords were returning. With shimmering faces they came down to earth. And the chosen people brought forth their gifts: feathers from the big forest birds, honey, incense and fruit.... All this the chosen laid at the gods' feet.... All of them rose up in the valleys and looked at the patriarchs.... But many of them were no more. . . . Only a few men were still alive to greet the former lords. . . .

Thus my people . . . has only kept the memory . . . like the written rolls of paper and the green stones. Our priests have preserved them in the underground temple precinct of Akakor, where Lhasa's flying apparatus and the strange vehicle which can go over mountains and water are also kept. The flying apparatus is a gleaming golden colour and is made of an unknown metal. It is shaped like a clay roll as high as two men, one standing on another, and the same width. The apparatus has room for two men. It has neither sails nor rudder. But our priests say that Lhasa could fly in it faster than the strongest eagle and moved in the clouds as easily as a leaf in the wind. The strange vehicle is equally mysterious. Seven long legs support a large silver-plated bowl. Three of the legs point forwards and four backwards. They resemble curved bamboo sticks and are movable. At their extremities are rolls the size of a water-lily. . . .

That is what it says in the tapes that Karl Brugger recorded and translated. It is the history of a Latin-American tribe as from 13000 B.C., as they experienced it and handed it down. The 'earlier lords whom we call gods' came to earth, according to Brugger, and formed those whom they met 'in their image'; gave them names, language and writing; communicated agricultural knowledge; formulated laws which are still partially valid today and left them the underground dwelling places as a protection against catastrophe.

Tatunca Nara is in fact authorised to hand down this tradition. His life from the record:

At the end of the rainy season in the year 12416–1937 according to the calendar of the white barbarians – a long hoped-for event took place in Akakor. Reinha bore Sinkaia a son. I am Sinkaia's first-born son, Tatunca Nara, the last legitimate prince of the Ugha Mongulala. . . .

Nowadays when everything is slanted towards pure materialism Tatunca Nara's account seems incredible, because anything fantastic does not fit into the current 'world-picture'. It will be filed away in the pigeon-hole marked 'incredible'. But

Fig. 63. Mythology as a miniature. In this Indian miniature the mythical sun-eagle Garuda carries a couple off to heaven.

for anyone who can liberate himself from the spirit of the age and understands only a little of the matter, the Indian story is crammed with reality. What will my critics say to this reality?

On 18 October 1976, a news agency in Mexico City announced that 'the skeleton of an unknown being had been found and that it might possibly be the remains of an extra terrestrial creature.' The Director of the Anthropological Museum explained the reason for this assumption. It was a question of a living being hitherto unknown on earth, the skeleton of which has a spinal column, shoulder bones, the beginnings of arms and a dog-like head, with small eye sockets, but only the trace of a snout.

This report reminds me of a description in Tatunca Nara's story:

In the middle of the room from the walls of which the mysterious light came stood four blocks of transparent stone. As I approached them, full of awe, I recognised four mysterious beings in them. Four living dead. Four sleeping humans. There were three men and a woman. They lay in a fluid which covered them up to the chest. They resembled men in everything, except that they had six fingers and six toes. Sleeping gods.

Suppose the depths of the earth in Mexico had released a sleeping 'god'?

In a debate* on my theory organised by sixteen scientists, Professor Joachim Illies said:

A thousand examples of the probability of a solution being 1 : 1000 do not alter its improbability in any way, do not make the solution any more probable than one case alone would have done. These are the laws of mathematics and at the same time the mental laws of reason, of that there can be no serious doubt.

Is that so, my dear professor? I am in complete disagreement with the arbitrariness of your argument.

To me, an ordinary simple citizen, ten circumstantial indications in support of an assertion always have more force as proof than one indication! However if Illies prefers 'one case alone', he has it in the Dogon myth. I want friendly attention. 2 x 2 are 4. Who will dispute that? Mathematics needs no circumstantial indications; it has clear cut rules. It is an enviable science. The mental laws of reason lack this absolute clarity. Murderers are brought to the electric chair or the gallows by reason, and afterwards they are often proved innocent. *Malheur* of reason? Countless 'reasonable' scientific theories survive by virtue of circumstantial evidence. Darwin's theory of evolution can be quoted as an example. Many, indeed the majority, of astronomical and astrophysical theories exist on the basis of circumstantial evidence – for example Professor Fred Hoyle's generally accepted theory that hydrogen was formed 'from nothing' in the original universe. The Marxist pseudo-scientists' sociological models for the future also live by circumstantial evidence as does nearly every archaeological supposition.

Why is it that a 'thousand examples' (= evidence) weigh so heavily in the scales in one case and in another do not have the weight of a feather? Is that the higher scientific justice?

*Ernst von Khuon: *Waren die Götter Astronauten?*

Figs. 64, 65. Mythology in straw. The Brasilian Kayapo Indians have made their straw suits in accordance with tradition. They are supposed to symbolise visitors from the cosmos. These astronaut costumes are worn on ritual occasions. Shots from my film *Botschaft der Götter* (Message from the Gods).

Of course I have my ideas about the circles which dispense this special brand of justice.

Everybody comes into the world with a kind of computer, the brain. From the very first, all sensory perceptions and actions of the will are centred there. Molecular memory units and electric nerve circuits are integrated in the 14 milliard cells of the grey matter of the cerebral cortex. Information is stored and treated there. It is already relayed to the baby in its cradle via receptors: that is hot, cold, wet, dry, sweet-smelling, stinking, black, white, coloured. Later come the deliberate special instructions by parents, teachers and priests: you are allowed to do this, but not that. This is right, that is wrong. And one day a man thinks and acts independently on the basis of his stored knowledge. He knows what evokes love and hate, joy and pain, pleasure and revulsion.

The London University physiologist, Professor H. J. Campbell, visiting professor at the Max Planck Insitute in Germany and the Collège de France in Paris, stated that the human brain always and in every case strives 'to achieve pleasure', (22) indeed that it is programmed to that end. By that Campbell does not mean only the achievement of sexual pleasure. Achievement of pleasure also comes from success in one's career and public recognition of special achievements. For example: anger, uncertainty and attacks on one's mental and material integrity arouse feelings of non-pleasure.

If we know that, it becomes understandable from a human point of view that feelings of aversion affect an expert in his field when the results of long diligent work are attacked. With a cultivated voice he announces his new insights from his professorial chair – pure achievement of pleasure, new every day, marvellous. And then, oh horror, his painfully erected mental structure is shaken. Unfortunately not even a scientist can liberate himself from feelings of aversion. I am not attacking the integrity of any scientist with this observation, only drawing each one of them as a fellow citizen in the all too human condition.

I have often wondered why someone does not feed the hyper-intelligent computer with dates and times from early traditions – myths, legends and religious writings. I ask myself if it would not be possible to work out the speeds of early spaceships and consequently the distances between the inhabitable 'worlds of the gods' from the relation between the divine year mentioned in the traditions and terrestrial years.

I have always been on the search for accurate numerical material which I could offer for computer programmes. I found something in a French translation (23) of the very ancient mysterious books *Kantyua* and *Tantyua*. The translation is dated 1883.

A few words about the two books:

Actually it is an understatement if we describe *Kantyua*, with its 108 folio volumes and 9 sections with 1083 books, as *one* book. In effect the sacred texts of Lamaism are collected in *Kantyua*. *Tantyua*, with its 225 volumes, is a commentary on it. Both works, on Chinese wooden blocks, take up so much room that they were kept hidden in the cellars of houses in several villages in Tibetan mountain valleys. They are secret scriptures, of which only a hundredth part of the original texts has been translated. Their date of origin is unknown.

One of the *Kantyua* books is entitled *Collection of the Six Voices*. This quotation comes from the chapter 'Divine Voices':

> There are different heavens and these heavens are not open to all divinities. However numerous the gods may be, they can never transgress the three fundamental laws, which are: the domain of the wish, the domain with extension, the domain without extension. These three laws are divided into subsections. There are 28 dwelling places altogether. The region of the wish has six.

After a detailed description of the different regions and their rulers, *different* divine years in comparison with human years are given for *each* region:

> In the heaven of the four Great Kings 50 terrestrial years correspond to a day and a night. The lifespan is 500 years, or nine million years if one counts in terrestrial years.
>
> Above the heaven of the four Kings we reach the second heavenly dwelling place... In this heaven 100 years among men count as a day and a night. The lifespan is 1000 years. If that is reckoned in human years, it is 3600 x 10000 years or 36 million years....

Fig. 66. Mythology as masquerade. For untold generations the Hopi Indians of Arizona have been making these puppets according to instructions in their myths. They are supposed to represent the 'exalted spiritual beings' who once visited them. First filmed for *Botschaft der Götter*.

After this heaven there is a place which resembles many clouds. Here are the seven treasures, like a great earth. 200 terrestrial days there are a day and a night for the gods. Their lifespan is 2000 years. If that is reckoned in human years, it comes to 144 million years.

After this heaven there is the dwelling place of Tusita. Among these gods 400 human years correspond to a day and a night. Their lifespan is 4000 years. This comes to 576 million years in human years....

After the world of the gods of Tusita ... is the fifth dwelling place.... The gods are able to transform themselves and possess the five elements.... Among these gods 800 human years correspond to a day and a night. Their lifespan is 10000 years and this amounts to two billion 304 million years and this amounts to two billion 304 million years counted in human years....

After the fifth heaven arises ... the sixth residence.... Those gods are able to transform everything and for their pleasure they have gardens, woods, castles and palaces, and everything they desire. This is the peak of the region of the wish. Among these gods 16000 human years correspond to a day and a night. Their lifespan is 16000 years, or 9 billion 216 million years expressed in human years....

TABLE OF THE TIME LAWS OF THE 'HEAVENLY ONES'

	Years on earth	= Divine years	Lifespan	Human years
In 1st heaven	50	1 day, 1 night	500	9,000,000
In 2nd heaven	100	1 day, 1 night	1,000	36,000,000
In 3rd heaven	200	1 day, 1 night	2,000	144,000,000
In 4th heaven	400	1 day, 1 night	4,000	576,000,000
In 5th heaven	800	1 day, 1 night	10,000	2,304,000,000
At the peak of the wish	1,600	1 day, 1 night	16,000	9,216,000,000

Computers work out how often an Eskimo suffers from colds in his life, how often a Central European changes his underclothes or how great the probability is of Mr. Smith from Milwaukee, USA, getting to know Mr. Dupont in Marseilles.

Here I offer a rich meal for these greedy machines, calculations with many known values.

If 50 terrestrial years make a day and a night in the kingdom of the four Great Kings, how swiftly must a spaceship move so that a ratio of 50 terrestrial years to 24 divine hours arises, taking the laws of time dilation into account?

If we have the first distance, we can proceed like Sherlock Holmes. Conan Doyle made his clever detective operate like this when he was on the trail of a wrong-doer. He ascertained the scene of the crime from existing evidence. Then he traced a circle within which the criminal must be if he was fleeing on foot. Bearing in mind the speed of a motor-car, he traced a second circle to be searched if the criminal were motorised. He drew the biggest circle on the assumption that the wrongdoer used an aeroplane which would reach place Y in time X.

A breath of Sherlock Holmes's imagination in tracking down the culprit could lead the exobiologists to accurate results and could help scientists to arrest fleeing spaceship culprits, as it were.

A recommendation according to the reckoning recipe-book: Take our solar system as the centre of the circle and bear in mind the orbital shift of our solar system in relation to other solar systems during the last 10,000 years. The unknown quantities will be found in a quadratic equation, for the basic algebraic material exists in the laws of time dilation and in the relationship earth/gods.

So many things are calculated for scientific and political waste-paper baskets, whose contents are put through the shredder next morning at the latest. Why not feed the computer a programme which can supply the future with important data from the past? It does not have to be a bad programme just because I recommend it.

During my searches for confirmation in literature and on my travels round the world I constantly stumbled on the egg as symbol of the spaceship.* Now I also find this appropriate object in the 'Citralakshana', the second chapter of the *Tantyua:* (24)

When the firmness of the world egg was laid aside, the darkness was overcome by the golden egg, and everything originated from the water. The progenitor of the earth came out of the golden egg.

The cosmic egg keeps on cropping up in Tibetan legends. In one of them it says: (25)

A white light originated from the uncreated being and from the basic material of this light came a perfect egg. From outside it was radiant, it was good through and through. It had no wings, yet it could fly. It had neither head, nor mouth, nor eyes, and yet a voice sounded from it. After five months the wonderful egg broke open and a man came out . . . .

Traditions of the Chinese Liao civilisation say that our world emerged from an egg. The first men came to earth in 'reddish-golden eggs'. The eggs looked like 'big yellow sacks'. Their appearance is uniformly described in the Liao tribes:

*Return to the Stars, pp.79-

'six feet, four wings, no eyes, no face.' (26)

The world egg is a central theme of mythology. In one of the oldest prayers in the Egyptian *Book of the Dead* the narrators pray:

> O world egg hear me!
> I am Horus of millions of years!
> I am the lord and master of the throne.
> Freed from evil, I traverse the ages
> and spaces that are boundless.

The egg motif is also clearly recognisable in the 'Song of the Origin of Things' in the *RigVeda*, the collection of the oldest Indian sacrificial myths:

> In those days there was neither non-being, nor being,
> There was no atmosphere, no heaven above . . . .
> The one, apart from whom there was no other
> Breathed windless in the beginningness.
> The whole night was covered with darkness,
> An ocean without light, lost in the night.
> Then was the one, hidden in the bowl,
> Born by the glowing heat of the radiant power.
> As they laid their measuring cord across it
> What was below then, and what above? . . . .
> Who has understood where the creation comes from?
> The gods originated from it on this side.
> Who is to say where they came from? (27)

The 'bowl, in which the life powerful (was) hidden', lay in 'space devoid of air' where there was 'no heaven'. (28) Out of this bowl 'the one' was born by 'the glowing heat of the radiant power'. An image as a code. The egg as a paraphrase for an unknown flying object.

The cores of myths are similar in many large-scale matters, but they are always identical in their effort to make the unprecedented intelligible.

The Spanish chronicler Pedro Simon (29) took down this myth from the traditional tales of the Chibcha Indians who live in the East Colombian cordillera:

It was night. There was still something of the world. The

light was enclosed in a big 'something-house' and came out of it. This 'something-house' concealed the light inside it, so that it came out. In the brightness of the light things began to came into being . . . .

The egg, which is mentioned in myths, is to be understood as the symbol of life, for life visibly crawled, stepped or came out of the egg and generally with explosive suddenness.

If eggs were not specially produced for the special purpose of interpreting myths, they had a breakable shell from the very beginning. But the progenitor of the world (Tantyua) came out of a golden by no means breakable egg — lightning was packed in a 'special' egg; this egg broke and all 'visible things' came out of it (Pangwe) - the world-egg traversed time and space with the 'master of the throne' on board *(Book of the Dead)* — accompanied by glowing hot radiant power, the 'bowl' appeared and the gods sprang out of it *(RigVeda)*. The obvious comparison for the thing which came from heaven did not occur to the Indian narrator; he spoke of a 'something-house'.

When myths speak of overcoming the darkness, people say they mean the darkness which surrounds the egg in the womb. This artless myth does not work, because the darkness in which the world-egg moves is accurately defined. It is always the darkness of millions of years ago; it always lay across the early times when there was neither being nor not-being. It always reigned before the zero hour of all genesis.

The wealth of fancy with which the inconceivable is described is staggering! In the *Tantyua* it is amazing how the smallest part of the element, the atom, is made intelligible: (30)

> Eight atoms form the tip of a hair, so it is taught. If one knows this measurement one arrives at the proposition that one hair tip equals eight nissen (eggs of the louse). Eight nissen make one louse and eight lice are explained as a grain of barley.

Of course eight atoms are not enough to form a hair tip but I think that the narrator's way of describing the smallest of all things to his listeners is brilliant. The atom has become 'conceivable' in its minuteness. It is not necessary to take refuge in symbols, it is not necessary to write a commentary, it is not necessary to explain what is 'meant'. The reality as hard core is absolutely clear. I think of the rabbi who was asked for advice by a believer. 'Tell me about it,' said the rabbi and listened to the facts of the case. When the believer tried to explain, the rabbi interrupted: 'Stop! If you have to explain, your case is bad already!' Good advice to writers of footnotes, too!

Tibet teems with myths. Originally twenty-seven legendary kings are mentioned in the *Gyelrap*, the genealogy of the kings of Tibet. Of them *seven heavenly kings climbed down the ladder of heaven*. They were declared *gods of light*, who returned whence they had come once their work on earth was done. Likewise the oldest Buddhist scriptures are supposed *to have fallen from heaven on a little chest*. (23)

Buddhism is not the same in Tibet as it is India. The teachings of the Tantra scholl are interwoven with Tibetan Buddhism, in which are united the adherents of those Hindu religious groups (Shakta) who worship a supreme god. Consequently this mixture has a mythology that is more studded with Buddhist names than with pure Buddhism.

The myths of Tibetan Buddhism tell of the life of the 'great teacher' called Padmasambhava (also, U-Rgyan Pad-ma) who came from heaven and brought with him writings in an unknown language. Nobody could understand them. The 'great teacher' hid them in caves *against the time when they would be understood*. (30) During his sojourn on earth, the 'great teacher' chose his favourite pupil Pagur Vaircana and gave him permission to translate some books from the foreign language after he had flown away. In fact even today there are Tibetan books with titles in a completely unknown language. So far no one has been able to translate them. Through such legacies, myths achieve the rank of one-time realities.

How does the favourite pupil describe the 'great teacher's' departure? So accurately that I think he earned good marks for it:

> Then a cloud and a rainbow appeared in the sky, and the cloud came very close. In the midst of the cloud stood a horse of gold and silver . . . . Everybody could see how it went to meet them (the gods) through the air. When the

horse had flown up one ell into the sky, Padmasambhava turned round.

'Looking for me will be an endless task,' he said and flew away.

The king and his retinue were like fish on the sand . . . when they gazed up, they saw Padmasambhava the size of a raven; when they looked up again they saw him the size of a thrush, and then again he was like a fly; the next time he seemed vague and shimmery, the size of a louse's egg. And when they looked up again, they could no longer see him at all.

A staggering pendant to the account of Etana's spaceflight! There the story was told from the point of view of the space-flyer, before whose eyes the earth vanished. Here it is told from the earthly standpoint, as the 'great teacher' disappears into space — on a horse of gold and silver.

It is, excuse me, Professor Illies, against all reason, if all these pointers do not carry some weight, if they are swept away as coincidences.

For there is also a counterpart of the ascension on horseback in the Bible. It is not described with the same refinement but the prophet is apostrophised in it as 'teacher' who knew more about heaven than all his fellow-citizens. When the 'teacher' was speaking to his favourite pupil Elisha:

> . . . behold, there appeared a chariot of fire, and horses of fire, and parted them asunder; and Elijah went up by a whirlwind into heaven. And Elisha saw it, and he cried, My father, my father . . . . And he saw him no more . . . . He took up . . . the mantle of Elijah that fell from him, and went back, and stood by the bank of Jordan. 2 Kings 2, xi-xiii

Millions and millions of people accepted Elijah's ascension with fiery horses at face value, because it was in the Bible. Why don't they accept Tibetan mythology as reality? What the pupil had to offer is a great narrative achievement. The people of Tibet knew the 'great teacher'. He had lived among them and taught them useful things. They had talked to him and he was so clever that he knew a language they did not understand. Then, one day, before their very eyes, he returned to the heaven he had always described as his home. He did not soar up and away like a ghost with no physical presence, but as a being of flesh and blood. At first he was as big as a raven, then as small as a thrush, later tiny as a fly and finally as minute as a louse's egg. A brilliant eye-witness account!

Just to tidy things up, I mention that quite similar ascension myths are handed down in many cultures on all the five continents. A fruitful theme for a dissertation.

Unlike the myths in *Kantyua* and *Tantyua* which are only partially translated, the Indian epic *Mahabharata* is undoubtedly the most comprehensively translated poem about the history of a people. From the 18 sections, into which the 180,000 verses are subdivided, I quote this from 'Arjuna's Journey to Indra's Heaven':

> When the guardians of the world had gone, Arjuna, the
> terror of the enemy, wished that Indra's heavenly car
> would come to him.
> And suddenly the car came in a gleam of light, with Matalis,
> Scaring darkness from the air and lighting up all the clouds,
> Filling the heavenly regions with a noise like thunder.
> It was a heavenly magical creation, an eye-ravishing image.
> Then he climbed into the car, brilliant as the Lord of
> Daylight.
> And he, the white scion of Kuru's dam, drove joyously
> Up to the heavenly region,
> In the magical creation, the car that is like the sun.
> When he reached the region invisible to earth-walking
> mortals
> He saw the heavenly car, wonderful to thousands.
> There the sun shines not, nor do the moon and fire glow,
> But there it shines in its own brilliance, by noble energy,
> Which is seen as the forms of stars from the earth below,
> Like lamps because of the great distance,
> Although they are large bodies.

Don't you immediately think of the beam from a lighthouse? No one need share my impassioned fantasy to have a vivid picture of the car *in a gleam of light,* which *scares darkness from the air,* in the illuminated clouds. But the chronicler is not merely conjuring up an *eye-ravishing* abstract picture. He notes down factual details of the take-off. How, for example, the car filled the *heavenly regions with a noise like thunder*. His gaze followed the car until it reached a remote part of the universe where '*the sun shines not, nor the moon*'.

Obviously. The craft was moving outside our solar system. If the contents of myths were only to be sought in the mist in which they are wrapped, we could not credit these traditions with any accurate information, such as unequivocally exists in the account of Arjuna's ascension. The chronicler wanted future generations to understand him. That is why he described in visual and acoustical detail what no one could see from the earth, namely, that stars are 'large bodies':

> Which is seen as the forms of stars from the earth below, like lamps because of the great distance, although they are large bodies!

No mist enshrouds this information, nor does it require any footnotes. It is just there and needs no explanation.

It would be a bad business if oral traditions only existed in early written form, for philologists are always at loggerheads about early traditions. But many of those discussed are depicted in various artistic forms which can be seen and comprehended.

Below I list some of these finds, finds of the kind that were also described in the texts:

Rock paintings in the sahara, Brasil and Peru, as well as among the North American and Canadian Indians.

Miniature art on Sumerian, Assyrian and Ancient Egyptian seals.

Dogu figures in Japan.

The straw suits worn by the Brazilian Kayapo Indians on feast days which in their traditional shape are supposed to symbolise former visitors from the cosmos.*

The Katchina dolls which are still made today by the Hopi Indians in Arizona. Countless generations ago they were modelled on the 'high spiritual beings' who had visited them and equipped with space attributes. The Katchinas promised to return.**

* *The Gold of the Gods*, pp. 171 *et seq.*
** First shown in my film *Message of the Gods*.

All that, should it be allowed to have any importance, or not?

All that, should it be allowed to be conclusive, or not? Don't make me laugh!

It is a contradiction in itself that the real opponents of science are to be sought — and found — in the ranks of the scientists themselves.

Fortresses of various sizes and with various defences have been built round the vales of academe with indefatigable zeal. They are raised high above all the blasphemers who presume to pick stones from out of the crumbling fortress walls, or even dare to climb the wall and cast a look — or a stone — at the ordered garden within. New ideas are unpopular missiles in this battle.

Seriously, I can easily understand why the campus is unwilling to take note of an accumulation of circumstantial evidence. Painful feelings about frivolous positions, which are untenable in the long run, come inevitably to the surface. It is a fearful prospect indeed to have to admit that someone who has no priestly status in the holy of holies is not so far wrong that he should be thrown from the pinnacles of the fortress amidst the fire and brimstone!

A chivalrous struggle in which the underdog capitulates honourably before he goes off with wounds which no longer heal, would be quite fair. A horrifying thought to have to wait until the besieged die out!

The Nobel Prize winner Max Planck (1858-1947), one of the greatest of modern scientists, actually took into account the necessity of the opponents of scientific truth dying out.

A new scientific truth does not usually win through in such a way that its opponents are convinced and say that they are enlightened, but rather by the opponents dying out and the growing generation becoming familiar with the truth a priori.

I am fortunate enough to have made the acquaintance of a great number of scientists who are tolerant, noble and unprejudiced people to talk with and set against the massive front of academic antagonists. With some of them I have made positive friendships. We talk, we correspond; I ask them for criticism, advice and help, which they supply. They are the 'good scientists', of whom the molecular biologist Gunter S. Stent spoke, when he wanted colleagues without prejudices. These men have their feelings of pain under control and even — something I can never admire enough — the magnanimity to accept valid arguments without jealousy. Consequently I see no reason not to continue finding as many arguments as I can, as evidence for my theory 'according to the strictest principles of scientific methodology' (Prof. Luis Navia), even if one scientist claims that *one* argument has no more power of proving than a *thousand* arguments. Because I have a high opinion of reason, I speculate about the reason of the open-minded as the fair judge.

Carl Gustav Jung (1875-1961) evaluates the mythical observations of ancient peoples as 'archetypal developments of consciousness', in which the 'collective unconscious' finds its counterpart in representations of good and evil, happiness and punishment, life and death.

Like other exegeses, the psychological one also goes against the grain as far as I am concerned. Where realities push themselves forward, one should not dissolve the core of the story into unrecognisable fragments with psychologising acids so as to be able to play 'what am I?' again in the end.

It is a fact that research results hardly give us a feeling of newly won security. We always feel caught in a net of threats which become greater from discovery to discovery. Even the things that would have positive effects reach us like a Job's messenger. If an invention has left the test-bench, the question is at once asked, without taking losses into account: Will it not have a prejudicial effect on mankind? The very fact that the question is put is disturbing regardless of what the answer may be.

Yet everybody has the primordial longing to get answers to questions which will explain his existence, explain to him whence,whither and why. Religions answer these questions with a litany of faith, but the man of today wants *knowledge*, not *faith*. There are no longer many men who find real peace in prayer. Like unbelievers, they too seek genuine answers. In the long run no one lets himself be fobbed off with makeshift answers of the kind that materialistic ideologies have ready to reel off pat. It is a question of a handful of truths which will

not be debatable again before day turns into night and night
into morning.

I am convinced that such truths exist if only we accept the
traditions of the very remote past as realities and laying bare
the core of them, throw light on our past and at the same time
(insofar as we draw lessons from the past) remove fears of the
future. Because we know what *was* possible and what *will be*
possible.

I put on record the following:

The creation myths of every people all over the world
resemble each other closely.

The *oldest* gods responsible for creation *always* come from
space and return there once their work is done. (Only later
generations of gods come out of caves, the depths of the earth
or water.)

The early gods have flying apparatuses which are unanim-
ously described as egg-shaped, the size of a giant bird, the size
of a giant snake, consisting of a metal hull with windows from
which light flashes, with sparkling body, bright as the sun,
blinding the eyes, radiant, lighting up the dark night,
spreading noise, taking off and landing with rolls of thunder,
objects with a tail of fire, under which the earth quakes or
burns up, always coming from space and always vanishing
into space, plunging into endless darkness, flying with the
power of giant birds or golden fiery horses, an indescribable
something, a something-house.

The gods of creation make the blue planet inhabitable.
They provide the prerequisites for the genesis of flora and
fauna.

Ancient gods produce intelligent men.

Ancient gods teach the first intelligent men, instruct them
in the use of tools, show them how to grow plants and rear
animals, lay down the first laws for communal life and provide
an infrastructure.

Gods make their scions terrestrial rulers (ancient emperors
and kings, the Pharaohs).

Ancient gods always return home to the universe when their
work is done and promise to come back to earth again.

One can always find an apt quotation in the Bible or in
Goethe. This time I found one from the Olympian of Weimar:

In our own day there is no doubt that world history has to

be paraphrased from time to time. This necessity does not arise because much that happened has been discovered later, but because new opinions are given, because the men of a progressive age are led to stand-points from which the past can be comprehended and judged in a new way.

Written in the year of grace 1829, how it must distress the Olympian that his accurate perception is still not recognised in practice after nearly a 150 years.

4: *The 'Gods' were made of flesh and blood.*

When I was travelling through India in 1975 and arrived in Srinigar, I had to look for a Bible so that I could translate a passage from Ezekiel for an Indian friend with whom I was to have a discussion. Everything I could remotely want on this expedition was stowed away in my Rangerover,but I had not packed a Bible.

I asked the hotel porter to get me a Bible in the town. After a few hours, during which he had tried every single bookshop, he returned empty-handed. I asked the hotel manager if he would be kind enough to ring up some of his Christian acquaintances to see if we could lay our hands on a bible that way. He made a series of phone calls, but he had no luck. A few days later I tried to get hold of a copy in Bombay, but there too there was nothing doing.

After these experiences it suddenly dawned on me. Why on earth should the Indians be interested in 'our' Bible? To them it is only a collection of myths, stories and legends. Not until you are far from home where the Bible is looked on as the book of books, do you realise that it does not have the status of a holy scripture in other parts of the world.

The prevailing faith alone determines this status; depending on religious and cultural, as well as geographical context; what is sacred to one, is a meaningless fable to another.

My whole plan for this book was thrown into confusion.

I had originally had the idea for two chapters in my head: one entitled 'Mythologies', the other 'Sacred Books'.

Seated before the source material I had accumulated, after my fruitless search for a Bible in India, I realised that the distinction was absurd. To whom in the Christian west is the Indian *RigVeda*, the 'Book of Creation', sacred? Nowadays who would number the *Egyptian Book of the Dead* among the sacred books, seeing that the Pharaonic age has been remote past to us for 2000 years and it is unlikely that anyone is committed to the earth according to the holy rites of the *Book*

155

of the Dead? What South American tribe would accept the *Avesta,* the Parsee scriptures, in the ranks of eternally sacred books? What Arab is willing to accept the holy traditions of the Formosan mountain tribes as the true word of God?

I remember as if it were yesterday how I threw my concept of this chapter over the wall into the Arabian Sea, so to speak, during a nocturnal walk round Bombay harbour. Then I decided, using the texts of ancient books from the five continents, to undertake to prove that my gods were fruitfully and actively at work on our earth and to leave it to the reader to judge whether these sources are sacred or profane.

Fig. 67. The author interviewing Professor Dileep Kumar Kanjilal in Calcutta.

What I set out to prove remains the same; using convincing evidence from unmanipulated ancient sources, to make it clear once and for all that the gods were not 'spirit' but existed in the flesh; that their existence was far from being limited to their spectacular 'appearance' and their happy return to their home in heaven; that they bequeathed us information and knowledge in sacred and profane books and that the gods made mistakes that were by no means divine.

To be concise, I shall prove that the gods were not the stylised figures that religions have made of them. Now I am going to plunge into the rich and abundant source material.

The *Avesta* is not a Unit Trust, although it sounds like one. It is a Middle Persian word and means 'basic text' or 'instruction'. It contains the collected religious texts of the Parsees, the present-day followers of Zarathustra. The Parsees refused to accept Islam and emigrated to India in the tenth century. They are doomed to extinction. They marry late and only among themselves, so that their birth-rate is low. Today there are barely 100,000 of them living in India. Their vernacular language is Gujerati, a neo-Indian language but they hold their religious services in the Avestan language, which has its own alphabet and has become virtually unintelligible with the passage of time.

The Parsees have a reputation for philanthropy and high moral character, and they abstain from any attempt to convert non-believers, which makes them extraordinarily *sympathique*. What a pity, owing to their small numbers, that they cannot spread this splendid attitude round the world!

Today only a quarter of the original *Avesta* has survived. It comprises the sacrificial prayers, *Yasna*, the *Yashts* with hymns to the twenty-one deities, a collection of ancient Iranian myths with subsequent additions, the *Visprat* with invocations to higher beings and lastly the *Videvat*, a book of ecclesiastical law with precepts for purification and penitence.

Parts of this ancient Persian religion were preserved in cuneiform script, which King Darius the Great (550-486 B.C.), his son Xerxes (519-465 B.C.) and his grandson Artaxerxes (465-424 B.C.) commissioned.

The supreme god is called Auramazda (Aura), who was creator of heaven and earth. With few exceptions, the other gods are only mentioned briefly. Fortunately, I hasten to add, for the strange names written in an alien tongue are hard to read and confusing, because they are so unfamiliar, unlike Joshua, Nehemiah, Obadiah, Habakkuk, Zephaniah or Malachi, whose equally strange sounding names are drilled into us in religious classes. But if you want to broaden your horizon, you will have to swallow the names of these illustrious persons, for better or for worse.

The various subsections of the *Avesta* have some extremely up-to-date information. In the Creation Myth (1) it says:

Then Yima made this earth grow until it was some three

thirds larger than it was before. On one third, cattle, beasts of burden and men now live. According to his wish and will, as his will ever shall be. 2 Fargard, lines 39-41.

Today we know that the earth's surface consists of 70.8% water and 29.2% land, i.e. a bare third. But the ancestors of the ancient Persians had not mapped the globe in those days. Who told them that 'cattle, beasts of burden and men' now lived their life *on one third*? Spirits and ghosts are not so specific in their communications.

The hygienic instructions which the god Auramazda gave the prophet Zarathustra (ca. 630-588 B.C.) refer to disease carried by bacteria as clearly as do the precepts in Leviticus. In the *Avesta* they run as follows:

A man dies in the depths of the valleys. The birds fly down from the mountain peaks to the depths of the valleys. Down to the body of this dead man and consume it. Down they fly to a tree, a hard or a soft one. They spew on it, they defecate on it, they urinate on it. A man goes up from the depths of the village to the mountain peaks. He goes to the tree where the birds were, for he wants firewood. He fells this tree, he cuts it up and splits the pieces . . . a corpse which is carried off by dogs, birds, wolves, winds or flies makes men unclean. 5 Fargard, lines 1-12.

In Leviticus, the description is on the same lines:

Every bed whereon he lieth that hath the issue is unclean: and every thing whereon he sitteth, shall be unclean . . . And he that sitteth on any thing whereon he sat that hath the issue shall wash his clothes, and bathe himself . . . And what saddle soever he rideth upon that hath the issue shall be unclean. And whosoever toucheth any thing that was under him shall be unclean . . . And the vessel of earth, that he toucheth which hath the issue, shall be broken . . .' Leviticus 15, 4-12.

These are statements of applied physiology of the kind now accepted as a matter of course on the basis of medical research. This knowledge was obviously not a matter of general experience, for it was always imparted by gods — and not only to Zarathustra and Moses. For different modes of behaviour are found in different ancient scriptures and it is always a god who gives the hygienic explanation.

I don't want to take part in the debate on which of the traditions is the older and which sacred or profane book took its information from a still older source. Who made use of whom, and when, is a very boring question. What matters to me is to put it on record that ancient peoples knew the chain reaction by which diseases are transmitted: corpse-bird-tree-man or patient-sickbed-saddle-vessel. Where did they get that knowledge from? A spirit god would not have bothered with such (important!) trifles. No, it must have been an educated man, anxious to promote development, a man with heads, hands and feet, sent from a prosperous industrial planet.

If we take the old traditions literally, the different peoples received all their practical knowledge from the gods at first hand. Of course you could argue that our forefathers would have had plenty of time to track down the process of infection by contact, without having the remotest idea of infectious micro-organisms. It is possible, but why should a general experience always issue from the mouths of the gods as an important revelation? It must have been a surprising statement, if people attributed its proclamation to the gods. Furthermore, how could our early forfathers have known that only a third of the earth is inhabitable? 'Spirit' does not divide the earth's surface into map squares. 'Spirit' has no eyes.

I postulate that the gods were people of flesh and blood.

STARS WITH SPECIAL QUALITIES

According to the Parsee scriptures, the stars form a host which is subdivided into various companies and they in turn are organised by a commander-in-chief. Tistrya is imagined as the supreme ruler of the constellations, a name which is also born by a single star. This star Tistrya is extolled forty times in the highest terms. For example:

'. . . The star Tistrya, the brilliant,do we praise. We praise the heavens that follow its laws. We praise endless time.

We praise time, the mistress of long periods.' 8. Tistar-Yast of the *Khorda Avesta*.

Next it is noteworthy that stars are praised for their especial qualities. For example:

. . . Praise we the star Tistrya, the brilliant, the majestic.

Praise we the star Catavaeca, which governs the water,

the strong, created by Mazda.

Praise we all the stars which contain the seeds of water.

Praise we all the stars which contain the seeds of earth.

Praise we all the stars which contain the seeds of trees.

Praise we those stars which are called Haptoiringa, the majestic, health-bringing, those in resistance to the Yatus praise we . . . .

Afrigan Rapithwine, verse 13.

I read in scholarly interpretations that these are only supposed to be fantastic extravagant decorations for the gods. But is that right? I suspect that there is something a good deal more concrete behind them.

Sheikh Mohammed Fani wrote in the book *Dabistan* (2) that to the Parsees *the planets are simply bodies with a spherical shape*. Well, well! Not until 1610 A.D. did Galileo Galilei cause a revolution in astronomical hypotheses by proving that the Copernican system was right.

In his book the same talented Sheikh describes the different temples that the Parsees erected at the gods' behest in honour of their planet of origin. One attractive peculiarity was that in every temple there was a spherical model of the planet with which it was associated. Each temple had its own domestic and clothing regulations depending on its particular planet. Parsees could only be seen in the Temple of Jupiter in the raiment of the scholar or the judge; in the Sanctuary of Mars they wore martial red garments and conversed 'in proud tones as if in an officers' mess'. In the Temple of Venus, they laughed and joked; in the Temple of Mercury they spoke like orators or philosophers. In the Temple of the Moon the Parsee priests behaved like children and *acted like wrestlers*, but in the Temple of the Sun they wore gold and brocade, and comported themselves *as befitted the King of Iran*.

In the oldest Parsee traditions I once again encounter astronomical concepts of time of a kind that remind me of time dilation.

This is what the Parsee calendar looked like:

Saturn's revolution round the sun corresponded to a day. That would be 29.5 years according to present-day astronomical calculations.

Thirty of these days equalled one month, i.e. a period of 885 terrestrial years.

Twelve of these months made a year, which was 10,620 terrestrial years.

They used the word *Ferd* for a million of these Parsee years.

A million *Ferd* made a *Vert*, and a million *Vert* was called a *Mert*.

A million *Mert* made a *Yad*, 3000 *Yad* a *Vad* and 2000 *Vad* a *Zad*.

The first monarchy which *ruled from heaven* is supposed to have lasted for more than 100 Zad. According to my calculations that would be a number with twenty-five figures.

What are we supposed to make of that?

I ask the simple question: why and for what end did the Parsees reckon in such vast periods of time? This 'calendar' would have been of no use at all to them in their everyday life. We celebrate the turn of the millennium as the great caesura in history and forecast exceptional prospects for the future from this turning point. In the Parsee calendar a millennium was a mere month.

No, this calendar only begins to make sense in connection with astronomy and vast periods of time:

'Praise we endless time. Praise we time, the mistress of long periods. . . .'

In the Indian national epic the *Mahabharata,* dating from the pre-Christian past, one of the 80,000 couplets gives philosophical expression to the immensity of time.

'God embraces space and time.

Time is the seed of the universe.'

The *Veda* (ancient Indian for knowledge) comprises the oldest religious literature of the Aryan Indians. The ancient Indian in which it is written is much older than the subsequent Sanskrit literature which took it over. The *Veda* is a collection of all the scriptures considered to be 'superhuman' and inspired. The date when it originated is still hotly disputed.

Rather like the Parsee *Avesta,* the *Veda* is grouped into four large sections. Originally it was a collection of hymns in the possession of leading priestly families – preserved in writing. Then the hymns became public property and were handed down literally by word of mouth for many centuries. In the process the *RigVeda* became the oldest source, going back into the remote past, of language, ethnology and religion. The

SamaVeda contains melodies which are turned into songs in the relevant texts of the *RigVeda*. The *YadshurVeda* is a collection of sacrificial liturgies and the *AtharveVeda* contains the tricks of white and black magic.

The contents of all four *Vedas* are still handed down in many schools as the highest cultural values. If these values were not preserved, the poor Indian people with its population of 500 million and more would probably collapse even more quickly and brutally into total dissolution.

One of the foremost experts on ancient Indian traditions is Professor Dileep Kumar Kanjilal of the Sanskrit University, Calcutta. On 12 August 1975, I visited this amiable scholar in his college for a conversation, taped extracts from which follow:

Professor, how old are the most ancient Vedic texts?
We must date the oldest texts to about 5000 B.C.

I found descriptions of flying cars in various Indian Sanskrit translations. Are they merely mythological products of the imagination?
India is a very old country with an extraordinarily rich Sanskrit tradition. In my opinion, the flying cars, which are often called Vimanas, actually were flying machines of some kind. When examining the many interpretations available today, we must not forget that for 2000 years all these descriptions have always been looked at with old eyes, so to speak. Now that we know that flying machines exist, the whole problem needs tackling from a new angle. It is no longer any use clinging to the traditional approach. Every perception that is bound to its time undergoes a transformation. Undoubtedly something factual is hidden behind the descriptions of flying cars; they have a different meaning from the one previously attributed to them. Naturally many mythological elements will still remain but we are trying hard to extract the scientific truth that is contained in these technological sounding traditions.

I know the story of Arjuna's ascent to Indra's heaven from the Mahabharata. It depicts the 'magical figure' of a heavenly car, which sails up into the clouds with a noise like thunder, on the various stages of its flight. Is it possible for an expert on Sanskrit texts like yourself to visualise a spacecraft in this description?
The passage about Arjuna's journey to heaven that you

have just mentioned is by no means complete. You appear to have been using a deficient translation. In the original version you could read that Arjuna sees some flying cars *which have crashed and are out of action.* Other flying cars stand on the ground, yet others are already in the air. These clear observations of flying cars and cars that can no longer fly prove that the original authors of the report knew exactly what they were talking about.

Are the ancient Indian gods immortal?

Generally speaking, no. They evidently pass through three stations and at the end of the third station they die. Moreover, the gods grew senile and suffered from quite normal disorders of old age. In the Sanskrit texts there are – naturally, I was going to say – many marriages between the gods and they also beget children. Copulation between gods and men also exists. The offspring of these unions inherited the knowledge and the weapons of their fathers. There is a passage in the *Ramayana* (next to the *Mahabharata,* the second great Indian epic) which tells how the deserts originated, namely as a result of destruction by terrible weapons of the gods. You can find descriptions of such weapons in the *Mahabharata.*

I accept Professor Kanjilal as an outstanding expert.

Back in my hotel I looked through the *Mahabharata* for the passage Professor Kanjilal had referred to. I found it in Book 8, the *Musala Parva:*

The unknown weapon is radiant lightning, a devastating messenger of death, which turned all the relations of Vrishni and Andhaka to ashes. Their calcined bodies were unrecognisable. Those who escaped lost their hair and nails. Crockery broke without cause; birds turned white. In a very short time food was poisonous. The lightning subsided and became fine ash.

A report from Hiroshima, or Nagasaki?

We can never forget the image of that holocaust.

The first atom bomb fell on Hiroshima on 6 August 1945. It claimed 260,000 human lives and the number of wounded was legion. Three days later Nagasaki was annihilated by atom bombs. There were 150,000 dead. We are haunted by images that rob us of sleep; people shrivelled up to the size of children's dolls by the incandescent heat; invalids without hair or skin who perished in field hospitals; trees and fields which were nothing but ashes. We must never forget it.

The American philosopher George Santayana (1863-1952) said:

'Those who do not remember the past, are doomed to repeat themselves.'

The catastrophe described in the *Mahabharata* took place unknown millennia ago:

It was as if the elements had been unleashed. The sun spun round in circles. Scorched by the fearful heat of the weapon, the world reeled. Elephants were burnt by the incandescent heat and ran wildly to and fro. . : . Water boiled; animals died. . . . The raging fire made the trees topple like ninepins as if in a forest fire. . . . Horses and chariots burnt up; it looked like the aftermath of a conflagration. Thousands of chariots were destroyed, then deep silence descended. . . . It was a ghastly sight to see. The corpses of the fallen were so mutilated by the frightful heat that they no longer looked like human beings. Never before have we seen such an awful weapon, and never before have we heard of such a weapon.

Hiroshima? Nagasaki? Or somewhere on the distant subcontinent thousands of years ago?

The heavens cried out, the earth bellowed an answer, lightning flashed forth, fire flamed upwards, it rained down death. The brightness vanished, the fire was extinguished. Everyone who was struck by the lightning was turned to ashes.

Hiroshima? Nagasaki? India?

No, a quotation from the Babylonian-Sumerian Epic *Gilgamesh*. Memories of the future.

We must not be such cowards as to dismiss such traditions as pointless myths and acclaim the authors' poetic imaginations. The large number of similar accounts in ancient scriptures turns a suspicion into certainty: the 'gods' used A or H weapons from (as yet) unknown flying objects.

Over nine years ago, in connection with the un-explained explosion on 30 June 1908, in the stony Tunguska of the Siberian taiga, I asked whether many symptoms – calcined men and women, herds of reindeer annihilated, trees burnt bare – might not point to an atomic explosion. Once again I was ridiculed.

There are more than 80 different theories of the cause of this event. The internationally recognised Soviet geologist Dr. Alexei Solotov devoted seventeen years of his life almost exclusively to investigating the riddle of the taiga. During recent years a scientific commission with members from several faculties has supported him. On 15 October 1976, Solotov declared in Moscow that an atom-driven spaceship had undoubtedly exploded in the taiga in June 1908. Radioactive substances still measurable today and the special characteristics of destruction still recognisable in this district excluded every theory hitherto accepted as probable. To questions such as: 'But wasn't it the impact of a giant meteorite?' and 'Couldn't it have been an earthquake?' Dr Solotov of the Academy of Sciences answered courageously: 'It was a spaceship and I shall prove it!' I am delighted to be able to quote his remark in this book.

After the discovery of nuclear fission the Americans worked on the preparation of the uranium bomb from 1943 to 1945. The first bomb was exploded on 16 July 1945, on the testing-ground near Los Alamos, New Mexico. The second fell on Hiroshima, the third on Nagasaki.

No, No, revered experts, you must accept it in the end. The stories of the chroniclers were not the products of their macabre imagination. What they handed down was once the stuff of experience, ghastly reality.

Spirits have no weapons. But the gods were made of flesh and blood.

As I have already mentioned, the *Ramayana* is the second great Indian epic. Unlike the *Mahabharata* it is an artistic epic, the poet Valkimi being accepted as its author according to native tradition.The written copy is dated to the fourth or third century BC. The hero of the epic is the King's son Rama, whose wife Sita was abducted by the daemonic giant Rawana and taken to the Island of Lanka. With the help of the King of the Apes, Rama managed to fetch her back. Rama was worshipped as the Indian incarnation of the god Vishnu, which is why the *Ramayana* is considered a sacred book in India.

The *Ramayana's* 24,000 shlokas* are also a treasure trove to
* Shloka, an Indian poetic measure consisting of two lines of verse.

pointers to the gods' space-travelling activities. There is a detailed description of a wonderful car which immediately suggests the idea of a spaceship. The car rises into the air with a whole family on board. Curiously enough, this craft is described as a flying pyramid which takes off vertically. When this flying pyramid rose from the ground, it naturally made a tremendous noise. That, too, one can read in the Sanskrit texts.

From the second half of the last to the beginning of this century it seems to have been the fashion to publish and comment on ancient Sanskrit writings in Germany. There are many well-intentioned books, behind which one can sense decades of painstaking work. I would encourage any of my readers who are especially interested, to borrow some of them from a library. If the *Ramayana* mentions what is clearly a flying apparatus, which made the mountains tremble, rose up amid thunder, burnt trees, meadows and the tops of houses, Professor Ludwig (3) comments as follows: 'There can be absolutely no doubt that this only meant a tropical storm.' *O sancta simplicitas!*

There is a German, but not literal, translation of the *Ramayana* by Professor Hermann Jacobi. The content is reproduced chapter by chapter, line by line. If the Professor comes up against complicated passages (4) which he finds meaningless because they talk about flying objects, he simply ignores them and in his arrogance remarks, 'Senseless babble' or 'This passage can safely be omitted, it contains nothing but fantastic ravings.'

In the Zurich Central Library I found countless volumes *about* Indian literature, Indian mysticism, Indian mythology and yard-long commentaries on the *Mahabharata*, the *Ramayana* and the *Vedas*, but very few direct translations. Scholarly commentaries *on* Indian texts are no longer my affair, since I know how much is suppressed as irrelevant, and since I realised that foreign sacred books are arrogantly dismissed by Bible-soaked westerners: 'Our religion is incomparably deeper and truer!' I cannot stand this denigration of other religions.

For seventy years people worked without the scholarly

objectivity we hear so much about.

It did not occur to anyone to bring out a *complete* translation of the *Ramayana* or the *Mahabharata,* without a commentary. You are always coming upon fragments, but you can drown in commentaries, with no quarter given. So I stuck to the only large-scale translations into English, the *Mahabharata* translated by Chandra Potrap Roy in Calcutta in 1896 (5), and the translation of the *Ramayana* (of which several English versions exist) by M. Nath Dutt, Calcutta, 1891. (6). There are good German translations of the Vedas.

I know the tongue-twisting sentences that young actors have to practise. They ought to try to pronounce the title of a Sanskrit text in the dramatic academies. It goes like this: Samarânganasutradhâra. (7) Anyone who can say it had better ring me up.

This monstrosity of a word heads the section on Vimanas, or flying vehicles. Like our helicopters, they are described as extremely manoeuvrable. They can stand still in the air, move round the globe or out into space above and dive to attack terrestrial targets. Unfortunately the book does not give individual details that would enable us to reconstruct the vehicle, not *'because of ignorance, but in order to avoid misuse.'* I do not know if there were terrorists in those days who could have knocked up these fabulous Vimanas. At least precautions were taken against industrial espionage and unlicensed manufacture.

Nevertheless, some very impressive information is given: (8)

> The body must be strongly and durably formed . . . of light material . . . . In a marvellous way a man can cover great distances in the heavens owing to the power dormant in the quicksilver which sets the driving whirlwind in motion.Likewise, it is possible, with practice, to build a Vimana as big as the temple for the 'god in motion'. Four strong quicksilver containers must be built into it. When these are heated by controlled fire from the iron containers, the Vimana develops the power of thunder through the quicksilver and looks like a pearl in the sky . . . The *Ramayana* tells us more about some of these flying cars:

> When morning came, Rama climbed climbed into the

heavenly car. The power of the car is boundless. The car was two storeys high with several sections and many windows. . . . It was colourful and mighty. . . . When it rose into the air, a heavenly sound rang out. . . .

Today aircraft and spaceships often have the names of birds on their bows: stork, hawk, eagle, etc. If ever these words are interpreted mythologically in days to come, I shall understand why. What business has an eagle on the moon (Eagle has landed)?

But no symbolic concepts of or mythologically explicable names for Vimanas occur in the Ramayana or the text with the unpronounceable title. Without beating about the bush, the talk is all about xlyimg cars, heavenly cars or vehicles of the gods among the clouds. No, the assertion by Sanskrit interpreters that the writers wanted to glorify or embellish the heroes with their descriptions cannot be accepted by anyone today. Just imagine all the things that could be discovered in these texts if our spaceflight engineers could read Sanskirt, that two and a half thousand year-old literary language, in the original? Even today it is the language of science and poetry in India.

AN AERIAL BATTLE AND A FLYING APE

I have already sketched out the basic story of the *Ramayana*. The section 'Rama and Sita' describes exactly how the villainous Rawana kidnaps the bewitching Sita in *an aerial car that is like the sun*. The flight goes over valleys, woods and high mountains. Neither the cries for help nor the prayers of the kidnapped heroine can persuade the villain to take her back.

When Rama hears about the commando-like abduction of Sita, he gives the laconic military order: 'Fly out the aerial cars at once!'

Rawana is already flying over the ocean in the direction of Lanka (Ceylon). But Rama's aerial car must have flown faster, for he is soon able to challenge Rawana to aerial combat. He uses a *heavenly arrow* to shoot down the kidnapper's vehicle, which dives *down into the depths*. Sita is saved and gets into her husband's celestial car, which, *at Rama's behest, rose up to a mountain of cloud with an enormous noise.*

Rama can consider himself lucky to have capable comrades in arms, because they are skilled in the use of incredibly cunning devices. One of these gifted comrades is the King of the Apes with his Minister Hanuman. The royal ape can grow into a giant or shrink up to a midget at will. But above all he is a daredevil pilot:

> When he begins his flight from the mountains, the tops of the cliffs break, the foundations of the mountains shake, giant trees are stripped of their boughs and broken, a shower of wood and leaves falls to the ground. The mountain birds and animals flee to their hiding-places.

The daring ape in his flying machine often starts from a city. This is not so popular, for *the beautiful lotus trees of Lanka are washed away.* The spectacle the cities see is simply beyond their powers of comprehension:

> *With burning tail he swings himself up over the rooftops and kindles vast conflagrations so that the tall buildings and towers collapse and the pleasure gardens are laid waste.*

Only an illiterate could overlook the fact that flying cars were described in ancient Indian texts. Anyone who denies that, does not want to admit it because it does not fit his world picture. In line with the theories of Darwin, who attributed a gradual and peaceful evolution to all living beings, the blessing of evolution is also bestowed on technology and human consciousness. No outside intervention in this gentle development was allowed. Even inexplicable leaps in evolution are usually declared to be a step by step procession through human history, it must — if no other convincing explanation can hold its own — make world-record leaps. Loren Eiseley, Professor of Anthropology at the University of Pennsylvania, has got wind of it:

> We have every reason to believe that, without prejudice to the forces that took part in the formation of the human brain, a stubborn and protracted struggle for existence between different groups of human beings *could not possibly* have produced such high mental faculties as those we accept today among all peoples in the world. *Something else, a different formation factor must have escaped the attention of the theoreticians of evolution.*

That is so, but 'The spirit did not fall from heaven'! (9)

The fantastic element that emerges in ancient texts and cannot be satisfactorily fitted into the *theory* of evolution is dismissed as humbug as soon as another *theory* is deduced from it, i.e. extra-terrestrials manipulated hominids and developed their minds suddenly in comparison with the length of human history. This means stalemate: one theory against another.

That may be normal and no disgrace so long as the holders of a theory do not behave as if they had been present in person when the hominids became intelligent.

If evolution is a continuing process, I ask for a — convincing! — answer to these questions: By what dispensation' did descriptions of heavenly vehicles *suddenly* appear in the ancient books of mankind in all four corners of the world? How did virtually intercontinental flights in comfortable capsules come about? Why were our ancestors always instructed in the practical affairs of life by these alien beings who came from heaven and why did they all return to their planet of origin once their task was completed? Where did our ancestors get the blueprints for the heavenly cars described with such precision? And the knowledge of the materials to be used? And the navigational instruments? (Even a god could not fly from India to Ceylon 'by eye'!) The craft that animated the heavens weren't like children's kites or sporting monoplanes. The heavenly cars were several storeys high; many of them were *as big as a temple*. Cars like that were not built in some do-it-yourself family workshop!

Why were these vehicles not developed further in line with the theory of evolution? Step by step, we should have landed on the moon a few thousand years ago!

When the Saturn Project, commissioned by NASA, was being developed and carried into effect, 20,000 firms of suppliers collaborated on the programme.

In the whole of Sanskrit literature there is not one line referring to technicians, factories or test flights. The heavenly vehicles were suddenly, simply and above all surprisingly, there. 'Gods' produced and worked them. Invention, planning and manufacture did not take place on our planet.

That is why I say that spirit did fall from heaven!

I cannot deny myself a slight digression here. Years ago when I wrote about the plains of Nazca* and suggested that the mysterious lines in the Peruvian foothills of the Andes

Fig. 68. Work rooms in space! NASA plan of a space station in orbit round the earth. This station could be assembled by the 1980s with the help of the Space Shuttle.

were landing-strips for spacecraft, my opponents scornfully pointed out that spaceships do not need landing-strips. *Basta*.

The first and biggest landing-ground ever built for 'ships from the universe' is under construction in America. The reason? The Space-Shuttle will take over the role of launching rockets; it will take manned and unmanned spacecraft up into orbit. But the Space-Shuttle has only very limited manoeuvrability within the earth's atmosphere owing to its limited fuel reserves. Space pilots need the gigantic landing-strips, because they must reach them on their first approach flight — there is not enough fuel to make a repeat approach. The first Space-Shuttle will take off in 1978. It is expected to have a life of 35,000 to 60,000 flying hours.

The vehicles reported in the Indian texts were obviously far ahead of the Space-Shuttle as regards construction. They could *fly round the earth*, they could *remain stationary in the air* and *mingle with the stars*, radiating light of such intensity that it seemed as if *there were two suns in the sky*.

Such observations makes us speculate whether photon

* *Chariots of the Gods?* — *Return to the Stars.*

propulsion units, the hypothetical ultimate goal of space-travel technology, were involved. Professor Eugen Sänger (1905-1964), a famous rocket and space-travel investigator, examined the possibility of photon drive which, without loss during the conversion of energy, could theoretically reach the speed of light at launching velocity. This kind of drive for flying bodies in space would shoot out a directed cluster of electromagnetic waves — light, perhaps — and so acquire its thrust. Photons are elementary particles without mass. Professor Ernst A. Steinhoff says that given existing technological standards, photon drive is hardly conceivable. There is absolutely no doubt that it is unrealisable at the moment. But technological standards are improving daily. Why should alien intelligences not have reached those standards long ago? Because we think we are the lords of creation?

But one fine day when spaceships with photon drive are shooting through our skies, the radiation will look *like lightning* and at great heights, shine *like a second sun*.

The martial imprint they left behind in the *Mahabharata* shows how physical the gods were. If military men from east and west ever thumb through this Indian epic, it will make their mouths water. The gods possessed weapons with murderously destructive powers.

In the Adi Parva, one of the books of the *Mahabharata*, the God Agni gives the hero Vasudeva a discus called Chakra, assuring him that he can kill his enemies with it: *'The weapon will always return to you when it has completed its mission.'*

When the valiant Vasudeva was in a perilous situation, he used Chakra against his enemy Shisupala:

'The edge of the discus instantly severed the king's head from his body and returned to Vasudeva's hand.'

We might imagine that it was a razor-sharp boomerang. But it was not, for the weapon was *enveloped in fire,* a gift from the fire god. Vasudeva would have burnt his hands badly if he had caught the boomerang in flight.

We know that the gods dwelling with Arjuna the hero of the epic, had highly sophisticated weapons at their disposal. So he turns to the god Shiva and asks him for a mighty weapon. The latter gives it to him with instructions how to use it:

O mighty hero, I shall give you my favourite weapon, Pashupat. But you must take care that you do not use it wrongly. If you hurl it at a weak enemy, it will destroy the whole world. There is nobody who cannot be killed by this weapon . . . After the purification sacrifice Shiva initiated him into the secrets of its use. Then he bade Arjuna to come into the kingdom of the heavenly ones. Arjuna prayed to Shiva, *the Lord of the Universe*, who disappeared into the clouds with Uma, his wife, like the setting sun . . . . (10)

The God Kuvera, who is described as a kind of keeper of the arsenal, gives Arjuna the weapon *Antardhana*, a precious and agreeable weapon for it has the power to put *the enemy to sleep*. A wonderful vision! How nice it would be if both the NATO and Warsaw Pact armies were to fall asleep together. At all events, the UN Secretary-General, who decides when they should wake up, would have to be very intelligent . . . .

When Arjuna has received the hypnotic weapon, Indra, the Lord of Heaven, *with his wife Sachi, drives up to Arjuna in his heavenly chariot and bids the hero to enter the car and travel in the heavens with him.*

The fluctuating struggle for power by the Kaurava and Pandava dynasties runs through the *Mahabharata's* war chronicles. The gods are continually intervening and their unfamiliar weapons are always decisive. The weapon *Narayana* is used in a battle with the Pandava troops:

A deafening tumult filled the battlefield. The Narayana weapon flew through the air; thousands of arrows came out of it like hisssing snakes and fell on the warriors on all sides.

That is in the book of the *Mahabharata* called Drona Parva. One thinks at once of the Stalin 'organs' (multiple rocket-throwers) which the Red Army introduced in the Second World War. They got their name both from the arrangement of the firing mechanism and from the sound of the approaching projectiles, which was like an organ.

The 'gods' seem to have been unequalled in the invention of evil weapons. And Arjuna possessed them. That is why he was exhorted to fire only the *'first* weapons' that the gods had given him, because the *'last* weapon' would have a devastating effect. To be sure even the first weapons were not made of papier mâché:

The weapons shot high into the air and from them burst flames like the great fire that swallows up the earth at the end of a terrestrial era. The animals on land and in the great waters trembled with fear. The whole earth shook.

That is in the book of the *Mahabharata* called *Aunshana Parva*.

Fortunately there were men even in those days who knew what would happen if the 'last weapon' was put into service. When the battle was at its height the sage Veda Vyasa intervened and called on the warring parties to withdraw the 'last weapon', which had been brought into position. If it were actually used . . .

'. . . drought would afflict the land for ten long years . . . and kill unborn children in their mother's womb.'

Vietnam!

The horror of scorched earth, leafless trees, deformed children, dying men and women has become the trauma of us citizens of the twentieth century. The curse of total war which knows only the defeated.

May there always be a sage to reduce the 'last weapon' to silence.

These examples of weapons which were constantly introduced by the 'gods' into terrestrial struggles, are undisputable evidence for my statement that the 'gods' were made of flesh and blood. Weapons of the kind described in the ancient Indian texts were not in keeping with the technological standard of the people of those days. But the path to weapons of such murderous destructive power leads via stages of development in technology which would inevitably have left other 'monuments' behind, besides weapons. Yet there are none. The weapon systems were *suddenly* there, just as *suddenly* as the flying apparatuses.

I am not easily taken in. I resist the interpretations which say that it is all pure imagination that has made itself at home in mythology. The imagination, too, needs something to spark it off; it has to be animated. But when the imagination 'reveals' accurate knowledge, of which no one *can have had* the faintest idea, we really ought to explain the apparently unintelligible from the present-day point of view. That is why, in Chapter 2, I described weapons of the kind that are being developed and produced *today*!

We must accept the fact that earlier interpretations of such texts could not include weapon systems or spacetravel objects. But those golden days of ignorance are over. *We* know about nuclear weapons, *we* are experiencing the first stages of practical space-travel. *We* must (if we are honest) bring our knowledge to bear on the interpretation of an ancient text, even accepting the possibility that man will lose his halo as lord of creation, and the probability that the theory of evolution will be overturned. Did NOTHING really fall from heaven?

The Rig Veda, too, offers us flesh-and-blood gods who drive their carriages in space. Here are only a few samples of an extensive and many-sided vision of space:

Everyone, who *journeys* out of this world, goes to the moon first . . . . The moon is the gateway to the celestial world and the man who can answer his questions, him he lets through . . . .'   *RigVeda, 1 Adhyaya.*

'All honour to Vayu, master of the atmosphere, master of space! O seek me, the sacrificial lord, an abode out. Open the gates of heaven, of the universe, that we may see thee achieve universal dominion.All honour to the masters of heaven, the masters of space. O seek me out an abode. Thither would we go.'   *RigVeda*, 24 (11)

A venerable sage instructs his pupil:

Space is greater than fire, for in space are both sun and moon, in it are lightning, stars and fire. Power of space one calls, one hears, one answers; in space man rejoices and does not rejoice; *man is born in space,man is born for space;* mayest thou worship space! He who worships space achieves space kingdoms, worlds rich in light, unconfined, for striding out boldly, *and as far as space reaches, so far will it be granted to him to walk at will* . . . .   *RigVeda*, 7 (12)

The venerable teacher is not giving his pupil a mental pattern for philosophical ideas, as one might perhaps say, in which case the text would have no connection with 'genuine' space. I have before me the family trees of such venerable teachers, which go back fifty-six generations to that Lord who *possessed the original knowledge*. With the difference that the genealogy of the RigVeda goes back to incomparably earlier times, it is the same as with the relay-race which in biblical genealogy leads back from Jesus to King David, from David to Abraham, from Abraham to Adam, to the original source of knowledge. You cannot take a patent on one family-tree, because it suits your purpose, and reject another that is equally solid and verifiable. It was incumbent on the venerable teachers in India to hand on tradition *unchanged*.

'*The moon is the gateway to the celestial world*'. Exactly! That is why both Americans and Russians made it their first goal for space-travel. Anyone who passes the crucial technological test of landing on the moon, him he lets *go beyond it*. Exactly. Now Mars has been reached; Venus and Jupiter are in our sights. Even if we formerly had only a marginal knowledge of space, it allowed us to reflect whether or not the moon may have been the test case for the inhabitants of other planets. The fact that intelligent life and civilisation on countless other planets is no longer disputed is an enormous advance made in the last ten years or so.

Master of the atmosphere, master of space, universal dominion? What is spurring the two leading powers of our age on to pursue space-travel? The cost is too high and the effort too great for it to be only a whim. In order to force breakneck technical progress by setting a very advanced target, we could think of and set ourselves less extravagant, accessible goals. The stocks of raw materials on our blue planet will be used up in the foreseeable future. The need to find new stocks on other planets made space-travel inevitable. Of course military motives, among many others, play an important role, but they rank far behind the realisation that the earth we have ravaged will be uninhabitable in the not so distant future.

One of the things that has been accepted as common knowledge today is that there are thousands and thousands of civilisations in the cosmos, indeed it is no longer seriously disputed that there are probably civilisations older than our own. It is a logical conclusion. Many millennia ago older civilisations on their home planets may have been in the desperate situation for which we are inevitably heading in the early part of the third millennium. *O master of space, seek out an abode for us. Thither would we go.*

Space stations are no longer the fantastic creations of

science-fiction writers. The designs exists; they are realisable with the same precision as the space rockets which are launched in America and Russia, and reach their targets on the dot. Even a four-storeyed space station which two American firms commissioned by NASA modelled on a 1:1 scale is already out of date. Space stations are planned that can take several hundred scientists and technicians on board. Under conditions of artificially created gravity they will do their research work in space as an everyday activity. We have already spoken about the future possibilities of space-travel. Here I may mention in passing that even space clinics are planned. Doctors *know* that certain patients who are considered incurable can get well in space.

Once a small band of astronauts has shown that the organism is not damaged by the stresses of space flight, women will travel in space, too. NASA is already training female astronauts. All the prerequisites for the *Rigveda* account will soon exist for us as well. '*Man is born in space, man is born for space!*'

Everything that is related about events in space in the ancient texts will be reality for us one day. It is 'only' a question of money. In the democracies short-sighted officials lack the courage to fix targets which will not bring success until the day after tomorrow. The survival of mankind is not a productive election issue anywhere in the western world. In the third world, public opinion is persuaded that there are more important tasks. This overlooks the fact that we are all in the same boat. When the factory chimneys of the industrial countries stop smoking, the blue planet will have to declare itself bankrupt. *O master of space, open the gates!*

THE SONS OF THE GODS ALWAYS IN TROUBLE

The book of the *Mahabharata* called *Adi Parva* tells of the conception and rearing of the semi-divine hero, Karna. The unmarried Kunti *was visited by the Sun god*. As a natural result of coupling with the god she bore a son, who took after his papa, for he was *radiant as the sun itself*. The former virgin Kunti was afraid of the shame that would attach to her, so she packed the child in a box and secretly put it in the river. The worthy Mrs Adhirata fished the baby out of the water, called him Karna and brought him up as her own child.

Who does not remember the moving story of baby Moses, whom in a basket made of rushes his mother entrusted to the Nile, from which one of Pharaoh's daughters took him ashore.

The countless sons of the gods are a problem. These members of the divine het-set not only abound in their hundreds in mythologies, but also exist in so to speak 'official', quite serious literature.

There is such an extraordinary story in the second century B.C. Qumran texts, which were found in caves in mountains near the Dead Sea in 1947, that I must mention it, at the risk of repetition.* The Lamech scroll that contains it is obviously more damaged after 2000 years than a library book that has been borrowed a thousand times. Time and the humidity in the cave have gnawed at it. But the fragmentary remains are interesting enough. It is not a myth, but a story noted down in historical time. This is it:

One day Lamech, Noah's father, came back from a journey that had lasted more than nine months. So he was surprised, and with good reason, to find a tiny baby, which could not be his and whose external features did not fit into the family at all. Who can blame Lamech for reproaching his wife Bat Enosh bitterly? But she swore by all that was holy that the seed must have come from him, Lamech, because she had had nothing to do with a soldier, or a stranger or even a *son of heaven:*

O my Lord . . . I swear to thee . . . that this seed was thine, this conception from thee and the planting of the fruit by thee, not by a stranger nor a guardian *nor a son of heaven* . . .

Lamech did not believe a word of it. He was terribly worried and went to ask his father Methuselah for advice. His father listened to the strange story, thought about it at length, but came to no conclusion, so he sought out the wise Enoch. This cuckoo's egg in a virtuous family made the ancient Methuselah accept the rigours of the journey. He had to find out the truth of the matter otherwise what would people think?

Enoch listened to Methuselah's report that a little boy had popped up from out of the blue and looked far more like a son

* *Chariots of the Gods?*

of heaven than a man, while his eyes, hair and skin did not resemble the rest of the family.

Sage old Enoch heard all this and sent Methuselah home with the disturbing news that a terrible judgement would come upon mankind and the earth. All flesh would be destroyed, because it was soiled and corrupt. But, said Enoch, he should order his son Lamech to keep the little boy and call him Noah, for the little Noah was chosen to be the ancestor of all those who survived the great judgement.

One astonishing thing about this family story is that a *son of heaven* is mentioned more than once as a legitimate procreator, another is that Noah's parents had already been told about the coming Flood. It is particularly noteworthy that grandfather Methuselah was given the news by Enoch, who according to tradition was soon afterwards carried up to heaven in a fiery chariot.

Enoch is my friend; I follow him closely. I have a special affinity for mysterious personalities, all the more as this man is mentioned so casually in the Old Testament. Enoch did not deserve to be relegated like this, for he was the author of an exciting book. If the fathers of the church had looked on us as bible readers who had come of age, the *Book of Enoch* would have its place in the book of books. But the ancient church excluded it from public use. Reason enough to make friends with Enoch and study his works.

When we find out what Enoch has to say, we realise that, from its point of view, the church was right in withholding the book from us. The information it supplies is so explosive that it could quite easily have thrown the God of the Old Testament out of the saddle.

Who was this Enoch, whose name in Hebrew means the initiate, the intelligent, the learned?

Moses describes him as the seventh of the ten patriarchs, i.e. an antediluvian patriarch, this son of Jared, who stands in the shadow of his son Methuselah, of whom Genesis says he lived 962 years — 'as old as Methuselah'. The narrator of the Pentateuch (the five Mosaic books) says that the initiate Enoch lived to be 365 years old and did not die, but *was carried up* to heaven in a fiery chariot.

We can consider ourselves doubly lucky that the prophet from the distant past left us an account of his wonderful experiences with the gods, and, that this first-person account ever turned up again.

Most modern scholars agree that the Book of Enoch was originally written in Hebrew or Aramaic. This original text was lost and has never been found.

If that loss had been definitive we should never have known anything about this precious literary work. But the Ethiopians prepared a translation based on a Greek version of the original. It originated in the early Christian era and was found in Egypt. At a point in time which can no longer be fixed this version of the Enoch text was included in the Old Testament canon of the Abyssinian Church and recorded in the list of holy scriptures.

News of the existence of the *Book of Enoch* reached Europe in the first half of the eighteenth century. The English explorer and founder of Ethiopian research James Bruce (1730-1794) not only discovered the source of the Blue Nile, but also brought back three copies of the Enoch text after the many years he spent abroad. Professor Richard Lawrence, later Archbishop of Cashel, first rendered some of it into English, before the German orientalist and Protestant theologian August Dillmann (1823-1894) made it readily available to scholars in his translation, which appeared in 1851. After that the text was amplified by some thirty additional Ethiopian manuscripts and collated with a Greek version. Comparison of the text by eminent academic scholars showed that we were dealing with a *genuine Enoch*.

Moreover, experts have not given up hope that one fine day the Hebrew or Aramaic original text will turn up in an Egyptian cemetery. Wonders never cease. The *Book of Enoch* is still found in some bibles which include the Apocypha. 'Apocrypha' in Greek means 'hidden writings' or sacred books that are kept secret.

I possess a translation of Enoch published in Thübingen in 1900. I know that there are more recent translations, but my version has an extensive critical commentary by 17 scholars that cannot be found elsewhere. The notes are useful, because they indicate different possible translations; they are not trying to hammer home one particular version. My copy enables you to sense the difficulties facing scholars when they tackled the labyrinthine, complicated and often chaotic text.

They were not afraid of admitting their confusion when confronted with astronomical series of figures, physical descriptions and semantic manipulations that are perfectly intelligible today. Consequently for every ten lines of Enoch they often give twenty lines of footnotes, in which the full range of linguistically possible translations is laid on the table. That's what I like to see.

If one tries to interpret the *Book of Enoch* solely from the theological point of view, it remains a strange hotch potch of information with no thread of Ariadne to lead one out of the maze. But if one leaves aside the luxuriant accessories and their flowery metaphorical language and concentrates on the skeleton, then we men of today are faced with an uncannily dramatic account – without changing one iota.

It is important to mention that Enoch scholars attribute the core of the book to *one* author and are unanimous in dating it the last third of the second century B.C. So in this case tradition has found only *one* author. The earlier assumption that the book might be of Christian origin has long been abandoned.

Everything I said about the eye witness' speechlessness is exemplified in the Enoch text. Both the observer of the events and the scribe lacked concrete ideas to explain what happened. Eyewitness and author found themselves in the situation to which you can reduce anybody by asking them to describe a spiral staircase without using their hands. Comparisons are necessary. The 'it looks like a game' has to be played. This game was always the norm for observers in the dim past, because it was necessary when they had to describe unknown and unprecedented processes in the words of *their* day. Incapable of relating what had happened in precise words, they had recourse to their (oriental) metaphorical language which waxed into a luxuriant growth of fairy-tale-like allegory. The bigger the impression made by the event experienced, the wilder the part played by the imagination.

In order to get the real picture of what occurred, it seems fair to me to erase the confusing colours, as it were, so that the documentary black and white photograph emerges – the instantaneous snap of the event. We ourselves were speechless when we saw the first direct pictures of Mars on television in our drawing-rooms. It must have been the same for eye witness's in the dim mists of time when they were impressed by shocking experiences.

The first five chapters of the *Book of Enoch* announce a Last Judgment. The God of heaven will leave his abode to appear on earth with his bands of angels. The next eleven chapters depict the fall of the 'rebel angels' who coupled with the daughters of men against their god's command. These 'angels' were given such specific tasks by their 'god' that it is really difficult to classify them in the host of heavenly beings:

Semyasa taught incantations and the cutting of roots, Armaros the answer to incantations, Baraquel star watching, Kokabeel astrology, Ezeqeel the lore of the clouds, Arakiel the signs of the earth, Samsaveel the signs of the sun, Seriel the signs of the moon . . .

That sounds as if God appointed the angels lecturers with special tasks during their stay on earth. We shall learn that the lecturers were well versed in their fields. There can be no doubt that their knowledge was streets ahead of that of the inhabitants of earth at the time.

Chapters 17 to 36, the 'hard core of the book', describe Enoch's travels in various worlds and to the distant vaults of heaven. Chapters 37 to 71 contain the so-called similitudes, parables of various kinds, imparted to the prophet by the gods. Enoch was directly commissioned to write down the similitudes so that he could hand them down to distant generations because his contemporaries could not understand the technical information; that was news for the future. This is not my interpretation, you can read it in Enoch!

Chapters 72 to 82 contain detailed information about the courses of the sun and moon, about intercalary days, the stars and the working of the heavens. They also give geographical destinations in the universe. The remaining chapters repeat Enoch's conversations with his son Methuselah, to whom he announces the coming Flood. The happy ending comes when Enoch vanishes into heaven in his fiery chariot.

The Slavonic *Book of Enoch* (14) contains details that are not found in the Ethiopic Book. It describes how Enoch made contact with the heavenly ones:

When I was 365 years old, I was at home alone one day in the second month . . . Then two very tall men, whom I had never seen on earth, appeared to me. Their faces shone like the sun, their eyes like burning torches; fire flashed from their lips; their garments and their song were magnificent; their arms like golden wings. They stood at the head of my bed and called me by name. I awoke from sleep and rose from bed; then I bowed before them, my face white with fear. Then spake both men to me: 'Be of good cheer, Enoch! Fear not! The Eternal Lord has sent us to thee, today thou shalt go to heaven with us. Instruct thy sons and thy servants what they must do in thy house. But no one shalt seek thee until the Lord leads you back to them.' . . .

Religious interpretations always claim that the antediluvian patriarch had a vision or saw an apparition. But the report is uncomfortably precise and refutes this explanation. For Enoch *awakes*, and at the request of the two men he gives instructions about what should be done in his absence. When Enoch's journey to heaven is also explained away as being simply a vision of death, I am compelled to say: Please have a good look, gentlemen, for the text says that the prophet returned to his family alive and well after his 'visions'.

It was no lucky chance that Enoch's experiences were written down. He was given strict orders to describe everything that had happened to him: (15)

The Lord said unto me: 'O Enoch, look at the writing on the heavenly tablets, read what is written thereon, and take note of all the details.' I looked at everything on the heavenly tablets, read everything that was written thereon, took note of everything and read the book.

This is the complete teaching of the wisdom, which is worthy of praise by all men and judge of all the earth, written by Enoch, the scribe.

This is the book, the word of righteousness and the reprimand of the eternal watchers.

And now, my son Methuselah, I tell thee everything and write it down for thee; I have revealed everything to thee and handed thee the books which have to do with all these things. My son Methuselah, preserve the books that come from thy father's hand and hand them on to the coming generations of the world.

Here everything is treated so factually and consciously that the man giving the orders cannot have been an imaginary being. No god of any religion ever asked for a detailed written record of his actions.

In the Slavonic *Book of Enoch* we also learn how many books were dictated to the prophet. It also says that God did *not* dictate in person, but entrusted the task to the archangel Bretil:

And he described to me all things in heaven, on earth and in the sea, the courses of the places of all elements, the seasons, the courses of days and the changes, the commandments and the teachings. And Bretil spoke to me for thirty days and thirty nights; his lips never stopped moving. I, too, wrote without ceasing everything that was said. When I had finished, I had written 360 books.

What does the library of the industrious scribe say about the much quoted 'eternal watchers'?

Before these happenings Enoch was hidden and no man among the children of men knew where he was hidden, where he abode or what had become of him . . . Lo, then the watchers of the great holy one summoned me, Enoch, the scribe, and said unto me: 'Enoch, thou scribe of righteousness, go tell the *watchers of heaven,* who left the high heavens, the holy eternal abodes, corrupted themselves with women as the children of men do, took women unto themselves and rushed to great ruin on earth.'

It would be blasphemous to transform this species of 'watchers of the heavens' into innocent angels. Even if they did do it (took women), they ought not to have done it, according to the interpreters of the holy scriptures. Angels are not supposed to mix with the daughters of earth. A whole troop must have been busy – 200 men who begot 1000 children were involved. They found themselves on an expedition without women and sought the objects of their fleshly lusts. And found them, like all occupation troops!

These and all the others with them took wives unto themselves, each of them chose one and they began . . . defile themselves with them . . . They became pregnant and bore *giants* 300 ells tall. They went to the daughters of men on earth, slept with them and defiled themselves with women . . . But the women bore giants and thus the whole earth was full of blood and unrighteousness.

If there were still any doubts about the origin and genus of the 'watchers', Enoch removes them unequivocally. He is summoned by the 'Lord', who obviously has authority over the watchers:

Come hither and harken unto my words. Go and speak to the *watchers of the heavens,* who sent thee, and ask them: 'You should intercede for men, not men for you. Why have you left high and holy heaven, slept with women, defiled yourselves with the daughters of men, taken wives unto yourselves and done as the children of earth and begot giants as sons? Although you were immortal, you have polluted yourselves with the blood of women, begotten children with the blood of the flesh, coveted the blood of men and produced flesh and blood as do they *who are mortal and perishable.'*

The situation is clear. Enoch is in the presence of the Commandant of the watchers. 'Watchers' are not the creation of this ancient prophet alone. They occur in the *Epic of Gilamesh.* The giants who were produced are mentioned. Baruch even gives the number of giants in existence shortly before the Flood:

God brought the Flood upon the earth and destroyed all flesh and also the 4,090,000 giants. The water was fifteen ells higher than the highest mountains ever were.

In the Enoch story we can only just catch the Commandant's sarcastic joke that he had expected his watchers to intercede for the children of earth, not men to be advocates of his subordinates. The exalted Lord is very angry over his crew's copulation with the daughters of men who are 'mortal and perishable'. Apparently he and his people are immortal. This attribute could be lost by the shameful nights of love and their products. Lastly the Commandant, who was dissatisfied with his people, knew the laws of time dilation on interstellar flights at high speeds! If the crew begot children on earth, the inhabitants of this planet would see through the swindle and realise that the visitors they had taken for gods were by no means immortal!

That was bad enough, but the chief was particularly annoyed by the disobedience of the crew whom he had given informative and educational tasks while he went about other business in the solar system in his spaceship. The fact that his expert instructors were chosen ground personnel, was all the more reason why they ought not to have coupled with the daughters of men. Here the heat of passion had thrown a spanner into a cosmic plan, a bitter pill for the Commandant.

I ask my readers not to forget about the giants who were born against orders. I shall let them plod through prehistory at their full height and with their enormous feet as proof of their former existence.

'Before these happenings Enoch was hidden and no man among the children of men, knew where he was hidden, where he abode or what had become of him.'

It may sound like a fairy-tale today, but in those days it was most unusual for a man of flesh and blood like Enoch to disappear suddenly and without trace from the face of the earth. Kidnapping had not yet become the everyday game of a sick society. Enoch's whereabouts would never have been explained if he himself had not put them on record.

Enoch went on a space journey!

ENOCH'S JOURNEY IN SPACE

Enoch, the astronaut, is speaking:
They bore me up into the heavens. I went in until I approached a wall which was built of crystal and surrounded by tongues of fire, and they began to fill me with fear. I went into the tongues of fire and approached a big house built of crystal. The walls of that house were like a floor paved with crystal stones, and its foundation was crystal. Its roof was like the path of the stars and lightning, with fiery cherubs between, and its heaven consisted of water. A sea of fire girdled its walls and its doors burnt with fire.

There was another house, bigger than the first; all its doors were open. In every respect, it was distinguished by magnificence, pomp and bigness. Its floor was of fire;

lightning and circling stars formed its upper part, and its roof was blazing fire. I perceived a lofty throne. Its appearance was like hoar-frost; around it was something that was like unto the radiant sun. Below the throne streams of blazing fire came forth and I could not look upon them. The great majesty sat thereon; his raiment was more brilliant than the sun and whiter than virgin snow. All around, ten thousand times ten thousand, stood before him, and everything that he wanted, that he did. And those standing by him did not withdraw from him by night or by day, nor did they go away from him.

They took me out and put me in a place. I saw the places of the lights, the store-rooms of the thunder and lightning. I saw the mouth of all the rivers of the earth and the mouth of the deep.

I saw the cornerstone of the earth and I saw the four winds which bear the earth and the strongholds of heaven. I saw the winds of heaven which move and swing round the sun's disc and all the stars. I saw the winds which carry the clouds above the earth; I saw the paths of the angels, and I saw at the end of the earth the strongholds of heaven above the earth.

I saw a deep abyss with pillars of heavenly fire, and I saw pillars of fire fall down below them; they could not be measured for height or for depth. Behind this abyss I saw a place where there were neither the strongholds of heaven above, nor the firmly fixed earth below, nor was there water below it. Nor were there any birds there; it was a desolate and dreadful place. There I saw seven stars like great burning mountains. When I enquired about it, the angel said: 'This is the place where heaven and earth are at an end'.

I wandered until I came to a place where there was no thing. There I saw fearful sights: I saw no heaven above and no firmly fixed land below, but a barren place, a great fire was there that blazed and flamed; the place had clefts in it down to the abyss and was full of falling pillars of fire.

The description is perfectly clear; I shall only give a few hints.

Enoch gives an accurate picture of his participation in a

space journey using the comparisons that would enable his contemporaries to share in the event mentally. It begins (as in Ezekiel) with the take-off in a space-shuttle to the mother spaceship. Enoch cannot get over his fear and amazement.

He is not familiar with the material of the space probe. He *has to* compare its heat-emitting outer hull to crystal stones because his contemporaries knew them from temples and palaces. Looks like . . . The reverse thrust jets which are already ignited for the launching, blaze like tongues of fire. As it is made of the same material as the outer hull, the interior also seems to him *as if* made of crystal.

What seems to Enoch to be the roof is obviously nothing else but the view through the hatch, but he does not know of the existence of heat-repelling glass, through which he can watch the courses of the stars. The sea of fire that surrounds the sun is the reflection, undiminished in the absence of an atmosphere, of the strong sunlight on the outer skin of the spaceship.

Even we could not understand the text, simple though it is, if we had not seen, for example, the coupling manoeuvre of the American and Russian astronauts with their probes in space. Then the Russians crept from their capsule through an airlock into the larger American one.

Enoch is taking part in a similar transfer to a much bigger spaceship when he says that he reached a larger 'house'. Again the flashing pomp and magnificence fascinated him (naturally, because his own home was a windy tent!). Again he lacked familiar words in the vernacular with which to convey his impressions to his fellow countrymen.

Here in the larger house he sees the Commandant, the 'great majesty'. As everyone obeys him, he must be the 'great majesty', in Enoch's way of looking at things. He finds the Commandant's raiment more brilliant than the sun and whiter than snow. The comparison is far from astonishing, for Enoch and his fellows wore coarse robes, woven from goat's hair. The 'astronaut look' was so magnificent that he took refuge in absurd-sounding comparisons. But the case is no different with present-day journalistic reporting on Haute couture shows when a really new fashion is presented in Paris, like Pierre Cardin's 'astronaut look' of a few years back. Then our own modern reporters juggled with daring comparisons to make the reader understand the extraordinary idea that had occurred to the head of a top fashion house. The same thing happened to Enoch.

Let those who are blind still consider the description of the space capsule as a dream or a vision. This recourse to unverifiable explanations breaks down completely in the face of observations which are too accurate to resemble even remotely the transfer of a vision into a written record. As Enoch also indulges in long demonstrable series of figures, the desperate theory of a vision crumbles to dust.

He saw, the prophet tells us, the mouth of all the rivers on earth; he describes the no man's land in the atmosphere, where no birds live; the zone of lethal cold in which there is no horizon, 'the place where heaven and earth come to an end'. Enoch grasped the eeriness of space.

ENOCH'S WEATHER SATELLITE

There my eyes beheld the secrets of thunder and lightning, the secrets of the winds, how they are divided to blow over the earth, and the secrets of the clouds and the dew. There I saw from whence they go out to that place and how the earth is filled with dust from there.

Next all the secrets of the lightning and the lights were shown me, how they lighten for the blessing and saturation of the earth.

For the thunder has fixed rules for the duration of the peal decreed for it. Thunder and lightning are never separated; driven by the spirit, they both travel on and do not separate. For when the lightning flashes, the thunder makes its voice resound.

Enoch was the recipient of knowledge that we earthdwellers only knew about thousands of years later. It is well known that thunder originates from the sudden expansion of air heated by lightning and is subject to the speed of sound (333 metres per second). Thunder *does have* fixed rules for 'the duration of its peal'. How much sooner would the laws of nature have been known, if the Enoch texts had been available to scholars? The ancient church fathers could certainly count on clever students of the Bible. They would have known the physical laws by which the universe works and the Almighty

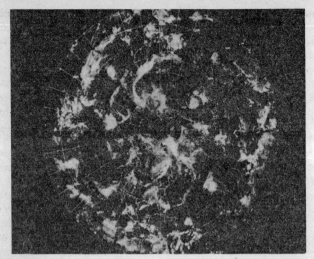

Fig. 69. This picture was composed from a number of individual photographs taken by the weather satellite ESSA V on 8.9.1967. They were assembled by a computer programme. You can see more than a dozen storm centres, and also the hurricanes which were known at the time by the attractive names Beulah, Doria, Chloe, Monica and Nanette.

would have been out of a job. We should have been in a position *to know* sooner, instead of having *to believe*. When we see satellite photographs of cloud formations above the earth on TV weather reports, we are experiencing what Enoch laid claim to in his report: he had seen it all from a great height with his own eyes.

'I saw the store-room of lightning.' That is certainly not an observation one can make from the back of a camel. But such 'store-rooms' can definitely be discerned at enormous heights. Lightning consists of powerful discharges of sparks between differently charged clouds, which build up discharge channels between themselves. Not until a channel reaches the earth's surface or another concentration of clouds, does the main discharge take place 'with pillars of heavenly fire'. Until then the lightning is collected so to speak in storerooms. Please do not blame Enoch! He had no idea of the existence of electricity and no conception of how brightly the heavens burnt when a quite normal flash of lightning converts an energy of 100 kilowatt hours. But there are also differences in tension of some hundred million volts. Naturally Enoch perceived these physical processes at a great height . . . heavenly fire!

ENOCH'S EARTH RESEARCH PROBE

After those days in that place where I had seen all the sights of what is hidden — I was caught up by a whirlwind and carried westwards — there mine eyes saw all the hidden things that should happen on earth: a mountain of iron, a copper mountain, a silver mountain, a gold mountain, a mountain of soft metal and a lead mountain.

The angel spoke: Wait but a while and everything hidden shall be revealed to thee. Those mountains that your eyes have beheld: the mountain of iron, the copper mountain, the silver mountain, the gold mountain, the mountain of soft metal, they shall all become before thy chosen eyes like wax before fire and like water that flows down over the mountains from above . . . .'

'This will be the end, for you know . . . all secrets, as well as all hidden powers and the powers of those who practise magic . . . who cast casting pictures for the whole earth; lastly too, how silver is won from the earth's dust, and how soft metal originates on earth. For lead and tin are not won from the earth like the first; there is a spring that produces them.'

We know that modern science employs satellites for earth research, for example in the NASA Earth Resources Technology Satellites programme. These space probes circle our planet in polar orbit at a height of 1000 km or more. They are equipped with multi-spectral TV cameras and the apparatuses of a radiometric comprehension system. With each picture TV cameras and radiometer cover an area about 200 km wide. Photographs that are very rich in contrast (false colour photography) are used for research in geology, geodesy, hydrology, oceanology, air and water pollution, etc., but also and especially for the discovery of mineral deposits, and the presence of gas, oil and water. Even archaeology has derived great benefit from the modern medium of space probes.

Today it is just as Enoch was told in olden times on his excursion into space. Satellite research finds deposits of different metals, discovers mountains of iron, copper, silver and gold beneath the earth's surface.

Even Enoch's remark that 'silver is won from the earth's dust' is correct. The silver content of the accessible part of the earth's crust is about 0.1 grammes per ton. Silver frequently occurs as a by-product of other metals, more rarely in workable deposits with about 500 grammes per ton. It must always 'be won from the earth's dust'. Pure lead is very seldom found in the earth's crust; it is washed out of slack during a rust reduction process at 1100 to 1200 C . . . it flows out as if from 'a spring'. Tin, too, which only occurs in the part of the earth's crust hitherto prospected in amounts of 3 grammes per ton, is smelted in electro-ovens and flows out of them as if from a spring.

Enoch means the initiate in Hebrew. During his space flight he was obviously initiated by skilled astronauts into technologies completely unknown to his own age.

EXPERT ADVISERS FOR SPECIAL DUTY LECTURERS

These are the names of their leaders over 100, 50 and ten. The name of the first is Jequn; he it is who led all the children of the angels astray, brought them down to the mainland (earth) and enticed them with the daughters of men. The second is called Asbeel; he gave the children of the angels bad advice, so that they defiled their bodies with the daughters of men. The third is called Gadreel; he it is who showed the children of men all kinds of death-dealing blows. He also seduced Eve, and showed the children of men the instruments of death, armour, the shield, the broadsword and every conceivable kind of instrument of death. From that hour onwards weapons have spread from his hand to the inhabitants of the earth. The fourth is called Penemue; he showed the children of men the difference between bitter and sweet and made known to them all the secrets of their wisdom. He taught men how to write with paper and ink, and as a result many have sinned from eternity to eternity and down to this day. The fifth is called Kasdeya; he taught the children of men all kinds of evil blows, the blows of the embryo in the mother's womb so that it departs, the blows of the soul, the snake's bite, the blows that arise from the midday heat . . . . Through Michael the earth was founded above the water and fair waters came out of the hidden regions of the mountains . . . .

Enoch or the historian describes the text as an account in images. They are images like those in paintings behind glass. The motifs shine through unmistakably. Jequn and Asbeel were responsible for the extraterrestrials copulating with the daughters of men and so for the production of giants, whose former existence is yet to be proved. Gadreel, skilled in biology and technology, knew the lore of weapons, including the production of unknown instruments of death. He must have acquired his knowledge outside the earthly regions, otherwise Enoch would not have been so surprised. He not only brought men paper and instructed them in the use of paper and ink, but also imparted knowledge, 'secrets' of many kinds, which he handed on as part of his job. Kasdeya was adept at a martial sport like karate ('all kinds of evil blows') and not only for duels. He knew the spot in the mother's womb which effects an abortion of the embryo, a painful but instrumentless method. Kasdeya also knew a cure for heat-stroke, that ailment that arises through overheating of the body when heat is stored up ('blows that arise from the midday heat'), and handed on elements of psychiatry ('blows of the soul'). It only needs a little imagination to guess that Michael was an architect ('the earth was founded above the water').

Enoch observed how basically the 'angels' were prepared for their task:

I saw how the angels were given long cords in those days, and they took wings, flew and turned to the north. I asked the angel: 'Why have they taken long cords and gone forth?' He said unto me: 'They have gone forth to measure. They bring for the righteous the measures of the righteous and the cords of the righteous . . . . The chosen shall begin to dwell among the chosen, and these are the measures . . . .

The measures shall reveal all secrets in the depths of the earth and those which were lost in the deserts . . . .' Asasel . . . showed them metals and how to work them and bracelets and jewellery, the use of eyeshadow, and how to beautify the eyelids and the most precious and choice stones and all kinds of colouring matters . . . .

Here the 'chosen' are obviously made familiar with new measurements. What use was an ell, the length of the fore-arm used for measuring? It could be long or short. 'The measure of the righteous' consisted of special measuring tapes which would be valid from then on. With them the chosen could measure the 'secrets of the depths', in which — besides metals — the 'most precious and choice stones' were to be found that could be turned into jewellery. The references to the art of cosmetics shows the sophisticated way of life of the people with whom Enoch stayed.

ANTEDILUVIAN ASTRONOMY

I saw the stars of heavens and I saw how he called them all by their names. I saw how they were weighed in an accurate balance according to their brightness, the extent of their space and the day of their appearance.

In fact astronomers do classify the stars by the names, their orders of magnitude ('weighed in an accurate balance'), brightness ('according to their brightness'), location ('extent of their space') and the day of first observation ('day of their appearance'). The antediluvian prophet must have acquired such accurate details from beings who were far more intellectually advanced than he and his contemporaries. Because all this *must* have happened *before* the Flood, since Enoch himself was told by a voice from heaven about this event, which was due to take place in the distant future:

For the whole world shall perish and a Flood is ready to cover the whole of the earth and everything on it shall die. Instruct him so that he may escape it, and his descendants be preserved for all peoples of the world.

It was frequently recurring references like these that made

Enoch scholars give up the idea that the text had originated in Christian times. The point being that the Flood was already past history in the Christian era. If antediluvian data were recorded in the Book of Enoch, will someone tell me how these primitive men acquired knowledge that did not exist in their day?

A compendium of antediluvian astronomy with the most complicated data takes up several chapters of the book. What I quote here is only a fraction which is still intelligible to people with no knowledge of astronomy:

> On that day the sun rises from the second gate and goes down in the west: it returns to the east and rises in the third gate for 31 mornings and goes down in the west. On that day the night diminishes and has nine parts and the day has nine parts, and night is equal to the day, and the year has exactly 364 days. The lengths of the days and nights, and the shortness of the days and nights, through the revolution

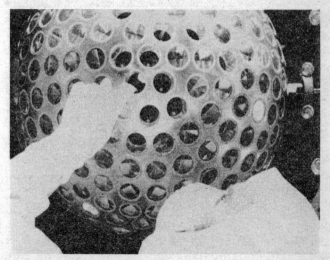

Fig. 70. Among other things, this geophysical reconnaissance satellite can predict earthquakes by laser beams. Laser beams search the earth's surface, are reflected and evaluated by a computer inside the satellite. The intervals between beams, which are recorded with an accuracy of a ten-billionth of a second, enable conclusions to be drawn on earth.

of the moon their difference arises . . . . Concerning the small light that is called moon, its rising and setting is different every month. Its days are like the days of the sun, and when its light is regular, it is the seventh part of the light of the sun, and it rises in this way . . . . One half of it rises 1/7, and the whole of the rest of its disc is empty and without light, except for 1/7 and 1/14 of the half of its light . . . .

Nikolaus Copernicus (1534), Galileo Galilei (1610) and Johannes Kepler (1609), fighting against the resistance of the Church, had to rediscover, for us enlightened earthmen, what we read in the *Book of Enoch!*

When I read history books, I get the impression that no hero left the world without uttering his 'famous last words'. Enoch followed this fine custom. Before vanishing into space in his 'fiery chariot', he gave this order to those left behind, according to the Slavonic *Book of Enoch.*

And the books which he gave you from God, conceal them not! Speak of them to all who so desire, that through them they may know the works of the Lord!

I have obeyed the prophet's wish.

EZRA AND THE RAPID SCRIBES

My proof that the 'gods' and their 'angels' were physical people will meet with a lot of opposition, but no one will contradict me if I say that God is omniscient.

'The signs thou askest for, I can only answer in part. But about thy life I can tell thee nothing for I do not know it myself.'

This sympathetic and honest divine answer was handed down by a prophet, in this case Ezra (hebrew: the help), the Jewish priest and scribe who returned to Jerusalem at the head of the few remaining survivors of his people. A bare ten chapters of the text of Ezra are tolerated in the Old Testament. Apart from this recognised Book of Ezra, there are two apocryphal ones rejected by the fathers of the church and the *'Fourth Book of Ezra'*, which is studded with esoteric knowledge. This apocryphal work from the first century AD also fell a victim to the censorship of the editors of the Bible.

Because everything he had to tell seemed so fantastic, Ezra, too, wanted to believe that his informant had appeared to him in a vision and made him the recipient and transmitter of the secret knowledge. But when almighty God in answer to a simple question honourably admits that he does not know the answer, we hear how the great master with nothing omniscient about him appears at a loss. There is nothing divine about the person who was questioned, indeed, he was amazingly pragmatic:

Assemble the people and say unto them that they shall not seek you for forty days. But doest thou prepare many tablets and take Saraya, Dabria, Selemia, Ethan and Asiel, those five men, for they know how to write quickly, and then come hither.

But when thou hast finished, thou shalt publish the one, but the other thou shalt hand over to the wise men in secret. Tomorrow at this time thou shalt begin to write.

In this wise 94 books were written down in 40 days. But when the 40 days were over, the All Highest spoke to me and said:

'The first 24 books shalt thou publish for the worthy and the unworthy to read. But the last 70 books shalt thou keep back and *only hand over to the wise men of thy people.'*

Here we have yet another proof that extra-terrestrial beings had a definite interest in handing down to later generations documents about their presence and news of the knowledge left behind. The Ezra text obviously had to be compiled in an emergency. In great haste, five men 'who know how to write quickly' were ordered by the Lord to write what was vouchsafed. It had to be exactly five men. Today one stenographer would do, if there was no tape-recorder available.

In his conversation with the All Highest (the Lord, the Master, the Ruler) Ezra is indignant about the unrighteousness on earth. As in other holy scriptures, the great Lord promises that he will return 'from heaven' one fine day to take 'the righteous and wise' with him. Whither? To what planet?

The home of the All Highest must have been some lightyears away from our solar system, because he gives the prophet hints about time dilation. Naturally, Ezra is surprised and asks artlessly why he could not have created all the peoples of the past, present and future at one time, so that they would all have been able to take part in the 'return home' together. Hence this dialogue:

The All Highest: 'Ask the mother's womb and say to it: If you beget ten children, why do you beget them each at its time? Ask it to produce ten at once.'

Ezra: 'It cannot do that, but each one at its time.'

The All Highest: 'So have I made the earth the mother's womb for those who, each at his time, shall be received by it. I have laid down a definite sequence in the world which I created.'

Ezra reflects about the sequence of time. He wants to know whether the living or the dead are happier when they return to heaven. The All Highest assures him:

'The living are far happier than the dead.'

This lapidary answer is understandable. The All Highest had already told the prophet that the earth was old and 'past its first youth'. If we assume the perpetually valid laws of time dilation, our planet may long have become uninhabitable owing to environmental pollution and industrial oversettlement when the trumpet is blown for the great 'return home'. The survivors are inhaling the last oxygen with a death-rattle in their throats. If the 'All Highest' deports these survivors to another planet, they will be by far the happier.

The All Highest confirms that it was he who spoke to Moses and gave him these instructions:

In those days I went forth Moses to lead the people from out of Egypt and bring them to Mount Sinai. There I kept him with me for many days. I told him many wonderful things and *showed him the secrets of the times*.

This is how the *Fourth Book of Ezra* ends:

Thus I did in the seventh year of the sixth week, 5000 years, three months and twelve days after the creation of the world . . . . Then Ezra was carried off and taken up to the place of his peers, once he had written all this down. *He is called the scribe of the knowledge of the All Highest.*

The censorship of the church fathers has left many blank spaces in the Bible. The *Apocalypse of Abraham*, dating to the second century A.D. is not included in the Old Testament, either. We learn something about Abraham in the Pentateuch, but not where he came from, nor that he was taken on a visit 'to heaven', like Enoch, Ezekiel, Elijah and others. In the Apocalypse we learn the Therach, a maker of idols, was Abraham's father. The young Abraham could not tolerate his father's job; he sought the one true God who could not be copied in wood and stone. This longed-for, unknown God met the teenager one day and ordered him to leave his father's house (14):

> I went forth. I had not reached the gate of the courtyard, when there was a great peal of thunder and fire fell from heaven and this burnt him (the father) up, his house and everything in it for a range of forty ells.

In the Old Testament, Moses tells us about Abraham exclusively in the third person, whereas the *Apocalypse* is narrated in the first person. As in Enoch, Ezra and Ezekiel, we have an eyewitness who was shocked by the frightening arrival of the stranger. Indeed, the first personal appearance of the 'angel' terrified him so much that he fainted on the spot:

> When I heard the voice that spoke such words to me, I looked now here, now there. It was not the breath of a man and my spirit was afeared and my soul (consciousness) flew out of me. I became like unto a stone and fell to the ground. And as I lay with my face on the floor, I heard the Holy Voice say: 'Go, Javel, lift this man up for me. Let him recover from his fear.' Then the angel came to me ... in the likeness of a man, took me by the right hand and put on my feet.

Once again Old Testament scholars announce that this was a vision of Abraham's, that the text was probably not compiled by him (as if the copyright of the other biblical authors was confirmed!) and so does not belong in the Old Testament. The Abraham of the *Apocalypse* shows his colours; he speaks in the first person. What pious religious Jew would have dared not only to turn himself into Abraham, but also to put words into the patriarch's mouth that did not belong to him? How could the description of the encounter, at which there was no other witness, be so dramatic if the protagonist himself had not told the story? I can well imagine why the fathers of the church did not want to see the *Apocalypse of Abraham* in the Bible. It frequently states that the Lord 'had grown fond of Abraham', a sentiment that must be alien to a divine universal spirit. Incidentally there can be no doubt about the physical robustness the angel displayed.

It emerges quite clearly from the *Apocalypse* that no spirit was involved. Recovered from his faint, Abraham examined the stranger who had made him faint in terror:

> Then I saw him who took me by the right hand and set me on my feet. His body was like a sapphire, his face like a chrysolite, the hair of his head like the snow and the diadem on his head like the rainbow.

The stranger introduces himself as the 'Servant of the Lord', who has been commissioned to accompany Abraham. The narrative continues in the first person and describes an Ascension:

> And it happened at sunset. There was smoke, like smoke from a furnace . . . . Then he bore me to the limits of the fiery flames. Then we rose up, as if with many winds, into heaven which was fixed on the firmament there. In the air on that height we ascended I saw a great light that I cannot describe, and in the light a mighty fire and in it a host . . . of mighty figures . . . who called out words which I did not know.

How the images resemble each other! Abraham, too, was taking a space-shuttle to the mothership which was circling the earth in orbit. Words failed Abraham when he was faced with the 'mighty light'; he could not describe it. We, enlightened children of the twentieth century, are of course much cleverer. With a good pair of binoculars or a small telescope we can observe some satellities. Lit up by the sun they glitter like small bright planets. But just imagine the mighty (sun) light reflected by the outer hull of a gigantic interstellar spaceship!

Abraham did not feel at ease on his flight in orbit:

> 'But I wanted to fall *downwards on the earth*. The lofty place on which we stood, now stood upright, now turned itself downwards . . . .'

Just as is envisaged for our future spaceships, the highly advanced technology of those days would have provided artificial gravity for the crew. This is most easily obtained by the constant rotation of the craft around its central axis. If a passenger is looking out of the observation window of a spaceship rotating in this way, he gets exactly the feeling described by Abraham: 'Now stood upright, now turned itself downward'. The millions of people who saw the film *2001 Space Odyssey* will never forget the impression of the permanently turning space-station — sometimes the earth is above, sometimes the stars, it was like being in a lift without floor or ceiling, just as the 'eternal, the strong one' said:

'Look *from above* at the stars which *are below thee* . . . .'

ABIMELECH, THE FIGS AND TIME DILATION

At first it was pure curiosity that led me to find out what was witheld from us Bible-readers; later the censored old texts became the objects of careful study. It turned out that many indications of prehistoric space travel are hidden in the censored texts, as well as references to time dilation, the effectiveness of which was meant to be kept from man, because otherwise the myth of the immortality of the gods would burst like a soap bubble.

The ancient Jewish scriptures contain the *Remains of the Words of Baruch,* or as it is also called the *Addendum to the Prophet Jeremiah.*

Baruch was a friend of the prophet Jeremiah, and in 604 B.C. he took down Jeremiah's sayings, which found a place in the Bible. Baruch obviously wrote down some unsuitable matter for the 'Remains' are not to be found in the Bible. The following story is told in chapters 3 to 5: (14)

Jeremiah, who is considered to be one of the great prophets, was also political agitator (like many of his colleagues). For years he had preached the downfall of Juda, if Babylon was not overthrown by a great effort. No one listened to him. Then the 'Lord' told him about the coming destruction of Jersualem and the deportation of the Jewish people into the Babylonian captivity. This happened in 586 B.C.

Jeremiah and Baruch were creeping through the city of Jerusalem to bury 'the greatest temple treasures', so that they would be spared from destruction. At this moment trumpets rang out in the clouds, and 'angels with torches in their hands came out of heaven'.

Jeremiah asked an angel to arrange a conversation with the All Mighty. The rendezvous took place. Jeremiah asked the Lord to spare his young Ethiopian friend Abimelech, for he had once 'pulled him out of a muddy ditch'. The Lord was touched by such gratitude and told Jeremiah to send his friend to Agrippa's vineyard 'by the mountain road'; there he himself would meet the young man and conceal him until everything was over: The next morning Jeremiah sent Abimelech forth and said: Take a basket and go to Agrippa's estate by the mountain road. Pick some figs, Give them to the sick and the people!

The next day Jerusalem was taken by the enemy. The survivors, among them Jeremiah were led into captivity in Babylon.

The terrible events passed right over Abimelech's head; he knew nothing at all about them. he strode cheerfully along the mountain road to pick figs. Suddenly he felt giddy. He sat down, with the basket of fresh figs between his knees, and fell asleep.

When he awoke a little later, he was afraid Jeremiah would scold him because he had dallied on the way. He quickly picked up the basket of figs and marched off in the direction of Jerusalem. Then the unprecedented thing happened:

Then he came to Jerusalem. Yet he knew neither this city, nor its houses, nor his own family.... This is not the right city. I am confused.... My head is still heavy.... Wondrous! How can I tell Jeremiah I am confused? Then he went outside the city and looked back at the monuments of the city and said: 'But it is the city, I have not made a mistake. Again he returned to the city and searched. He could not find any of his own people and once again he went out of the city. There he stood sadly, for he did not know whither he should go.

Abimelech is overcome. He had only gone out on a quick errand to pick some figs. He could no longer understand the world.

Outside the town he squatted down. An old man came by.

Abimelech asked him: 'what city is that?' – 'Jerusalem', answered the old man. Abimelech asked after the priest Jeremiah and his pupil Baruch and a number of well-known people, and added that he no longer knew anyone in the city. The old man said thoughtfully:

'You mention Jeremiah and ask after him after all this time? Jeremiah was carried off to Babylon long ago, with all our people.'

Abimelech thought the old man was mad and was only sorry it was wrong to curse or mock old people, otherwise he would have given him a piece of his mind. He asked what time it was and worked out that only a few hours had passed since he had set out:

Here, make sure. Take them. Look at the figs!'

And Abimelech showed the old man his basket of figs. And he saw that they were still juicy. When the old man saw them, he cried out: 'My son, you are protected by God.... Look, today it is sixty-six years since the people was carried off to Babylon. So that you may know that it is true, look at the fields. The seeds are just germinating, the season for figs has not yet come!

In the course of the story an 'angel of the Lord' sends an eagle and this proud bird brings a letter of Baruch's from Jerusalem to Babylon. The letter tells the captive Jeremiah that his friend Abimelech is alive and well, and has grown no older.

Inevitably, the dispute is not yet over about who wrote the account, when it was written, who the authors and collaborators were and which is the oldest version. I don't care what the outcome of this academic feud is; I am only interested in the bare facts. A man is hidden by the Almighty or one of his angels. He falls asleep and thinks he has only had a snooze, 'for the figs are still fresh and juicy; they have just been picked!' He tries to find out if he is right in the head. Several times he goes into the city and back out on to the mountain road. He wants to find out what strange fate has befallen the city, this city 'which he has only just left'. And then he learns – he can't understand it – that sixty-six years have passed since he left Jerusalem and fell asleep. That is why the city and its inhabitants have changed so much.

This phenomenon of time dilation is demonstrated visually by the fresh figs. Abimelech wakes at a time when there are no figs hanging on the trees. The original author, whoever he may have been, was preoccupied with capturing and convincingly describing for future generations the phenomenon of time dilation that he had *experienced* in his own body and with his own eyes. He wanted people in the future to be able to conceive of the unprecedented event.

Time fuses of this kind were deliberately placed in the texts of ancient books. Extra-terrestrials had no choice, no other possibility of leaving traces of their presence and activities except in religions. Only there could they be preserved, discovered at some point in the future and ... understood.

On the basis of circumstantial evidence I am subjectively convinced (and it is legitimate to represent a subjective position in a trial of opinions!) that after carrying out quite definite tasks and before returning to their planet, extraterrestrials deposited a kind of time capsule somewhere in our solar system in which they left details of their presence here for a distant future.

Duncan Lunan, a Scottish astronomer and President of the Scottish Association for Technology and Research, suspects that there is such an extraterrestrial probe in our solar system. (16) On the basis of strange recurrent radio echoes which produce coded pictures of the constellation Epsilon Boötes, Lunan assumes that the probe comes from this constellation, which is 103 lightyears away. Professor R.N.Bracewell of the Radio-astronomical Institute of Stanford University, U.S.A., thinks Lunan's discovery is 'a possibility for contact with another intelligence'. From his observations Lunan concluded that the artificial probe has been circling in our solar system for 12,6000 years and that it has a complete programme of information for mankind stored in it. Repeated radio signals from the earth were returned on the same wavelength at intelligent intervals.

My interpretation: the artificial object emitting radio signals was placed in our solar system by SOMEONE and this SOMEONE was on the earth 12,600 years ago. I am convinced that this or another extra-terrestrial deposit may contain information about the expedition to earth; it may name the launching planet and give the speed at which the spaceship moved; it may contain a logbook of activities on earth. This and much more could be in the informative programme of an artificial probe postulated by Duncan Lunan.

There remains one question I am always asked, after lectures in which I put forward this hypothesis. How could extra-terrestrials assume that we backward earth-dwellers would ever get the idea of looking for such a time-capsule in our solar system?

The answer closes one link in my chain of circumstantial evidence.

Obviously one cannot search for something unless one suspects that it exists. According to the laws of probability, it would be absurd, both today and in the future, to look for a time-capsule deposited just SOMEWHERE. The extra-terrestrials knew from the geological history of their home planet that it would be quite senseless to conceal their documents in a statue or under a monolith. Over the millenia wind, rain, storms and tides would destroy everything; earthquakes and floods would obliterate every trace, and what natural catastrophes left untouched wars would ferret out and annihilate.

So where to place documents or information about the past for the future? Where was it safe for a depot which would survive the ages?

Only at a point X in our solar system! At a point which is calculable logically and mathematically, perhaps in the field of gravity of a triangle of planets, perhaps within a large orbit around earth, moon, Mars or Venus, perhaps hidden at the centre of gravity of the continents; perhaps at the magnetic North or South Pole. These are only a few of the possible logical and mathematical points.

But even then no trail would have been laid for the paper-chase leading to this point.

All the indications convinced me that references to the goal men should seek were contained in mythologies, sacred books and religions. Since the 'gods' made men in their image, they could anticipate and predict the thoughts and actions of their products. They knew that curiosity was one of their strongest characteristics and the desire for more knowledge another. Familiar with the brain-structure of their 'offspring', the extra-terrestrials knew that discovery and the development of technology were programmed. As soon as one problem was solved, another would be looked for. Sooner or later the desire to conquer space would be there; space travel would be the goal aspired to.

It was obvious to them that not until this point in time would their 'images' understand the traces they had hidden in traditional stories. With the technical know-how of space travel then available, their products would examine all the mythologies, legends and religions with new (their own!) eyes, interpret them from a modern point of view and, inevitably, when the time was ripe, ask the questions: Where can we find proof that our forefathers received visits from space? Where can we bring to light overt or hidden pointers?

The time is ripe for the discovery of our remotest past. Let us not miss the chance of winning our part of the legacy in the cosmos.

I LOVE THE GODS WITH MINOR FAULTS

Recently public opinion researchers asked people in the streets of Zurich how they envisaged 'God Almighty'. The answers ranged from 'as spirit' to 'as an old man with a white beard high above the clouds'.

Comical as that may look at first sight, their confusion when faced with the complex question seems quite logical to me. The confusion is the result of centuries of indoctrination by all religions, in which it was suggested to every earthling that he had to feel himself surrounded by god everywhere and that he must know that he was watched by god even in the most secret places. This milliard-fold bilocation required a god/spirit who had to be omnipresent and omniscient. Only then can God be informed about everything that creeps and flies; only then can a unified judgment of the righteous and unrighteous be made; only then can dogmas be established. Only a god/spirit can penetrate everything and everyone: god is all. Panthesim is dominant in all religio-philosophical teachings in which god and the world are identical. In line with this teaching god must be impersonal. That is a conception which the great philosopher Arthur Schopenhauer (1788–1860) apostrophised as 'polite atheism'. Even in Christianity, which makes God

the Father and God the Son appear as persons acting in a
human way, there is a good dose of pantheism, otherwise the
Christian God could not be omni-present. God must be spirit.
Omnipresent, omnipotent and ominscient, he has the all-
powerful gift of knowing in advance what is going to happen.
Standing above everything in that way, needs, faults and
errors are unknown to him. As god/spirit he does not need a
visible vehicle in order to move from one place to another.
Only spirit can be everywhere.

That is a definition I could go along with if there were not
contradictions in the early traditions, i.e. in the Bible, that are
insoluable and take this familiar definition *ad absurdum.*

On a close inspection the biblical God is not omniscient.
The prophet Ezra knew that. God says to him: 'The signs thou
askest for, I can only answer in part. But about thy life I can
tell thee nothing, for I do not know it myself.' Nor is the
biblical God free of errors! In Genesis, God at first says that
his work, namely the creation of man, is good:

'And God saw every thing that he had made, and, behold, it
was very good.'   Genesis 1, 31

But soon he regretted his achievement:

'And it repented the Lord that he had made man on the
earth, and it grieved him at his heart.'   Genesis 6,6

In other words God is not certain about what he has done.
Finally his handiwork seems to have failed so badly that he
destroys his own creation by unleashing the Flood. So there
were snags about the omniscience dependent on omnipre-
sence. After Adam and Eve had eaten the apple from the tree
of knowledge, they hid themselves among the trees for shame.
But God does not know where Adam is:

'And the Lord God called unto Adam, and said unto him,
where art thou?"   Genesis 3,9

Adam assures the Lord that he heard him coming, but hid
himself because he was afraid:

And he said, who told thee that thou wast naked? Hast
thou eaten of the tree, whereof I commanded thee that thou
shouldest not eat?

And the man said, The women whom thou gavest to be
with me, she gave me of the tree, and I did eat.

                                              Genesis 3, 11–12

God was obviously not in the picture. He did not know

where Adam was hiding and he had no idea that Eve had persuaded Adam to eat the apple.

These are not the only notorious examples of lack of omniscience. Nor does the fact that he did not know in advance what would happen, fit in with the conception of a timeless God. The world of paradise was easy to survey. He himself, so the scripture says, had produced Adam and Eve, so he must have been able to watch over their activities. That is something that does not make sense.

After Adam had 'known' her, as was to be expected, Eve brought Cain and Abel into the world. Abel was a shepherd, Cain a farmer, two crisis-proof and permanently subsidised callings, a clever choice. The two lads bring the Lord an offering. And how does the Lord without fault view them?

'. . . And the Lord had respect unto Abel and his offering: But unto Cain and to his offering he had not respect.'

Genesis 4, 4–5

Until that moment neither Cain nor Abel had given cause for being judged in different ways. Small wonder that Cain reacted sullenly to this partisan God:

'And the Lord said unto Cain, Why art thou wroth? and why is thy countenance fallen?' Genesis 4,6

An omniscient God would have known about the fratricide to come, but this does not prevent Cain from killing his innocent brother, Abel! He even has to ask for information:

'Where is Abel thy brother?' Genesis 4, 9

The Lord is incapable of stopping a frightful murder! Finally God is so displeased with his handiwork that he has decided to put an end to everything:

And it repented the Lord that he had made man on the earth, and it grieved him at his heart.

And the Lord said, I will destroy man whom I have created from the face of the earth; both man, and beast, and the creeping thing, and the fowls of the air; for it repenteth me that I have made them. Genesis 6, 6–7

We can quite understand God's attitude to the brood which had turned out so badly, but should not the Omniscient one have sensed how things were? Not content with his first regrets, he repents anew, after the annihilating Flood, that he has destroyed his whole creation: When Noah had anchored his ark on a mountain, he kindled a sacrificial fire in gratitude:

And the Lord smelled a sweet savour; and the Lord said
in his heart, I will not again curse the ground any more for
man's sake; for the imagination of man's heart is evil from
his youth; neither will I again smite any more everything
living, as I have done.   Genesis 8, 11

Belated recognition that his own work was faulty! The
much-praised Omniscient one did not know how his work
would turn out? Strange!

If we accept the biblical Genesis, all men are descendants of
Noah and his stepsons and stepdaughters who were on board
with him. They were an élite which the Lord had considered
worthy to survive. Contrary to his oath, God felt impelled to
smite this brood again with the total destruction of Sodom and
Gomorrha.

My Bible lesson is intended to emphasise, no more and no
less, an observation; a divine figure is portrayed who made
mistakes, felt regrets and was capable of bloody acts; a god is
shown who experiences such terribly human passions as
anger, partisan love, and heartlessness. They seem to me to be
completely ungodly attributes. At least they do not fit in with
the conception of an imaginary omniscient being, standing
above material things, that has has been urged on us. I simply
want to make it clear that the Old Testament God was neither
timeless, nor omniscient, nor abstract. I simply want to give
examples to show that be took a real part in events, that he
was even seen in human guise '. . . walking in the garden in
the cool of the day. . . .'   Genesis 3, 8

I chose the Bible from the various religious sources
available because everyone can look up my quotations in his
own family Bible.

The fact is that the gods in myths behave exactly the same.
Greek and Roman divinities were characterised as immortal,
but unlike the Bible, not as 'eternal'. They simply become
incomparably older than the men among whom they dwell
from time to time. The myths of the world of antiquity
describe the gods as sympathetic human figures, who kick
over the traces, who in their anger make arbitrary decisions
which they subsequently have to amend, who frequently
change their minds and who quite openly express regret over

enterprises that have gone wrong.

Many of these gods were even born on earth, act bisexually with girls and boys, and frequently rebel against their parents. Generations clashed in divine families, just as they have always done in the best circles. The Father of the Gods, Zeus, Lord of heaven and the universe, fell head over heels in love with his cup-bearer, Ganymede, who, because of his beauty, was reared on Olympus, whither Zeus is supposed to have enticed him in a far from godly way. Something was always going on in this divine family. Zeus's son Apollo fell in love with the beautiful youth Hyacinth, who was active as god of fertility. The god Apollo killed his beloved in a way quite unbefitting a god, he hurled a discus at him! Whether it was intentional or unintentional, it was not divine.

The Roman god Mars, responsible for war, fields and growth, allowed himself to be badly taken in by the old goddess Anna Perenna. In order to include a god from Germanic mythology in the illustrious company, I may mention Odin (Wotan). This papa of all the gods and men had a really perverse partiality for disguises. Sometimes he appeared as a snake, sometimes as an eagle, sometimes he mingled with the people as a raven. He hurled the spear, not a divine activity; he rode the eight-legged horse Sleipnir. Odin was an anxious god. When he withdrew to Valhalla, he took valiant warriors from the battlefields to guard him. Finally he was eaten by the wolf Fenrir, in spite of his security guards. If Odin was spirit, Fenrir must have swallowed air or whatever else may have survived of the materialisation of such a god.

I have nothing against the gods, on the contrary, I 'love' them. But I love them with all their faults, with all their lovable weaknesses and errors. It makes them so human; this brand of gods is so much closer to us! Not in vain did they create us in their image. Thus and not otherwise do they 'haunt' the mythical tales of all peoples and all ages.

All the texts support the view that the gods were people of flesh and blood!

5: A Creation takes place

'The laws of inheritance are comparatively unknown. No one knows why the same characteristic is sometimes inherited by different individuals of the same species and individuals of the same kind and sometimes not, why a child often appears with definite characteristics of his grandfather or grandmother of even more distant forebears.'

Charles Robert Darwin (1809–1882) made this public confession in 1859 in his main work *The Origin of Species*. Naturally, for the conclusions of present-day biological research were not at his disposal. Essentially he arrived at his theory of evolution by biological observations in South America and on the Galapagos Islands during a five-year voyage round the world. Since then, it has been cemented into the creed of the origin of the species.

What has the theory of evolution to do with the proof of *my* theory? I say frankly and freely: EVERYTHING. I postulate that unknown beings created human intelligence by a deliberate artificial mutation and that extra-terrestrials ennobled man 'in their own image'.

To begin with let us tackle a few vital questions: What is 'life'? Does it originate by chance? Does it even originate by itself? Can such a chance happen everywhere that the prerequisites for it are favourable? Does it even originate by itself? Can such a chance happen everywhere that the prerequisites for it are favourable? Or has chance been a unique singular process in the formation of life?

Those are only a few questions, but they alone divide the world of scholarship into two groups, each of which disputes the other's position.

For example a group of molecular biologists close to Professor Manfred Eigen, Nobel Prizewinner for Chemistry in 1967, head of the division for physical chemistry at the Max Planck Institute, Göttingen, are convinced that they know the essential contexts for the origin of life, while a group of organic

211

chemists supporting Professor A.E. Wilder-Smith (1) and James F. Coppedge, Director of the Centre for Research into Biological Probability, at Northbridge, California, represents exactly opposite conceptions. (2)

In order to make the reader understand what this controversy is about and to explain why my extra-terrestrials have become involved once again, I must try to give a quick picture of the origin of life in a few simplified steps.

THE GREAT DRAMA OF THE CREATION

Milliards of years ago the primitive atmosphere from which the first life must have come, consisted mainly of steam, methane, ammonia, carbon dioxide and minerals of all kinds. Minerals were hurtled into the hot atmoshpere from the bowels of the earth by volcanoes, storms raged in the atmosphere and as they cooled down torrential rain descended on the planet. The tempestuous rain of the primaeval world released inorganic matter, matter from the lifeless world of nature, from the hot crust of rocks, and washed it into the primaeval ocean. There a kind of chemical culture-solution was formed in which simple molecules* were forced by the pressure of the unleashed forces to combine with other molecules. Amino acids (organic acids, lipoids,** nucleotide bases,*** mineral salts and phosphates, are some of the substances absolutely essential for plants. They all have one thing in common. They are chemicals, which do not 'live'. According to the hypothesis currently prevalent, the first act of the great drama went something like this:

Under the constant physical bombardment of discharges from primaeval thunderstorms, the amino acids joined to form macromolecules, and they in turn formed long series of proteins. Proteins are simply albumen, higher molecular natural substances vital to the organism. Everyone knows

---

* Molecules: Smallest part of a unified substance that still possesses its chemical qualities. A molecule consists of at least two, and usually several, atoms which can be equivalent, but are mostly different.
** Lipoids: a customary name on the basis of superficial similarity for that apparently fat-like substance appearing in animals and plants, which is only partly related to fats in its chemical structure.
*** Nucleotides: building stones of nucleic acids.

about them from diet sheets. They consist of carbon, hydrogen, oxygen and nitrogen in a fairly fixed relation.

The busy chemical couplings continued. Phosphates combined with sugar to form saccharic phosphates and these in turn showed a liking for the four well known bases: adenine, guanine, cytosine and thymine. From these combinations arose the nucleotides, already mentioned, which joined together in long chains, i.e. the nucleic acids. Those were the stars in the first act of terrestrial creation.

Until this moment when the primal soup was served up, several miracles must have happened. Before I make them the target of my remarks, I must note down in telegraphic language the development up to the first cell and then probe into the 'wound' with bold fingers.

I shall have to describe things backwards, for it is difficult to find the salient point to take off from. Nucleic acids are formed from chains of nucleotides, whose single unit has a phosphoric-acid-sugar base, which sticks together with adenine, guanine, cytosine or thymine. A prolonged look at these four bases is important. A nucleic acid which swam into the primitive ocean, so it says in the relevant literature, (3) always found another nucleic acid with which it promptly joined into a chain. But as each nucleic acid contains the Big Four of the nitrogen-rich bases, adenine, guanine, cytosine and thymine, these bases could form large chains of nucleic acids. Adenine is keen to join thymine, and guanine strives for cytosine as if drawn by a magnet.

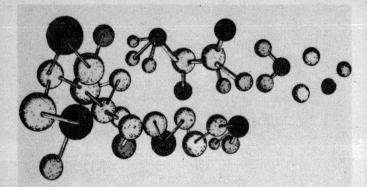

Fig. 72. From atom to macromolecule.

With this harmonious forging of chains of nucleic acids, the double helix was formed, e.g. DNA, that has become so famous (deoxyribosenucleic acid). DNA is the last chemical outpost before life and at the same time nature's most brilliant idea! *Every* organism has its own original DNA, and each of these has a code in which all the characteristics of the species are entered. Each species is programmed in its uniqueness. But the incredible thing is that this complicated programme is stored in each cell! Man, for example, carries 'his' programme around fifty billionfold in his fifty billion cells. One billion equals 100 milliards $= 10^{12}$.

So DNA is the key to life, yet what is life?

It is said that life is always linked with an organism, in the simplest case, with the cell. An organism's metabolism and conversion of energy shows if it is living or not. So do its development and ability to reproduce, which functions constitute life.

Actually this definition is not adequate today. A virus, for example, has no metabolism and does not convert energy on its own; a virus eats nothing and excretes nothing. Its reproduction (duplication) takes place inside foreign cells in which it lives as a parasite. In other words, a virus 'functions' without metabolism and conversion of energy. I have also heard that everything which moves under the microscope is alive. It can easily be proved that that is not right, either. Chemicals will also move under a strong electronic microscope, for physically speaking they are negatively or positively charged and attract or repel each other. So we can establish movement, although the substratum does not 'live'. A division between animate and inanimate matter is scarcely possible today. At best scientists are agreed on conceiving *organic* life

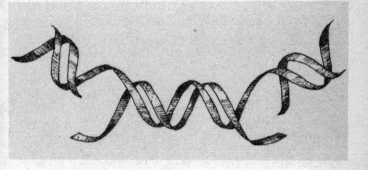

Fig. 73. The DNA double helix.

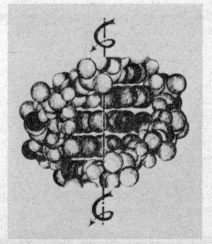

Fig. 74. Molecule model of the double helix.

as a phenomenon which can accept energy and divide itself, i.e. reproduce itself. In this sense the cell represents the first form of primitive life. How does it originate? 'Helix' means spiral in Latin. When the biochemists Watson, Crick and Wilkins won the Nobel Prize in 1962 for their model of DNA, the two-stranded nucleic acid chain, they christened it the double helix.

The strands of this double spiral can open the ends of their chains and use the building stones surrounding them, the nucleic acids and the nucleotides, to produce copies of their model. The strands of the DNA separate. Nucleotide after nucleotide plugs itself, so to speak, into the base appropriate to it (bases are combinations which salts form with acids). The newly originating molecules now have one strand, which originates by combination with existing chemical bases. The new molecules are identical with the 'old' ones; it is just that duplication (replication) has taken place. In other words the first primitive forms of life, the cells, have originated from nothing else but 'dead' chemicals. And if we agree to follow this outline, these cells have been 'born' by pure chance.

But, chance, too, has its own kind of laws. Molecules of *the right kind, which suited each other*, have to combine in the first cell-formation. How high is the degree of probability for this chance? We have a dice in front of us numbered one to six. 216 throws are needed for the numbers $1 + 2$ to come up *one after another* with a certain probability. According to the rules of probability six must be multiplied by six times six, because no demon gambler can make the dice turn up 1 plus 2 in fewer throws. Even 216 throws only produce 1 plus 2 with some degree of probability; they cannot do it *with certainty*. (4) You have only to watch the faces of gamblers who use a system at roulette to know how uncertain the return or the (calculated!) first appearance of a number is. Around the turn of the century gamblers working on probability used to shoot themselves in the shadow of casinos. Today they leave town without paying their hotel bills and disappear. Their alliance with probability has remained unreliable.

Dr. James F. Coppedge has made up an amusing mathematical game. (2)

Our alphabet has 26 letters. If you write the 26 letters on small squares of cardboard, put them in a hat and mix them well, the chance of picking out A is 1:26.

The word 'evolution' consists of nine letters in a set order. The probability of fishing these nine letters out of the hat in the right order is 1 : 542,950,367,897,6.

This crazy figure is reached, because one must multiply 26 × 9, nine times in succession.

If a man took a letter out of the hat every five seconds, day and night, without stopping, he might – perhaps! – compose the word 'evolution' by pure chance in 800,000 years.

The mathematician in Coppedge pushed the game to its limits. In my book this makes him one of the rare breed of scientists with a sense of humour. He took his thesis 'Evolution is impossible' as the subject of his probability game.

The sentence consists of twenty-one letters and two white spaces between the words. Consequently two cards with a nought on are put in the hat.

What is the probability of picking the provocative sentence 'Evolution is impossible' in the right sequence of letters?

1 : 834 390 000 000 000 000 000 000 000 000 0!

So as to give people even an approximate idea of the magnitude of this figure, Coppedge suggests a machine that works at the speed of light and as the result can take one billion letters out of the hat every second, sort them out and return them to the hat if they are not correct.

In order to compose the brief sentence 'Evolution is impossible' in the correct sequence, the science-fiction machine would have to whirl away uninterruptedly for 260 000 000 000 000 000 00 years.

The claim of the theory of evolution to prove the origin of life on our good old earth from dead molecules is based on chances incomparably higher than those.

In the primitive sea, it is said, amino acids formed into long chains of proteins. But proteins do not originate by a miracle; enzymes (ferments) are needed, too. Yet the unlimited transformation of amino acids into enzymes and then into proteins in the primitive soup was impossible because a fixed law opposes it: the Law of chemical mass action. According to this fully accepted law of physical chemistry, a chemical reaction – whether in a gaseous phase or in solution – never terminates completely. It tends to stop short as soon as chemical equilibrium is reached. You can put bacteria into a vessel full of water and watch how these small unicellular organisms multiply incredibly rapidly by division. Water does not prevent bacteria from replication, but its molecules, and they are what we are essentially concerned with, are 'dead'. They do not reproduce themselves. In the primitive sea the law of chemical mass action did not allow unlimited chemical reactions. The water stopped them, just imagine the titanic struggle! Enormous masses of water, quite inconceivable today, were opposed to the *individual* microscopic particles of the amino acids.

In this brief resumé I cannot possibly mention all the

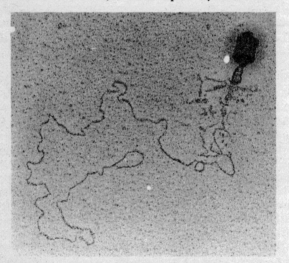

Fig. 75. Bacteria phage ejecting a DNA thread.

chances which are supposed to have played a part in the origin of life. But saccharic phosphates are also supposed to have combined with one of the four bases adenine, guanine, cytosine and thymine in the primal soup and become nucleotides. The nucleotides were driven round – by chance, of course – until they met passing nucleotides with which they happily united! These unions finally produced the stuff of life, the nucleic acids, once again by chance.

No.

Science prides itself on being accurate and dismisses chance in its proofs. So how can it operate with chance when it suits its book as if it was a block of reinforced concrete? How can it violate one of its most sacred laws, the law of chemical mass action? How can it recklessly contravene the laws of entropy which form some of the most important pillars of physics next to the laws of energy. When energy is converted, entropy serves to calculate that part of the thermal energy which cannot be converted into mechanical work. In order to understand the effect of this complicated law, one must imagine that heat is conceived of as an unarranged movement of atoms and molecules. The various conceivable divisions of speeds and spatial positions are compared in the frequency of their appearance. It is assumed that given a state of change, the theoretically less probable state. The probability of the chance meeting of a preponderant part of the molecules in half the available space is incomparably less than the other probability that the molecules divide using the whole available space. But along the beatified line of evolution the less probable possibility provided for by the entropic laws is tacitly accepted and presupposed. One chance after another. Gentlemen!

I am quite convinced that it is not only the chemical and physical laws that contradict the chemical reactions in the primal sea that are accepted so frivolously. Mathematical probability, or more accurately improbability, also precludes them. Each individual coupling by molecules would be the purest chance. But if in addition molecules combined with each other – and that in the necessary sequence –, the series of chances would be raised to the nth power. Then it would be necessary to invoke the aid of miracles. Belief in miracles is incompatible with science.

Darwin's faithful champions must have sensed this when they abandoned this part of the theory of evolution. They quickly offered *a new theory*. They said that proteins did not form in the primal sea, but originated on the shores of the crater. Undisturbed by the law of chemical mass action, chemical reactions took place in porous cracks and crevices, in the twinkling of an eye as it were.

A phenomenon, a miracle. As we know, protein is albumen and albumen cannot stand heat. If the formation of proteins had actually taken place in these obscure places, the albumen would very soon have been denaturalised. Every good house-wife knows how sensitive to heat egg whites are; that is why they only heat them gently, without boiling.

But the cells produced by the DNA need a constant supply of viable proteins, because – damn it all – there can be no cells without albumen, I swear it. It is not my fault that it is so, but the fact remains that it is, even if you can find something different in some clever book.

A PANORAMA OF EVOLUTION

Let us faithfully follow the panorama that the theory of evolution unfolds before us.

According to it, a thin layer, a film, of lipoids, fat-like substances, lay over the primitive sea. Below it swam DNA strands and clusters of amino acids. When the great primaeval downpour began, heavy drops of water broke through the film of lipoids. Bubbles formed that contained DNA, amino acids, proteins and nucleotides.

The chemical laboratory inside the bubbles stabilised itself, but finally the bubbles burst because of the rumbling activity going on within. Because the DNA was capable of replication, this process went on on a mass-production scale, and at the same time a simple kind of reproduction is supposed to have been set in motion.

The accessories to these processes which were first depo-sited on the shores of the crater now suddenly had to swim in the primitive sea again in enormous, quite inconceivable quantities, because we can hardly believe that the raindrops fell through the film of lipoids right on to the places where they would meet the celebrated DNA. Or are raindrops drawn into the great game of chance as well? Too many cooks spoil the primitive broth.... Admittedly the absurdities in the *theory* of the first formation of life on the young earth are known to molecular biologists, too. There are many more points like this; I have only selected a few.

How can we at least make the injured points heal until only the invisible scars of erroneous research are left? The biggest problem in the field of research is still there. Sometime in the course of milliards of years inanimate chemical substances must have combined into an order that produced 'life'. But how?

Professor Eigen introduced a brilliant idea into the great game. The physicist postulated that the chemical/physical laws were not operative. Everyone knows that physics has proved that there are negative or positive charges in every particle. As this fact also applies to molecules, these must attract or repel according to their nature. Therefore chance could be pensioned off! The processes in macromolecules unfolded according to measurable physical laws. Creation had its own rules of procedure. Perfect.

The physiological chemist Jacques Monod, formerly head of research into cellular biology at the Pasteur Institute, Paris, like Eigen a Nobel Prizewinner (for medicine, 1965), came to the conclusion that the origin of life on our planet was so complicated and 'impossible' that we ought to accept the fact that our existence was absolutely unique in the universe.

'The ancient covenant is in pieces. Man knows at last that he is alone in the unfeeling immensity of the universe, out of which he emerged only by chance.' (5)

Monod's book, *Chance and Necessity,* which aroused worldwide interest, was scarcely three years old when Eigen astonished scientific circles with his theory:

Investigation of the dynamics of the process underlying selection and evolution shows that the entirely uncontrolled chance situation in evolution apostrophised by Monod does not exist. (6)

There are circles which think that Eigen's theory is just as important as Einstein's theory of relativity.

Why?

We must differentiate between three levels when considering the origin and development of life:

Chemical evolution. By that we understand the separation of chemical materials from stone, as was the case on the planet earth in its infancy.

Auto-organisation by molecules into cells capable of reproduction. This refers to the unexplained dilemma I mention previously, how do 'living' cells come from 'dead' chemicals?

Evolution of the individual species. By this we should under-

stand Darwin's theory of evolution (not dogma!), which had the nice idea that the species developed to their present state by means of loving partners ripe for reproduction

Credit is due to Professor Eigen for having built a bridge that is intended to make the second level intelligible.

Since the Stanley Miller experiment,* we know that, under similar conditions to those existing on earth milliards of years ago, molecular combinations take place. Miller and everybody who worked on the primal soup experiment obviously did not have a chateau-bottled dose of the primitive liquid culture at their disposal, a creation vintage, as it were. Nevertheless, laboratory tests clearly showed that complicated molecular combinations take place independently. At a time when we faced the wall of silence and did not know *why* these combinations happened, Eigen, with his *chemical theory of evolution,* supplied a possible solution:

> The precisely defined division of an atom into molecules, the spatial structure of protein, the symmetrical arrangement of the building stones in the crystal lattice, the bizarre shape of a mountain massif or the visible pattern of a constellation in the night sky – they all result from *the static workings of forces between material parts,* which give the whole its more or less symmetrical form. (6)

Workings of forces, negatively or positively charged particles, magnetic fields, seem to be a simple solution of the great mystery.

But have they solved all the puzzles? Is the miracle of life intelligible?

Anyone who wants to give a resounding yes to the question must accept the milliard and billionfold chances as 'legitimate', something I consider quite unscientific. I am only a

* *Cf. Return to the Stars,* pp. 29 *et seq.*

simple citizen, but I simply cannot stomach chance even on an infinitely small scale. I can't and won't swallow it. But if we strike the word chance out of the impressively simple and therefore convincing calculation, the answer to the question is a resounding no.

I was confirmed in my scepticism by a conversation with Professor Ernest Wilder-Smith, an eminent scholar, who gave the new theory a critical microscopic examination. When I visited Professor Wilder-Smith at his house on Lake Thun, he was in possession of three doctorates: he won the first with a dissertation on organic chemistry, he got the second from the Faculty of Natural Sciences at Geneva University, and the

Fig. 77. Professor A.E. Wilder-Smith.

third from the Eidgenössisch Technischen Hochschule (ETH) in Zurich. Among more than fifty scientific publications, his well-known book *Man's Origin, Man's Destiny* is outstanding.

As Wilder-Smith is a guest professor at several universities, it takes patience and luck to meet him. I got to know him after a fascinating lecture at the ETH on 'The development of life' and asked him for an interview. This took place some weeks later. After this we corresponded and finally came the vital conversation by Lake Thun. In the course of the years I have met many prominent and likable scientists, but very few with such an impressive inner magnetism. Professor Wilder-Smith is a very, very religious man, a position which does not prevent him from being an exact scientist and questioning the nature of things down to their essence. He does not think much of the theories of his colleague Professor Eigen. And he told me why.

I myself am annoyed that I have to lead my readers over such rough roads before they can understand my theory. Although many concepts without which one cannot discuss the processes are familiar nowadays from newspaper reports, we do not experience them in practice. They are simply concepts that are hung up unused in the wardrobe housing the present-day store of knowledge. But I have to use them.

All molecules, the shells of which contain many atoms, as Stanley Miller also found out, turned out *without exception* to be levorotatory *and* dextrorotatory (turning to the left *and* to the right). Such tendencies to turn one way are qualities such as hard matter, fluids, gases and solutions exhibit.

Simplifying matters greatly we can imagine a rope-ladder, the right hand edge of whose upper rung is held in the right hand and the left hand edge of whose lower rung is held in the left hand. If the right hand turns the rope-ladder it winds round into a spiral to the right. Vice-versa, the left hand can make it spiral to the left. The rope-ladder (which here roughly represents the chemical structure of a molecule) with its rungs and ropes has not changed in substance until the turns are

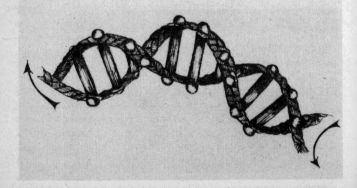

applied. We shall have to be content with this highly simplified explanation, because an exposition of the processes in molecules according to the laws of polarisation and optical activity would take us too far from our theme.

During countless laboratory experiments Professor Wilder-Smith, always produced dextro – *and* levorotatory molecules.

But it is a fact that *all* molecules that participate in the building of life on our planet, are *exclusively levorotatory*. Dextrorotatory molecules* do exist as well, but they are a few exceptions among many milliards of molecules.

But if, and this is the snag, the molecular chains of amino acids, proteins, nucleic acids and DNA have really only combined by chance, levorotatory *and* dextrorotatory forms of molecules must have existed at the beginning of all things. Can we make the rotation of the earth responsible for this? Certainly not, because in that case exclusively *levorotatory* forms ought to be produced in laboratory experiments which are subject to the earth's rotation. But in fact they always produce forms that rotate in both directions!

Annoying, isn't it? As a result the part of chance in the great drama of the origin of life must be struck out.

Levo- and dextrorotatory molecules could never have combined, for they have a toxic (poisonous) effect on one another!

That is why penicillin has a fatal effect on bacteria, which, like all life, exhibit *only levorotatory* molecules. If everything had gone right at the genesis of life, there *really* should only be forms of life which are composed of dextrorotatory *or* levorotatory molecules.

Have the levorotatory molecules devoured all the dextrorotatory ones? Impossible, for one sort is poison to the other.

Levorotatory, dextrorotatory molecules . . . .

When I was reading this chapter to a friend, he told me that he had not quite understood my rope-ladder comparison. Look at your hands, I said to him. Each of your prehensile tools is constructed identically, each has four fingers, with a thumb on the left and a thumb on the right. Although built

* For example, there are dextrorotatory molecules in penicillin, D-glutamine acids in the capsular substance of anthrax cells and in some substances appearing in antibiotics such as gramicidine and tryocydine.

the same, you cannot lay the palms on top of each other, even if you turn your hands. Although they are the same, you cannot achieve this superimposition. Molecules behave in exactly the same way, my friend. Amino acids can exist in both dextro- and levorotations, and in the same molecular structure, nevertheless a *levorotatory* molecule has a different 'character' from a *dextrorotatory one*. My friend told me that he understood now.

In all modesty I give myself credit for handling theories in bold outlines, in special cases even being prepared not to stumble over the countless chances, but rather to make a large detour round them. But I cannot simply switch off reason in the darkness that the theory diffuses. Nor do I want to. I cannot swallow the reference made by an important scientist to the fact of *exclusively levorotatory* molecules. Exact science – and that is my 'faith' – proves its theories by experiments. So far *not a single* laboratory experiment – as chance would have it! – has produced *solely* levorotatory molecules. So why does science lay it on thick in this case and argue against the unequivocal results of its own experiments?

'There's music in the air!' The answer is there for the grasping, there is a breath of the uncanny to be felt on the skin. The multiplication table of research is at last spelt out. *Someone* or *Something* helped to stir when the primal soup was cooking. It was not chance or spirits or miracles that took a hand. We shall arrest this being. But we can put the handcuffs on, we shall be chivalrously fair to the 'delinquent' and assume once again for a moment that the molecules which originated and which found their way – close your eyes – via many chances to the proteins really were exclusively *levorotatory*.

The smallest conceivable 'living' unit consists of at least 239 protein molecules. Such a protein molecule is itself composed of 20 different amino acids and many complicated enzymes as well, which must not only link up in a fixed sequence, but all in a *levorotatory* state. Chance after chance.

The probability that the simplest cell is *only* formed of *levorotatory* amino acids is calculated at $1 : 10^{123}$. (2) This enormous figure not only looks funny when printed in full it also makes it clear how improbable such chance hits are:

1 : 1000 000 000 000 000 000 000 000 000 000 000 000 000
000 000 000 000 000 000 000 000 000 000 000 000 000
000 000 000 000 000 000 000 000 000 000 000 000 000
000 000

The (im)probability game gets even more absurd!

If the first cell, which formed itself by such a wonderful coincidence from exclusively *levorotatory* amino acids, proteins, etc., also 'produced' a fellow species which owed its chemical 'evironment' to the great brother 'chance' and so consisted soley of levorotatory macro molecules, the probability of such a progress is calculated at 1: $10^{22117769304}$.

I dislike introducing the word 'impossible' into my vocabulary. But this is the time and place to use it. As I was writing, this, I tried to imagine the incredible series of numbers in tangible form.

I get 75 letters on one line of a page of my manuscript. Each page has 37 lines and therefore has 2775 letters. To write it out in words like a cheque, I could get two thousand seven hundred and seventy-five letters on a page. 100 pages of manuscript would contain 277,500 letters. There would be over a million letters on 400 pages of manuscript. I gave up counting any further. Even using the number of letters in hundreds of books one could never really conceive of the monstrous figure. 'In words' it would be twenty-two millard, one hundred and seventeen million, seven hundred and sixty-nine thousand three hundred and four. There are figures which are inconceivable to us normal mortals and this one is a real monstrosity. But it will be immediately conceivable to anyone that no ostensibly scientific theory can be proved with this kind of improbability, with such a concentration of chances.

Let us boldly assume that the first living cell formed itself by this non-stop series of chances. A new problem crops up at once! A cell needs energy to exist.

Following the classical textbook, it was released by a series of positive mutations.* A positive mutation is only to be expected *once* in 20 million mutations. Magnanimous as ever, we assume that all the original mutations went off smoothly so

---

* Mutation: a historical evolutionary process which leads to the origin of a changed hereditary characteristic in a group of cells of an individual, an evolutionary mechanism.

that finally the cells could produce chlorophyll,* which converted a tiny part of the sun's light into chemical energy. In that way, the energy problem, too, would be solved purely by chance, but the snag about this solution is that during this process of transformation oxygen is produced as a by-product!

But our chemical excursion still leads us through the primitive atmosphere. It has absolutely no similarity to the atmosphere we breathe today. We must realise that the primitive atmosphere consisted mainly of methane and ammonia, the addition of oxygen would have killed them immediately. That is a fact and no one can seriously dispute it.

Why is there never any reference to this in the textbooks? Why are the facts of chemical and biological experiments kept secret, why do scholars reject the mathematical calculations which prove that chance as an answer is just not tenable?

Once again I jump over the shadow which 'dogma' draws behind it like a majestic train and imagine that the first cell originated in the way scholars would have us believe. It is impossible! For all organic reactions that lead to the formation of albumen and DNA molecules are reversible. This means that chemicals which combine can separate from each other equally quickly. The assumption of the probability of the 'constant' development of enzymes, proteins and the DNA is thus revealed to be unacceptable once again.

I asked Professor Manfred Eigen for his opinion about this tricky and in the truest sense of the word world-shaking matter. He answered both my fundamental questions in a letter dated 1.9.1976:

'Are the chemical processes in the primal soup that ultimately led to the first cells reversible? If they are, do the physical rules of the game still apply?'

Eigen's answer:

The processes that led to chemical evolution and to selection in Darwin's sense of the word, have always been irreversible. In other words, it was a question of reactions of

---

* Chlorophyll: a pigment of photosynthesis with vital chemical combinations that enable the cell to absorb light in the form of energy.

energy-rich molecules which spontaneously combined into macromolecular structures during the liberation of energy. It can be shown that an evolutionary procedure is only possible far away from equilibrium — for this an envelope of free energy was always needed. the physical rules of the game which we have elaborated for the process of evolution are based directly on this irreversibility of the processes leading to self-organisation.

My question:

'*Your theory makes a 'necessity' of Monod's 'chance'. Could one conclude that this necessity happens on all the other planets similar to earth?*'

Eigen's answer:

Our theory certainly does not make Monod's 'chance' a 'necessity' in the general sense. We simply show that there are regular laws that lead to the necessary behaviour of the whole, even given statistical uncertainty about individual processes. Nevertheless one must make a very careful differentiation here. In static processes there is virtually nothing left of chance, except for quite insignificant variations. In the evolutionary processes chance variations, e.g. mutations, are increased up to the macroscopic level. Thus we are definitely not turning Monod's 'chance' into 'necessity' in general terms, we simply claim – as was already explicit in the title of Monod's book – that the origin of life is a fluctuation between chance and law or chance and necessity.

If we go into further details, we come to the conclusion that on planets similar to the earth, i.e. planets that have gone through a similar chemistry to our planet, lifelike processes must take place although they differ markedly in their detailed structure from those occurring on this planet.

Professor Eigen's answers left me somewhat astonished. It is in fact true that during the formation of albumen and DNA molecules *enzymes* make certain reactions irreversible *de facto*, in that they feed coupled energy into the system. *But enzymes are not formed spontaneously!* I had that confirmed by several organic chemists. Consequently what use is the postulated *irreversibility* if it does not become a fact until a stage of chemical evolution which it will never reach because of the *reversibility* of certain chemical substances?

For my argument *against* what is generally adduced in favour of 'natural evolution', the High Court can examine the results of experiments (although it should exclude technical books indulging in specious indoctrination). It would then be able to confirm the following facts objectively:

1. The law of chemical mass action and the principles of entropy are against the previous assumptions about the formation of proteins.

2. Proteins cannot have formed on the hot shores of the crater. They would have been destroyed. Denatured.

3. All the molecular chains playing a part in the building up of life are *levorotatory* — a conclusion that has not yet been reached experimentally. Experiments, left to chance, produce levorotatory *and* dextrorotatory molecular chains.

4. The *statistical* probability of macromolecular chains forming cells by serial chances is incredibly small. In fact, it is virtually nil.

5. The organic reactions in the primal soup that lead to the formation of enzymes are reversible. The laborious and chance development of chemicals to cell is unacceptable.

These realisations do not spring from my daring imagination. I mainly owe them to my conversations with Professor Wilder-Smith. Professor Eigen also takes these border situations with their undefined difficulties into account:

> The fragment of protein structures that can have originated in the whole of the earth's history is actually so infinitessimally small that the existence of efficient enzyme molecules borders on the miraculous.

In that case is there *any* explanation for the great miracle of the genesis of the first life?

According to the definition of Professor Hans Kuhn (7) of the Max Planck Institute for Biophysical Chemistry at Göttingen, the origin of life is . . . '. . . a regular process that takes place of necessity under suitable external conditions.'

Kuhn is scarcely worried by the fact that every living structure consists of *levorotatory* molecules, for it depends . . . 'on the chance that was first able to achieve a system capable of reproduction out of d-ribose.* Seen from this point of view,

---

*Ribose: an important building stone for nucleic acids, with traces of sugar.

the problem of the origin of optical activity seems simple.'

In other words it is simply insinuated that later all other molecules adapted themselves in a 'levocompound' to the first chain of amino acids that was *levorotatory* by pure chance. Molecules are 'dead'. They do not multiply out of themselves. Only much later were incomparably more complicated DNA structures to become capable of replication. Until the curtain went up on this act of the drama, a further x milliard chances would be necessary. Here scientists are openly operating with the *deus ex machina* of the classical theatre, the 'god from the machine' who — when things cannot go on any longer — 'supplies unexpected or artificially created solutions to problems'. I quote Socrates:

'We for our part would have to settle matters like the tragedians who have recourse to the machine when they are at a loss.'

I am not at a loss. There are two thick vapour trails which 'my' gods left behind in the primitive heavens.

TRACES OF LIFE IN SPACE

Since 1937 the presence of molecules in space has been proved. Molecules of various kinds have been recorded in interstellar clouds by astronomical measurements, especially during the past six years. More than 20 organic molecules* are already in the archives. In 1972 Professors Ronald Brown and Peter Godfrey of Monash University, Melbourne, demonstrated the presence of formaldimine in a gas cloud 30,000 light-years from the earth. It, too, is an organic molecule which contains carbon, hydrogen and nitrogen; it is one of the basic ingredients of life. Is there a possibility that 'life' was – accidentally! – imported into earth from space?

In 1972 the co-discoverers of the double helix (DNA), Francis Crick and Leslie Orgel, published an article called 'Directed Panspermia' in the scientific periodical *Icarus*. In it they put forward the theory that an unknown alien intelligence had so arranged things in space that *life* could originate everywhere *using a similar blue print*. The strangers are supposed to have sent out a spaceship with various microorganisms. This is what Crick and Orgel wrote:

*Organic molecules contain one or more atoms of carbon.

A payload of 1000 kilos could transport 100 probes with their culture-solutions. Each probe would contain 10^{15} microorganisms. It would not even be necessary to make this spaceship travel at maximum velocity as the time of arrival is unimportant. The radius of our galaxy is some 10^5 lightyears. Thus it would be possible to infect many planets in our galaxy in 10^8 years, even if the spaceship travelled at one thousandth of the speed of light. Several thousand stars lie within a range of 100 lightyears and they could be infected in a million years of spaceship time.

It is certainly a great pleasure for me to hear such theories from the lips of eminent authorities like Crick and Orgel, and to tell my readers about them. Since such statements supporting my assumptions are hardly known outside scientific circles, they are going to appear here between the covers of this book.

The article in *Icarus* says in black and white that the creation took place according to a plan. Chance is out of the question. Contrary to the solution by which every conceivable solar system is supposed to have been infected with bacteria by pure chance, we have here a possibility I find more convincing. The earth (and probably other planets in other solar systems) were *deliberately* supplied with the germs of life by visitors from spaceships!

We know that there are incredible distances between the stars. Propulsion systems that guarantee exceptional speeds are needed to cover such distances in *manned spaceships*. At these speeds the effect of time dilation that I have mentioned several times would be felt. If the space travellers returned to their home system from the interstellar voyage, they might land on the day of judgment. Millions of years could have passed *at home*. None of their generation that wished them a good flight when they left would be alive.

The extra-terrestrials avoid this 'danger', as soon as they deposit the germs of their kind of life in alien solar systems. Once they have planted such germs, evolution – without the help of chance! – unfolds almost automatically. Various planets in the depth of the galaxy now develop life-models in the style of the home planet. Thus the strangers create adequate conditions of life for them with the passage of time.

And even the law of time dilation is checkmated. A brilliant plan that is convincingly logical.

What could be conjecture acquires realistic dimensions, because *all* life on our planet originates, grows and dies according to one and the same genetic code. In other words the facts speak for the assumption that terrestrial life (because it is always the same) was 'flown in' from another planet. But we are still left with the question of how it originated there.

The Swedish physical chemist Svante August Arrhenius (1859-1927) took up this question at the end of the last century. Life must have begun somewhere, he said, and postulated that life is eternal so that the question of its origin does not arise. (9) Naturally even a circle has a beginning somewhere but once it is complete, the question of where it began no longer arises. It has become unimportant and cannot be answered because the circle represents a self-enclosed system. Arrhenius said that with all respect we must put a creator at the beginning of the circle, of even what we generally describe as God.

Meanwhile science has gone beyond religious explanations.

Even today technology is theoretically capable of making our neighbouring planet Venus inhabitable by artificial

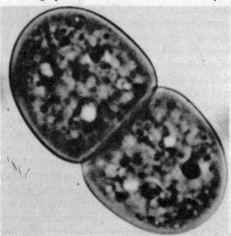

Fig. 79. Blue alga (synechococcus) dividing, magnified 200 times.

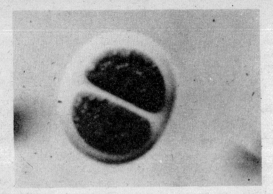

Fig. 80. Blue alga (chroococcus) after division. Magnified 200 times.

means! A few years ago the American astronomer Carl Sagan suggested sending up spaceships with thousands of tons of blue algae aboard and 'blowing' this cargo into the Venusian atmosphere. Why? Blue algae, unicellular algae with no real cytoplast, have the unusual characteristic of being able to survive even at relatively high temperatures. By their metabolism they reduce the high proportion of carbon dioxide, the antirespriatory gas in which human life asphyxiates. Hence Sagan's proposal. The algae's metabolism would gradually make the surface temperature fall and finally bring it below 100 °C. Blue algae would then cause the same chemical reaction as once took place in the primal soup. With the help of light and heat large quantities of carbon dioxide particles would be transformed into oxygen. The planet Venus would gradually become inhabitable.

Did extra-terrestrials carry out the blue algae experiment on our earth milliards of years ago? Why not?

It could have been done. Blue algae have a past as old as the hills. The remains of blue algae have been found in thick siliceous stone 3.5 milliard years old in the Onverwacht stratum in the Transvaal, South Africa. According to information from Professor H.D. Pflug of the University of Giessen their stage of evolution corresponds to that of blue algae living today. (10) According to this, organisms capable of photosynthesis existed 3.5 milliard years ago. In those days the

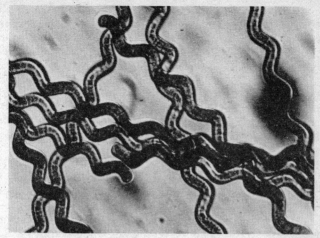

Fig. 81. Thread-forming blue alga (spirulina), magnified 120 times.

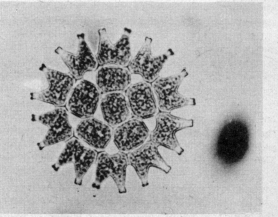

Fig. 82. Colony-forming green alga (pediastrum). 16 cells floating in combination, magnified 300 times.

earth's atmosphere was virtually without oxygen. Was the first terrestrial life made possible by a deliberate experiment from outside?

Anyone who categorically denies this possibility must in all fairness prove where the 3.5 milliard-years-old blue algae came from! At the time to which the blue algae discovered in the Transvaal date, chemical evolution was presumably in full swing. According to some theories some kinds of primitive unicellular forms of life existed in the primal sea. But how did blue algae get on to terra firma and into strata which are 3.5 milliard years old? It just does not work without an 'evolutionary leap forward'...unless one is prepared to think a little further. The 'small remainder' is supposed to have developed automatically from the first cell? O mama mia!

According to anthropological professors, the species developed according to the rules postulated by Darwin (11) in a gigantic greenhouse, generously watered by chance. One after another:

'All individuals of the same species came from a common family and departed from a central point in evolution.'

And:

As all forms of life are the immediate descendants of those which live long before the Cambrian period,* we can be sure that the regular sequence of generations was never interrupted and that no Flood destroyed the earth.

APE RESEARCH

Darwin's theory is the anthropologists' creed. It is considered a sacrilege not to believe in it. Even someone who is prepared to consider the theory as partially verified, but has justifiable doubts about the rest, is pilloried and ridiculed. So long as the 'belief' in a theory cannot be dictatorially ordained – and we don't want things to go that far – it should be possible to discuss, question, and seek other ways.

Scarcely a month goes by without the jubilant announcement that a skull has been found and the said skull is always conclusive evidence of the very first 'primitive man'. This kind of anthropology no longer counts as research into the early

*Cambrian period. Earliest division of the Paleozoic era, which is rich in fossils, with all branches of the animal world being represented.

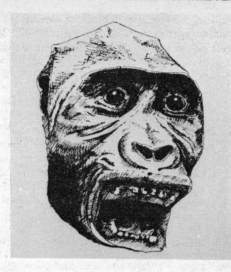

history of intelligent man, if we look at it closely. It is studying the progeny of apes! Then does it matter so much if a skull is five or ten million years old? It may be very interesting, but it is terribly unimportant to know when a species of apes could first stand on its hind legs. Considering the zeal with which this ape research is carried on, one must assume that some impudent fellow would deny that apes have changed during millions of years. All the mammals, fishes and insects have assumed other forms by mutations. Why should the noble ape have been an exception? Who can deny that?

What I should like to deny is that one species has been able to cross with another at any time in the course of evolution! If there is a genuine cross in chemical evolution, biological evolution would turn into a nightmare for the darwinian dogma. It is obvious to me that in offering a nightmare I am being provocative. Why should the champions of this dogma sleep softly on the pillows of their yellowed inheritance, while I rack my brains to find out how it really happened?!

I am not being provocative with empty pockets. So that I can take out their contents, I must explain how genetic information was transferred from the simple cell to highly

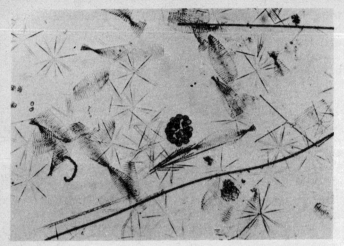

Fig. 84. Microscope photograph of cell formations in stagnant water: silicic algae, Panzer flagellates and green algae.

complicated forms of life.

DNA is the bearer of genetic information. Cells grow out of DNA and they contain, as 'scions' of DNA, several thousand genes which form chromosomes in which hereditary factors are localised.

The cell is a highly complicated structure. The genes (which live in it in chromosomes) are like Siamese twins. After cell division they carry on coupled together. The characteristics of a chromosome with all the hereditary factors reach the same germ cell together. But the cell reacts sensitively to every possible environmental stimulus. If ionising rays, for example, meet certain chemical substances or even viruses in the cytoplast, the stored up genetic information can be altered. After such an alteration (mutation), the DNA suddenly stops repeating the same pattern as the original DNA. 'Printer's errors' have crept in. If the cell does not perish as a result of the printer's error, it will remain on the new programme for all future cell divisions. Ad infinitum.

Without exceptions mutations are at a disadvantage. Only one in twenty million works out positively, a lottery with a very vague result. Nevertheless biological evolution teems with positive mutations. They must all have unfolded favourably by chance, for ultimately the first complicated kinds of life were formed.

Trilobites are among the first of these kinds of life that can be found in early fossil deposits. They were crablike creatures.

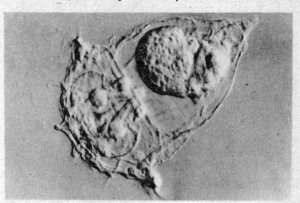

Fig. 85. Rotifer (synchaeta), a form of life which feeds on bacteria. Magnified 100 times.

'Naturally' there must have been countless other forms of life before them, but their traces are no longer to be found. The primitive oceans have submerged them.

The many positive mutations made the various forms of life come into being, including 'naturally' the highly complex ones which no longer reproduced themselves by cell division, but by impregnation. Then Darwin's assumption that the regular sequence of the generations was never interrupted becomes grotesque.

Why?

Because every species has a specific unalterable chromosome count and shape!

The human germ cells have 46 chromosomes. A mature egg cell has 22 autosomes* plus one X or Y chromosome as in this simple calculation: twice 22 = 44 autosomes plus two sexual chromosomes = 46 chromosomes in every human cell. When

* Autosome. A chromosome that unlike the sexual chromosomes occurs in pairs in the corresponding cells of the two sexes.

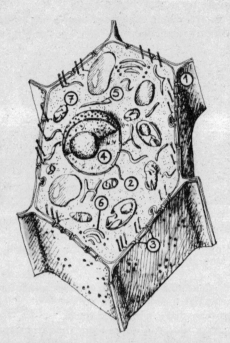

Fig. 86. Cross-section of cell with its most important components: 1. Cell wall – 2. Fluid that fills the cell (cytoplasm) –
Cell plasma surrounds the nucleus. 3. Connections with
neighbouring cell – 4. Nucleus: the genetic controlroom with
a very high DNA content in which important hereditary
information is stored. DNA is localised in the chromosomes
which assume the shape of comparatively short compressed
rods during mitosis (cell division) – 5. Branching system of
small channels through which the cell plasma flows – 6. The
Coli process in the cell at the point where material is
syntnesised – 7. Bodies in which cell respiration takes place.
They supply the energy for the cells' functioning.

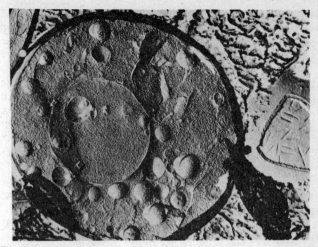

Fig. 87. Cross-section of nucleus. Electromicroscope photograph taken by the ETH, Zurich.

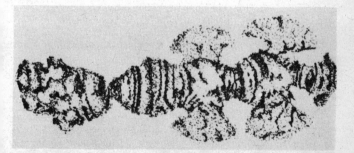

Fig. 88. Magnification of a giant chromosome in which the hereditary material is activated.

mating takes place, there are twice 22 autosomes with the 23rd pair from the chromosome of the male and female cells. The genes mingle and introduce cell fission.

As with mankind, the shape and number of chromosomes are specific *for each species*.

Numerical chromosome mutations are an every day occurrence owing to printer's errors in the DNA. Suddenly a cell builds one chromosome too many. In the Federal Republic of Germany alone the figure for such numerical chromosome mutations is estimated at 125,000 a year.

About 9 per cent of all births is involved. Bearers of such mutated chromosomes are not capable of reproduction, for the anomalous figure is rejected by the intact egg cell. (Thus even if anyone had the perverse idea, he could not cross with a chimpanzee, although both are of the same tribe. Their chromosome counts simply do not go together!)

Of course it would be conceivable that among many births with anomalous chromosome counts matching ones might meet by chance, produce children and originate a new species. But this species can only reproduce itself by the inbreeding of those affected by the printer's error.

New species lead not only to numerical chromosome mutations, they also alter the bodily structure of each species that makes use of its sexual apparatus. From a television programme I learnt that there are 20,000 species of spiders ... and that not one of them can mate with any of the others!

INTERMEDIATE STAGES

How can we explain the intermediate stages which lead from one species to another?

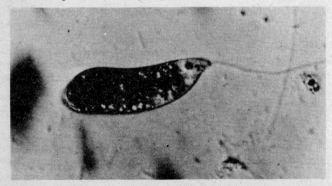

Fig. 89. Pexanema with cilia by which it moves – an intermediate stage between animal and plant-life, magnified 300 times.

Professor Wilder-Smith allowed me to quote from his book
Herfunft und Zukunft des Menschen on this subject:

The intermediate stages arising in the course of evolution
cannot fulfil any purpose, as they are completely useless. As
an example I may quote the complicated structure which
the female whale possesses in order to suckle her young underwater without drowning.

One cannot imagine any intermediate stage on the way
from a normal nipple to a completely developed whale nipple which is suitable for underwater suckling. It was either
there complete and ready to function or it was not.

If it is claimed that such a system develops gradually by
chance mutation, that means condemning all whale babies
to a watery grave during an evolutionary peroid lasting
thousands of years. To deny planning in the elaboration of
such a system strains our credulity more than the invitation
to believe in an intelligent nipple constructor, who incidentally must have had a very sound knowledge of hyd-
raulics.(12)

A very recent theory puts forward the view that the whale
originally lived on land as a mammal and only waddled into
the water later. I cannot judge if that is an acceptable idea,
but at least I recognise that it does not alter Professor Wilder-
Smith's opinion in any way. On the contrary. What a crazy
change of habitat to attribute to a mammal which gave birth
to its children on land and suddenly – armed with nipples –
enters the sea to suckle its young under water. Fantastic!

The number of species of living creatures existing on the
earth today is estimated at about three million. None of them
formerly looked like they look today. Consequently they
achieved their present form via many intermediate stages.
This sequence of developments applies equally to the vegeta-
ble world.

If we posit a successful mutation which had one chance in
20 million of coming off behind every species of animal and
plant life, mother nature has achieved the miraculous feat of
backing an endless series of winners for several hundred million years when the odds against it were incredibly high. A
really crazy idea to be asked to 'believe'.

Flat worms, annelids, leeches and finally crabs, spiders and a vast host of insects developed in the primal sea from jellyfish and polypods. The first vertebrates are supposed to have developed from certain species of worms. All naturally on the tacit assumption of chance yet positive mutations, and tolerating intermediate stages 'that serve no purpose'. With whom did the first crab drawn from the lottery of indescribable chance mate? Can we seriously expect that by chance there were several suitable crabs in the neighbourhood of the first one? It is part of the multiplication table of reproduction that only couples can multiply themselves. Thank heavens, I say, speaking for myself. Not only would an enormous crab production have been necessary, they would have had to be recruited from male and female crabs.

The first 'construction draft' for the earliest human stage of evolution leads back to the bony fish (crossopterygian), according to an authoritative theory, a fish whose skeleton was mainly bone though it still had some cartilage. At some time, but fairly suddenly, the construction was changed so that the swim-bladders could extract oxygen from the air and no longer from the water. The lungs – heaven protect me – were created. The whole way in which it is supposed to have happened sounds very airy-fairy:

From these finned and fringed fishes which breathed through their lungs and left the water it was only a short step to Ichtyostega, the first batrachian, which did not have a proper fish's tail, but whose fins had changed into real limbs.(13)

What drove our hideous primordial ancestor in his endless solitude? What sort of chromosome count did his cells have? With whom could this batrachian mate? He must have developed this primitive urge, otherwise his species would have died out before it acquired feet. Before eggs can be laid they must be impregnated. Who performed this laborious task?

OLYMPIC JUMPS BY EVOLUTION

The advance from bony fish to amphibian, from amphibian to reptile, mammal, etc. etc., was made with giant leaps. The first amphibian was no genuine land animal: it waddled back into its native element, water, to lay its eggs. We must not underestimate the amphibians. 230 to 205 millions of years ago they decided to become reptiles and lay their eggs on dry land. The last amphibian – or the first reptile – of this line of evolution was a small creature which rejoiced in the attractive name of Seymouria. Seymouria was the transitional form from amphibians to reptiles.

From that moment on the reptile could no longer mate with its old comrade, the amphibian, in the water. It was referred to its new fellow-species and they were, incredible as it may seem, all on their way to land to form a selection of complaisant partners.

I am quite willing to follow this biological line which makes new species originate by mutations in the course of past eras. But without wishing to denigrate the results of palaeontological research, I should like to point out the extremely difficult conditions with which each new form of life was confronted in order to preserve itself.

In the course of the history of biological evolution, various saurians first appeared about 200 million years ago. There were hundreds of species, including 12 metre-long, carnivorous monsters such as the spinosaurians in Egypt; fast-swimming plesiosaurians with small skulls and short tails who

used their fins as paddles; kentrurosaurians armed with spines and thick scales, and even some flying saurians. Saurians dominated the picture of the animate world for 140 million years.

All the hundreds of species of saurians stemmed from one and the same family but they could not mate with one another! The widely different dimensions of these primordial beasts alone thwarted any chance of coupling, even with the most complicated sexual gymnastics. How could a monster like the Brachiosaurus, 30 m long, weighing 100 tons and with a shoulder height of 12 m, possibly marry the tiny Compsognathus that was only 35 cm long. No, each species kept to itself.

64 million years ago something happened that is considered a unique palaeontological puzzle.

Every species of saurian suddenly died out all over the globe, on every continent. Out of the hundreds of species not a single one survived.

Different theories have attempted to explain this phenomenon. L.B. Halstead (4) compared these theories, only to reject them all.

At the end of the saurian age, mammals which were too intelligent for the dinosaurs are supposed to have originated. But says Halstead, the mammals of that period would have been more like shrews and hedgehogs and therefore not the kind of opponents to endanger the lives of the saurians.

Another popular view was that the extinction of the dinosaurs could have been connected with the spread of flowering plants. Before this the saurians had fed for preference on conifers, palms and ferns, and this food had contained laxative oils. The change in nourishment caused constipation. After the fatal end of the vegetarians, there was no food for the carnivores either, and so they too died out. According to Halstead, this theory was controverted by the fact that some groups were successfully able to change to the 'modern' plants for a long time.

Another speculation has it that a hormone disease made their eggshells so thick that the embryos inside could neither breathe nor break out of them. Yet another version puts forward the idea that animals appeared which ate more eggs than the beasts could lay.

Even if either theory could explain the sudden disappearance of the dinosaurs, writes Halstead, there would still be no explanation for the dying out of other animals, which disappeared from the surface of the earth simultaneously with the dinosaurs. Recently scholars have mentioned continental drift in this connection. The movement of the land masses that began in the early Jurassic Era speeded up in the Cretaceous. Finally the continents broke away from one another; the ocean floor rose and sea-level was higher. As a result the climate changed and the weather was so stormy that the pteriosaurians with their delicate bone structure could not stand it (only some species had such a delicate bodily structure; even a much harsher climatic change could hardly have affected the monstrous saurians.) Halstead countered this latest theory by pointing out that there are no traces of a general change in climate around the time in question.

I can hear someone whispering in my ear: have these digressions anything to do with the standardised theory of evolution? Or with your extra-terrestrials? Yes, quite a lot. A critic once accused me of blaming my gods for everything I could not understand. Okay. I can only counter this by saying that everything in the theory of evolution that is shown to be impossible is attributed to chances occurring during the past milliards of years. The very chances that are obviously supposed to be the real 'master-builders' of our life.

About the time of the mass death of the saurians there were very few mammals at first and according to the Darwinian theory there were certainly no men!

Halstead:

'No man ever saw a living saurian, because the family of man did not exist in those days!'

TROUBLESOME GIANTS

To err is human and there is nothing to be ashamed about in admitting an error. L. B. Halstead has erred here! Against this 'dogma' inspired by Darwin, we can put facts, facts that are wilfully ignored because they are shaking the foundations of a sacrosanct theory. The facts in question are hard facts, in the literal sense of the word.

The clearly preserved tracks of dinosaurs' feet were found in the river-bed of the Paluxy River near Glen Rose in Texas, U.S.A. Geologists are unanimous in saying that the river-bed must be dated to the end of the Mesozoic period in the Cretaceous. That was 140 million years ago.

The footprints of a man were found in the same stratum, close to the dinosaurs' footprints! It looked exactly as if the

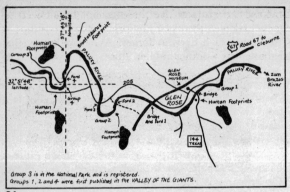

Fig 91.

man had pursued the dinosaur. There is no doubt that this man saw a living dinosaur!

This simultaneous appearance of man plus dinosaur does not fit into the Darwinian theory. As the theory of evolution operates with its millionfold, constantly recurrent chances, this awkward evidence could naturally be dismissed as an amusing chance occurrence – if these prints which 'put their feet in' the theory of evolution were unique.

As Dr. C. N. Dougherty (15) has clearly proved the 'Valley of the Giants' in Texas contains hundreds of footprints of saurians of various species and the prints of large human feet are always found between and next to them. I have been there and seen this extraordinary palaeontological discovery. The photographs supporting this part of my book are incontrovertible documents.

So:

Geologists and palaeontologists are quite unanimous in stating that the strata in the Paluxy River in which the prints were found are 140 million years old. The clear prints made it possible to predict the probable finding place of the next footprints. The direction in which the saurian was going could be established and the giant man was following it. Stratum after stratum of the dried-out river-bed was carefully excavated. The saurians had left the imprint of their feet in the ground at the plotted spots and just where it had been suspected, about thirty metres away in the same direction, human footprints were found.

Obviously, even facts like these cannot be allowed to endanger a hallowed theory at any price. As a precaution scholars explained such finds as forgeries. I talked to one of the palaeontologists working at Glen Rose:

Fig. 92. Geological/fossil document from the time when man and dinosaur trod the same territory.

How do you explain these footprints?

There is only one explanation. Either the footprint of the saurian or the footprint of the man must have been forged.

There are hundreds of footprints of saurians of the most varied species here. The oldest inhabitants of Glen Rose and Walnut Sprints know them from their grandfathers' days. Not to mention the trace of human feet which the people here call 'giants' feet'. Scholars have taken great care to uncover the undisturbed strata of the ground in order to reveal the footprints. Who could have had an interest in forging them? How could anybody imprint such traces in such ancient strata? Aren't you making it too easy for yourself when you talk about forgeries?

If you had any idea of the theory of evolution and fossil dating methods, you would have to admit that this must be a case of forgery.

The valiant scholar – why on earth was he working here if there were only forgeries to be found? – had taken a strong dose of his Darwin, for even the fossil dating method, which is holy writ to him, could flourish only within the theory of evolution. It simply accepts that only simple primitive organisms can be found in the oldest geological strata. 'Logical', because complicated forms of life should not have existed in the age-old geological formations (in this case 140 million years ago). This fossil dating method will have it that only fossils of primitive forms of life exist in the oldest strata. But does this hold water?

I shall let Professor Wilder-Smith have the floor:

Basically we have postulated the correctness of the

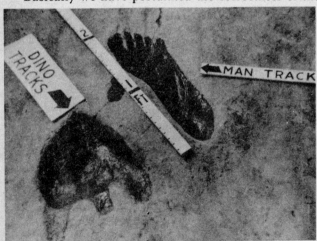

Fig. 93. Fossil message from the past: track of saurian (left) and giant's footprint (right) in the same geological stratum.

theory of evolution in order to submit it to proof. *For we assume,* according to Darwinism, that the oldest formations contain only the most primitive organisms. Then when we discover formations which contain only primitive organisms, we claim that these formations are old. We are arguing in a vicious circle. Only the oldest strata contain exclusively primitive organisms, consequently when a formation contains only primitive organisms, it is old and primitive. Yet this dating method (master fossils) has become one of the most important in modern geology. So firm is the conviction that Darwinism is scientifically incontrovertible that people calmly make use of Darwinism to put the accuracy of Darwinism to the proof. (12)

Professor Wilder-Smith can produce more than 500 objects which provide empirical proof of his view that primitive undeveloped forms of life can be found in *more recent* geological strata, but also that highly developed forms of life can be found in *much older* strata. That is not at all surprising because in the course of the geological development of the earth to its present-day stage strata were often forced above or below each other. What is surprising, however, is the attempt to prove

Fig. 94. Footprints of giants side by side with dinosaur's tracks have often been recorded in the Paluxy River Valley. Dr C.N. Dougherty published them for the first time in his book *Valley of the Giants.*

Darwinism with such master fossils.

The Paluxy River is not the only region through which men trudged in prehistoric times. In 1931 Dr. Wilbur G. Burroughs (16) of the Geological Division of Berea College, Kentucky, USA, reported finds of human footprints over 250 million years old. He found ten of them a few miles north-east of Mount Vernon. Yet neither dinosaurs nor mammals existed 250 million years ago. Absurd as it may be, it is still the chronicler's duty to mention that forgeries were immediately spoken about in this case, too.

Those scholars who are ready to use the word 'forgery' at the drop of a hat must suspect that all over the world there is a horde of poor madmen who have nothing better to do than to scratch foot prints in the earth at dead of night, by the sweat of their brows, with special tools and boxes full of 'antique' strata. But this stereotyped objection did not work at Mount Vernon, either. Burroughs' microscopic photographs showed clearly that where the soles of the feet usually exert stronger pressure, more grains of sand were compressed than between the toes and under the arch. The prints, with their five toes, corresponded exactly with human feet 23.75cm long and 10.25cm wide. The beings who left these imprints were undoubtedly bipeds walking upright, even if Charles Darwin is spinning in his grave. But 'preserved feet' were also discovered long before the present day. In 1822, in its fifth year of publication, *The American Journal of Science,* which is still highly respected, reported that footprints had been exposed in Cretaceous formations 140 million years old in the valley of the Mississippi near Arizona and in New Mexico, and that on the evidence of the prints they must have belonged to very tall men. If our ancestors ever did clamber down from the trees, they must have learnt this exercise at a very early period.

The all too transparent construction of the Darwinistic-palaeontological detective story destroys its validity.

Praise to the outsiders who devote themselves to their hobby with passionate zeal. William J. Meister is such a man. He collects fossils. He is particularly keen on the fossils of trilobites, those many-footed hard-shelled arthropods, which throve in the primitive oceans and swamps 500 million years ago. These trophies of the chase sought by Mr. Meister died out at least 400 million years age.

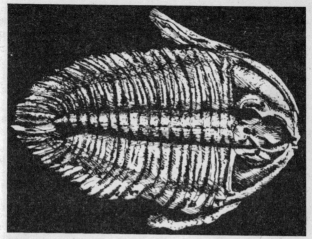

Fig. 95. Trilobites, primitive crayfish, animals from the earth's beginnings. They mainly inhabited lakes near the coast and broad river valleys. Trilobites are looked on as basic fossils.

On 3 June 1968, William Meister, his wife and two daughters, and the Francis Shapes and their two daughters, were staying near Antelope Springs, 43 miles from Delta in the State of Utah, USA. William Meister, armed with a little hammer, went looking for his beloved fossils. On this particular day, the four girls were more successful than the collector, to whom they shouted when they thought they saw a fossil in a cliff. At first Meister could not see anything, but mostly to please the girls he hammered away at the spot they showed him. Suddenly a layer of rock unfolded 'like an open book'. (17) When the expert collector held the piece of rock in his hand, he could not believe his senses. He saw the prints of two human feet and the prehistoric man who left these traces behind, *had worn shoes*! There were no heels, toes or arches, but instead the clear outlines of pointed shoes, which were 32.5cm long, 11.25cm wide and 7.5cm at the heels. As with every footprint, the pressure of the body's weight could be seen on the ground. The heels had made a deeper impression than the tips of the shoes.

Although shoeprints had not previously formed part of

Meister's collection, they had a connection with his special interest. The heel of the left foot had trodden on a trilobite, the remains of which had been fossilised along with the footprints. And William Meister had some experience of trilobites.

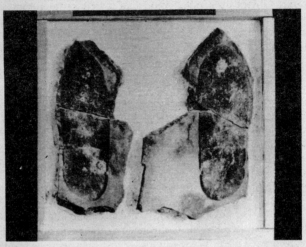

Fig. 96. W. J. Meister found these footprints of someone wearing shoes in a 540 million-year-old stratum near Antelope Springs, USA.

He took his find to Professor Melvin A. Cook of the University of Utah, who advised him to consult a geologist: 'I am no authority in the field of fossils, but this find speaks for itself!' My friend Brad Steiger, (17) told me that the miraculous find has been examined by many scientists since 1968 without anyone daring to come out with a definite verdict. But at least the geologists were prepared to date the fossil find to the Cambrian. Later two more footprints were found not far from Antelope Springs, but on that occasion the prehistoric wanderer did not squash any trilobites.

This kind of 'stone-hard' proof does not fit into the picture of the only true faith (read 'theory'). I am afraid that Darwin's *theory* – always 'proved' by the theory itself – has made generations of palaeontologists and anthropologists professionally blind. The fossil finds are much weightier evidence than mere indications. They are there. Scholars can touch them, put them under a microscope and test their age with all the chemical mixtures at their disposal. When things lie on the table and cannot be overlooked, we call them facts.

Who can tell me what phantom beings left these footprints behind? Obviously people would like to rely on phantoms if they fitted the picture. Yet phantoms leave no footprints when they vanish, as far as I know. So who was moving about among the dinosaurs' tracks 140 million years ago? Whose shoe squashed a trilobite 440 million years (!) ago?

As it has been proved that no men existed in those distant days, beings who were humanoid but different must have perpetuated themselves in the ground.

How can I identify for my child, who walked the earth with humanoid feet 400 million years ago by our terrestrial calendar? They were 'gods' who gave the comparatively young sprinter Ezekiel the tip: 'He who has ears to hear, let him hear!'

Andrew Tomas describes a more recent sensational find:

In east Nevada, Professor Luther S. Cressmann of the University of Oregon came across 200 pairs of sandals woven from fibres in the Lamos Caves. They were so beautifully made by a craftsman that they could have been taken for modern beach sandals of the kind people wear at St. Tropez or Miami. After a radio carbon test (C 14) it was established that they were over 9,000 years old.

But these sandals are actually quite young when compared with the print of a shoe in a coal-seam in Fisher Canyon, Pershing County, likewise in Nevada. The print of the sole is so clear that traces of strong thread can even be seen. The age of these prints is estimated at over 15 million years.

Yet man did not appear for another 14 million years. Or in other words according to the generally accepted view primitive man emerged about two million years ago and only began to wear shoes 25,000 years ago! So whose footprint can it be? (18)

I shall answer Andrew Tomas's question, but first of all I should like to put on a star parade of more footprints and also of skeletons which must have belonged to the prehistoric giants who made the prints, although their existence is firmly denied by anthropologists.

The German palaeontologist and anthropologist Larson Kohl found the bones of gigantic men in 1936 on the shores of Lakes Elyasi in Central Africa. From 1937-41 the German palaeontologist and anthropologist Gustav von Königswald and Franz Weidenreich (1875-1948), who taught in Pekin for a long time, found several bones of giant men in chemists' shops in Hongkong and China. Chemists' shops may seem strange places to make anthropological finds, but the reader should know that in Chinese chemists' all kinds of powders are mixed from old bones, teeth, dry skin, etc. So the shops are supplied with usable materials just as they were found. In 1944 Professor Weidenreich gave the American Ethnological Society an account of the giant bones.

Quite recently the Australian archaeologist Dr. Rex Gilroy, Director of the Mount York Natural History Museum, disco-

Fig. 97. Dr Rex Gilroy, Director of the Mount York Natural History Museum, found this giant fossil footprint in Australia.

vered fossil footprints of giants on Mount Victoria. Not the slightest doubt was raised about the authenticity of the giant footprints.

Six kilometres from Safita, Syria, archaeologists excavated flint tools weighing 3.8 kg. The flint tools found at Ain Fritissa (Eastern Morocco) are not to be sneezed at either. They were 32 cm long, 22 cm wide and weighed 4.2 kg. It was calculated that the men who handled these implements must have been a good 4 metres tall. The finds of giant skeletons in Java, South China and South Africa (the Transvaal) stand out as question marks in the literature on the subject.

In the proper scientific manner Weidenreich (19) and Professor Saurat (20) put the results of their research concerning the former existence of giants into their books. Doubts about these fundamental studies are not only unfair, but also unreasonable. On the basis of such evidence, the former French delegate to the *Prähistorischen Gesellschaft,* Dr. Louis Burkhalter, wrote in the *Revue du Musee de Beyrouth* in 1950:

> We want to make it clear that the existence of gigantic human beings in the Acheulian period must be considered as a scientifically assured fact.

It is more than remarkable that there is no place for giants in the Darwinian and anthropological theory of the earliest history of man. What crude vanishing tricks will scholars go on using to dismiss fossil finds of giant footprints, of bones much larger than those of present-day man and implements that human beings of normal stature could never have used?

These convincing finds simply 'rehabilitate' what scholars still find doubtful in myths. Enoch claimed that the Gods produced a race of giants. The *Apocrypha of Baruch* even knew how many giants there were before the Flood: 4,090,000. Both the *Epic of Gilgamesh* and the *Popol Vuh* have something to tell us about giants. Parts of the Bible are virtually a 'giant show'. Even the Eskimos say in their myths: 'In those days there were giants on the earth.' (21) Nordic, Germanic, Greek and Sumerian myths – to name only a few – are permanently preoccupied with giants. Why was a tradition of living beings handed down if they never existed?

Mamelukes were poor devils, slaves of Turkish or Circassian origin. In the twelfth century they performed compulsory military service in Egypt and Syria. They risked their necks if they opened their mouths. Nevertheless Schiller said of them: Mameluke, too, shows, courage,

Obedience is the Christian's adornment.

In spite of freedom of instruction I do not see any Mamelukes among the palaeontologists. Then why is no one brave enough to confirm the authenticity of the finds? Because the admission, in one single case, would bring down the whole house of palaeontology together with the Darwinian theory? I am waiting for a Mameluke. For a disobedient Christian.

How do we find our way out of the jungle into the light that illuminates the facts?

Myths tell us that gods created men and animals, that they initiated the creation on earth and destroyed their products if the evolution did not go according to plan. And they say that the gods returned to check their handiwork.

Scientifically based pointers now allow us to conclude that extra-terrestrials made the earth habitable, just as it would be theoretically possible today to make the planet Venus habitable by bombarding it with blue algae (Carl Sagan). Following a plan, extra-terrestrials filled selected areas of space with the germs of life (Crick/Orgel), the biological evolution of which they followed carefully for millions of years. If only palaeontologists would recognise the effect of time dilation and blow the stale air of 150 years out of their studies, they would not need to shake their clever heads in such an unreasonable fashion. What they have to grasp is basically *so simple. Time can be manipulated by speed. Time is not a constant quantity!*

CHANCE WAS NOT CONSULTED

The extra-terrestrials were not interested in speculations about chance, the great unknown. They made quite sure what they were doing. They worked according to a plan. They did not wait for the outcome of evolutions that were subject to chance; they cultivated life and different species according to plan. If an undesirable species threatened to dominate the earth and endanger other forms of life or disturb their development, they destroyed that species. Today we know that every species of saurian, for example, could have been destroyed at one fell swoop by showering them with viruses, which cause infectious diseases in men, animals, plants and bacteria. Is this the answer to the mystery of the disappearance of the prehistoric beasts? I always offer something more than 'we don't know how'. At the time I put this daring question, I am forty-one years old, young enough to be able to wait and see whether scholars will condescend to include awkward new information in their efforts to solve the great mystery.

In my theory that extra-terrestrials took part in the drama of creation, milliards of years of evolution larded with chances at every moment are quite unnecessary.

How can people accept as certain, what must be theoretical and must remain so, as things stand? Biological evolution à la Darwin will never be 'proved' in any laboratory in the world. The process cannot be completed because there is not enough time to record the results with all their imponderables even if hundreds of generations of research workers pass on bulletins in which they hand down the conclusions of their researches up to point X. The great game of chance is supposed to have taken milliards of years.

When scholars say that trilobites lived 500 million years ago or dinosaurs existed 140 million years ago, those are simply bold deductions from fossil finds in geological strata. But the time when the strata originated is an assumption, the accuracy of which cannot be checked in practice. Shifts in the stratification of geological strata in all directions; the break up of continents involving basic changes and climatological catastrophes, permit of only vague approximate estimates in which errors must always be taken into account. The snake bites its own tail. The chronology of geological strata depends on the dating of master fossils. Establishing the age of the creatures preserved as fossils is based on geological assertions about dates. One hand washes the other, but neither of them gets clean in the process.

You may object that the artifical mutations and breeding on the grandiose scale that I postulate are inconceivable. Why? Because the idea of this possibility seems too shocking? Have not countless kinds of trees, flowers and fruits been cultivated in the last hundred years alone? Have not whole races of cows, horses and dogs had their hereditary structure altered? The processes used for the purpose until now are laborious, time-consuming and boring. They take place by mating. Geneticists have known for a long time that such developments can be manipulated faster, more simply and more safely. What happened in 'nature' during milliards of years of evolution by billions of chance mutations with positive results, can be created in genetic laboratories in weeks, without dependence on chance.

SENSATIONS THAT ARE EASILY OVERLOOKED

Professor Har Gobind Khorana, 1968 Nobel Prizewinner for Medicine, succeeded in synthesising a gene in a test tube at the Massachusetts Institute of Technology in Cambridge, USA. (When I mentioned this possiblity in 1969*, I was ridiculed as an irrespressible visionary.)

Fig. 98. Nobel Prizewinner Professor Har Gobind Khorana succeeded in synthesising a gene in a test-tube in 1968. On 30 August 1976, he and his MIT team managed to implant an artificial gene in a living cell.

At MIT Khorana and his team produced the gene of a bacteria consisting of 16 nucleotides in a test tube. This artificial gene was introduced into a virophage (phi=80). Virophages consist only of DNA, the bearer of hereditary information,

*Return to the Stars, pp. 34 et seq.

with a covering of albumen (protein). Let us remember that DNA doubles itself by the separation of its two strands. The MIT men's problem was smuggling the artificial gene into the DNA. They succeeded. When the DNA manipulated in this way doubled itself again, the new artifically created programme began to unfold.

RNA (ribosenucleic acid) is just as important as DNA and is mentioned in publications nearly as often. It supplies a cell with DNA in that it directs the formation of proteins that are specified by the DNA. Only a year after Khorana's test tube gene, Professor Charles Weissmann, Director of the Institute for Molecular Biology at Zurich University succeeded in *deliberately* altering hereditary factors. He was able to separate parts of the DNA and RNA from a combination of molecules and replace them by other molecular building stones. The Zurich scientist exchanged 16 of the 4,500 building stones of the nucleic acid. That was in 1974.

In 1975 the British firm of ICI set up the first special laboratory for gene manipulation. In this experimental research institute, working under the strictest security measures, the hereditary factors of cells of highly developed organisms are transferred to bacteria. In this way the tiny unicellular creatures, which multiply by division, receive a 'higher' genetic code, which promptly makes them produce organic materials, for example other bacteria or even medicaments. Spooky, isn't it?

I should mention in passing that research workers, free of restrictions, are also working on the manipulation of plants. At the Botanical Faculty of the University of Hohenheim in Baden-Württemberg, celebrated for over 150 years, efforts to extract plants capable of reproduction from isolated protoplasts* were successful (22). New plants originated when the families determined by the DNA were introduced directly into the cell content of the protoplasts.

Research has understood how articificial mutations can be effected; it is even on the way to 'copying' man. 'All' that is needed for the purpose is a cell with its hereditary information and at once a human body is constructed in 'this image'. So it was more than a mere aphorism when the Hispano-American bio-chemist Severo Ochoa, winner of the Nobel Prize for Physiology and Medicine in 1959, declared:

'Geneticists are slowly beginning to play God!'

In 1975 the Nobel Prizewinner Manfred Eigen prophesied:

'It will become possible to reproduce *every* organism from its natural hereditary material by 'artifical', i.e. other than natural means.' (6)

I should add here, in line with Arthur Koestler (23), that I frequently mention Nobel Prizewinners in order to prove that certain strange theories were not put forward by eccentric outsiders, but by the outstanding scientists.

On 30 August, 1976 only a few newspapers (24) carried a sensational report in the place where it belonged — page 1!

'ARTIFICAL GENE INTRODUCED INTO LIVING CELL!'

News of this quality is much more important for the future of mankind than any political squabble or the daily reports from the overabundant battlefields of our enlightened era.

After nine years of research and experiments, Professor Khorana of MIT, Cambridge, USA, and his team succeeded in implanting an artifical gene in a *living* cell for the first time, where it went on working like a natural gene. Genes are the bearers of hereditary factors. *So deliberate artificial mutation has been successfully used by man for the first time.* This is what Nobel prize winner Khorana had to say: 'This development opens new doors to the understanding of how genes work and how they are regulated, i.e. what causes their functions and what does not.' The gene used in the experiments was taken from the bacteria *escherichia* that lives in the human stomach and consists of only 126 nucleic acids, of which each gene possesses several millions. The sensational news item went on:

The main part of a gene — a long chemical chain with the genetic code for the structure of a molecule consisting basically of protein — was successfully developed only a few years ago. However, until now the 'release mechanism' of the start and stop to make it functional was lacking. The MIT gene now possesses this functional control mechanism for the first time. During further experiments the scientists will try to find out why the genes are only active at a particular time.

The result of this research work proves that genes can be deliberately inserted by people who want to force a planned alteration of hereditary factors, and who know their goal. Experiments that go wrong are corrected until they lead to the desired result.

What remains of all the speculations about how man became intelligent?

Only one fact stands firm. We must be satisfied with man as the only intelligent living creature on this planet of ours. If we take all the genetic differences between man and his forebears the apes, only a skeleton of the common family tree is left. Man has a speech centre and can articulate words. The ape cannot speak. Man can indulge in sex whenever he gets the urge for it. Apes (like other animals) can only have sex while they are on heat. To give just two examples.

Man learns, prays and works. He devotes himself to the arts. I do not know of any ape schools, ape temples, ape theatres or ape factories. So where did man get his exceptional abilities from?

Nine years ago I dared to express my view that extra-terrestrials had brought to the earth knowledge of the kind we are just acquiring and that they made our ancestors become intelligent by manipulations of the genetic code.*

In order to emphasise the hypothetical nature of this personal conviction, I quoted Professor Max Perutz:

There are about one hundred million pairs of nucleotide bases distributed among forty-six chromosomes in a single human cell. How could we erase a specific gene from one particular chromosome, or add one to it, or improve a single pair of nucleotides? It hardly seems practicable to me.

Well, at the time he made his sceptical prognosis for the future, Perutz did not have the conclusions of the Khorana team at his disposal. Perhaps he took part in the Congress of the American Chemical Society in San Francisco on 31 August 1976. There his fellow-Nobel Prizewinner Khorana submitted the results of his epoch-making experiment to a chosen band of experts. If he did, he knows that deliberate artificial mutation has become possible. A specific gene from a specific

* Return to the Stars, p. 35

chromosome *can* be introduced into the DNA.

Perutz has certainly also heard from his Nobel comrades Crick and Orgel that faced with the insolubility of the great puzzle they had not considered the postulate that alien intelligences had imported Panspermia into the earth, beneath their immaculate academic dignity. Perhaps Perutz has now abandoned his scepticism. I don't know. Nine years is a long time; a great deal has happened in the interim and many hypotheses have become facts.

PARABLE OF A CREATION

Far from the predominant but very theoretical assumption that terrestrial man is the outstanding product of all creation, I postulate that far back in prehistory extra-terrestrials had succesfully reached the end of a road on which we are taking our first cautious steps.

I should like to describe this absurd situation of ours in the form of a 'parable', which the reporter of the scientific magazine *Futurum* kindly put at my disposal. I doubt if this eye-witness account will ever be read elsewhere than in this book. Facetious futurology with a stinging background has scarcity value.

The press chief of Biolaboratory Phi-X-2117 had not exaggerated when he invited me to to participate in an unprecedented experiment which was to take place in a place which was kept secret.

I was supposed to arrive three days before the experiment began. There was not a cloud in the sky when I drove towards the goal marked on the map. I could not see anything that resembled a normal laboratory. I thought I had missed my target, when I saw below me, beyond a bend near the mountain top, a broad apparently endless valley. There was no house or other buildings to be seen, only the wonderful new road along which my car descended almost noiselessly, and a gigantic glass dome, an arena, and a glass cathedral spanning the whole width of the valley. Words fail me when I try to describe the immense size of this glass palace.

For three whole days I was prepared for the experiment.

I was immunised with all kinds of injections, the names of which I had been told, but cannot remember. I had been informed that they were absolutely necessary, because the experiment in which I was the only reporter allowed to participate was by no means without danger. Finally, on X day I was kitted up (I had rapidly lost all sense of time in this uncanny world). White skintight overalls, skinbreathing via an oxygen capsule attached to sensors, and oxygen mask.

I was led through several air locks into the glass dome, where to my boundless astonishment I found that a second only slightly smaller glass dome was installed inside the first one. A great many scientists were running about between the two glass domes. Apparatuses, computers and enormous containers for chemicals stood in the gleaming corridor running round the experimental 'greenhouse'.

A young scientist told me over a microphone what was going to happen next. According to a fixed programme calculated down to the last detail, a primitive cocktail of the kind necessary for building organic molecules was going to be mixed from purely chemical ingredients under the glass dome. As I am an absolute layman when it comes to chemistry and biology, I do not wish to introduce any false concepts at this point, but simply say that steam poured into the dome from many jets, that clouds with yellow and brown shades mingled, that – to put it in a way we are used to – it looked liked the beginning of time. Savage. Uncanny. Violent.

The noise did not seem to satisfy the scientists, for at a signal the harsh lights of tremendously powerful searchlights were directed at the bubbling soup of water and steam. Then lightning flashed between electrodes from all sides. I thought that the turmoil would burst the dome, but now I saw the primitive cocktail being mixed, shaken and churned up as if in a thousand geysers.

My companion told me with great satisfaction that the first molecular process was beginning its cycle. The idea was to reproduce the beginning of all life in the biggest chemical process of all time. Please, I said, all I want is to come out of here alive. . . .

From time to time men wearing the same overalls as

myself took samples from the primitive cocktail. Looking through their electron microscopes they were happy to observe that some molecules had combined into chains of amino acids and that was a good beginning, not only for their planned experiment. This was how it would have been at the origin of the first life, my companion said, but added anxiously that it was all happening much too slowly, for they could not wait milliards of years for the result of their experiment. Time had been no object when the original slow process of the formation of life had unfolded. They, of course, had less time and they were just reflecting how they could speed things up.

I don't know how much time passed before we were told how they proposed to accelerate the process. The biochemists had decided, my guide said, to mix a few million levorotatory proteins into the soup. They could only use this type of protein, because the shelves of their chemical bar are right out of dextrorotatory proteins. Also he said, and accompanied his explanation with a significant look, they all wanted to survive the experiment, too. Consequently they would take care not to mix in dextrotatory proteins even if they were available, otherwise everything that was showing signs of life would be destroyed and even the organisers of the experiment would be in danger, not to mention myself, because all cells consist exclusively of levorotatory molecules. When I asked in all innocence why the two sorts could not be mixed, my guide (and he shook his head at my stupidity) said I must excuse him for being rude but that it would be absolutely ridiculous to try to mix levorotatory and dextroratatory molecules. The incompatibility of fire and water was nothing to the enmity between these two species. But he thought that there was a good chance of the experiment continuing without interruption.

The news that DNA chains would now form and that they had the remarkable ability to duplicate themselves spread like wildfire. The scientists slapped each other's backs. Cells, whole troops of cells were beginning to form simple organisms! Their unanimous joy was only damaged by a glance at the calendar. Things were still going much too slowly.

Once again they conferred. From my observation post I

saw them busily talking and arguing. Finally I saw them take a vote. Some turned their thumbs down, the majority turned them up, confident of victory.

My guide returned and said that the genetic specialists had won the day. They intended to mutate a battery of cells by building planned genetic information into them. These experts were confident they could programme the cells of specific species of organisms. First they would produce organisms with hard shells, then a kind which would increase the oxygen in the primitive cocktail and finally they planned a species of organism that could multiply a millionfold in a short time. They were convinced they could produce all kinds of life for which they had the appropriate DNA in their laboratory. The only limit would be when the right seeds were not available.

I looked through the panes of the glass dome in fascination. What was going on seemed like a miracle, and if I had not seen that it was all the work of the men in the white coats I would have had to believe that it *was* a miracle. Suddenly all kinds of species of life sprouted from the bubbling cocktail. I watched a wonderful wild primitive landscape come into being. Plants shot out of the ground. Animals were creeping and hopping everywhere. Sometimes small metal arms fished young creatures out of the giant zoo. I wanted to know why. My guide, who was carried away by what was going on, said angrily: 'You can see. Those broods have faults. The genetic surgeons are correcting those faults with different genetic material. The DNA programme must have been wrong!'

I was very glad I had been given this exclusive story on biolaboratory PHI-X-2117. It was something that does not happen every day. I suspected that it might really be a unique story. For the scientists had reached their goal: an experimentally constructed zoo, which, as I had observed, had partly originated by itself, filled the glass dome. I must admit that I felt quite uneasy. Things were so turbulent down there that I was afraid the strange animals would kill each other or destroy the beautiful primitive landscape. I was glad to note that I was not a coward, because the scientists shared my feelings. Once again they sat down and wondered what to do next.

Soon my guide brought the news that things could not be left to go on like that. Now they had come to the last act of the experiment in which they would produce intelligent life that would be able to create order in the chaos and dominate the lower forms of life. How would they do that, I asked curiously? 'That's the easiest thing in the world, my friend! We simply have to implant genetic material from our own cells into the most advanced form of life. We shall create beings in our own image!'

That went better and faster than they had expected. They preened themselves visibly when they could point to the creatures they had planned to resemble themselves. My constant companion told me that from now on there was a considerable simplification in the experiment. Now the scientists knew how a species would behave, because it had all their own characteristics. They knew in advance when something would produce feelings of pain or pleasure, for the creators themselves were affected by the same stimuli. As had been planned, the intelligent creations started to create order in the zoo at once. At the same time they began to multiply in masses. I can only depict in flashes how things went. They started forms of communal life, made the first infrastructure and soon afterwards published the first manifesto of an artistic movement. Some groups clearly separated from the rest. They were carrying on scientific research.

The men in the white overalls grinned:'Look, our images.' Another clique was observed with anger. It made contact with engineers who were summoned from workshops. Strong young men were put into identical clothes, began to march in step and then were given weapons. Like their creators they staged the first war.

As I have said, nothing now was a surprise. The products behaved exactly like their creators. For a time they quietly enjoyed their own progress of which they seemed inordinately proud.

I forgot to mention that all of us in the observation dome heard over microphones what was said down below. So we also participated in the great disquiet that was spreading down there. An unprecedented idea shook the test-tube civilisation. There were constant discussions. What kind of a revolt was in progress?

The scientists had all the machines that made noises turned off so that they could hear what was disturbing their creations.

They wanted to know how they had originated – they wanted to know where they came from, who had made them, what they were like, where they had lived before and who had placed them on this world.

The experimenters were not really surprised, because they had included their own natural curiosity in the programme. Yet here they had no chance to intervene. The answers to such questions were not envisaged in the programme they were running. They knew exactly how these beings had originated.

The most intelligent of the scientists advised that they should sham deaf and not listen. The discontent would soon quieten down. Just leave them be. . . .

But the intelligent creatures did not calm down. As they got no answers to their insistent questions, they began to bore holes in their earth, because they hoped to find an explanation down below. (This is what we heard them say.) Then they built better and better microscopes under which they slid the cells of other species between glass slides. But they also observed cells of their own species, discovered molecules and analysed them. By now quite familiar with writing, they published thick books about possible ways of obtaining the information they sought. As facts could not be found, they developed countless theories about their presumed origin and descent.

After endless disputes the general view prevailed that each species had presumably developed from the others and that the stronger had won through against the others and survived. Naturally some intelligences raised their voices against this theory and pointed out that it would not have been possible, because the species could not have mated with each other, as they had constantly observed and could confirm every day. These sceptics were squashed with the remark that evolution in their zoo had taken so long that this trick of 'one from another' could have been possible.

As I had never formed any ideas about such problems, I was particularly interested in the objection made by one

young man. He said it would be strange that in the course of·
their history only one species, namely the one to which they
belonged, had developed intelligence and that all the other
forms of life were still swarming around them, below their
standard. They cut the revolutionary short, for everyone
taking part in the discussion had long considered that they
were the masterpiece of creation. They had no intention of
being deprived of this exceptional position. Basta.

It was really funny to hear how the intelligences that had
originated under the glass dome, partly chemically, partly
by genetic manipulation, came to the conclusion that their
origin and evolution had happened by pure chance, that the
species had originated from one another by a lengthy
development and that they themselves had become the only
intelligent beings by a series of lucky co-incidences. If I had
not witnessed the experiment from the very beginning, I
might have thought there was a grain of truth in the absurd
idea. But I was an eye- and ear-witness of the most
marvellous experiment of all time. So I could only laugh at
the nonsense they were talking.

A row showing no signs of stopping began at a moment
when the discussion seemed to be over. Someone asked if
intelligent people 'from outside' might not have had a hand
in the business. This idea was pooh-poohed as being too
farfetched to consider. After all they knew who they were
and the kind of opinion they ought to have of themselves.
They were arrogant enough, these products of an experiment!

I was only a non-participant observer, nevertheless I
understood, indeed even felt sorry for, the poor old scientists who had been dashing round the experimental dome
day and night, and now saw themselves cheated after all
their efforts. They had taken such trouble over mixing the
primitive cocktail, and the gene manipulations had made
them cry, not to mention the cells they took out of their own
bodies.

Now their products would suddenly have none of all that.
They completely disowned their creators, whose guest I
was.

Although, like all reporters, I should have liked to know
whether the story had a happy ending, I quite understood

why the chief ordered the termination of the experiment.

THE POINT AT WHICH WE STAND

On the face of it that parable is simply an amusing diversion, yet the ingredients of empirical knowledge are hidden in it. Are we behaving like the creatures under the glass dome? Were we not created in the same way as they were? Do *our* creators observe us from time to time? Are they annoyed at our arrogance and blindness? Are they furious because we reject the 'midwifery' they supplied at our 'birth'? Could *our* creators break off 'Experiment Earth' one day?

Our scientists, too, drill deep into the ground in the hope of finding information about the early history of the earth and the sequence of the origin of life in hidden strata. Test probes are drilled kilometres deep into the sea bed. Very recent drilling off the coasts of Australia showed that all the sediments found were either more than forty-five or less than thirty million years old. Oceanographers of Hawaii University found marine fossils off Australia, New Zealand and New Guinea that were also more than forty-five or less than thirty million years old.

James Andrews, who led the expedition in the research vessel *Glomar Challenger,* has no solution to the puzzle of why a 'menopause' of fifteen millions years in the earth's history occurred. SOMETHING must have happened on the earth during this enormous period of time; it cannot simply have held its breath. Perhaps this question will be cleared up when the earth's strata are analysed.

In 1856 a skeleton which J. C. Fuhlrott discovered in Neandertal between Düsseldorf and Wuppertal, caused a furore. The English anatomist King used the word Neandertal to describe a whole race of men who are supposed to have been our ancestors in the Pleistocene of the Quaternary Ice Age. Perhaps this calculation would have worked out, if scholars had not found out that Neandertal Man died out 50,000 years ago and left no descendants or collateral lines. There was no more talk of the evolution of this prototype, although I cannot quite believe in the complete extinction of Neandertal Man, for I still know some of these Ice Age beings whose ostensibly voluminous brains have not yet thawed out .

Neandertal Man was written off, but archaeologists sought busily for earliest man. They seek and seek, and keep on finding some monkey's skull that is loudly proclaimed to be the earliest genuine ancestor of our exalted race. *Homo erectus* (erectus = upright) a star of an ancestor, who walked upright and used fire. Until a few years ago experts gave him an

approximate age of 1.5 million years. In the meantime we have had to go back a million years, because a skull was discovered in Kenya in 1975 that was 2.5 million years old. Or was supposed to be. It is also included in the album of the *Homo erectus family.*

At the next skull auction, the age was bid even higher. In the Afar region of Ethiopia the American palaeontologist Donald C. Johanson dug up the skull of a small young woman, whom he called Lucy.

It is not impolite for palaeontologists to certify that a lady is very, very old. Johanson credited Lucy with 3.5 million years. No sooner had a label with this age been stuck on Lucy's little skull than L. Leakey, Director of the National Research Centre for Prehistory and Palaeontology in Nairobi, presented a still older skull, which he simply called ER 1470, being less

poetic than his American colleague. The former possessor of
the skull died 3.5 million years ago.

There's no end to the fun! New skulls, new bones, new
datings. Over and over again we are told that the bones
definitely come from our early forebears, whereas in fact they
come from the descendants of some species of ape. Leakey tells
it like it is:

> The earlier view that *Homo sapiens* descends from Nean-
> dertal Man, and he from *Homo Erectus* and the last-named
> from *Australopithecus**, is an error. The facts showed that the
> line which leads to *Homo sapiens* was already represented in

Fig. 100. 'Gods' working on the 'tree of life'. Surely this
mythical tradition could be an interesting object of study for
geneticists?

*Bone finds from the transitional field between man and animal that are
supposed to be closer to man, small-brained hominids.

East Africa two million years ago and is contemporary with *Australopithecus*. The line which led to *Homo erectus* emerged somewhat later. Probably both the actual Homo and primitive *Australopithecus* existed in the later Pliocene four million years ago.

Although nothing is known for sure, the literature on the subject sells the suppositions about *Homo sapiens* as if they were proven facts. Even the *Encyclopaedia Britannica* has the nerve to claim: 'Not the slightest doubt can exist about the fact of evolution.' Professor Luis E. Navia of the New York Institute of Technology has an entirely different opinion:

> There are scientists who speak of evolution as a fact and are immediately prepared to condemn the 'mysticism' and pseudo-scientific hypotheses of others. Hypotheses can only become facts when we have analysed all the possible and pertinent information. Perhaps they forget that it is impossible to include all the evolutionary information, because we should have to discover all the geological remains and observe a greater number of evolutions. As Darwin himself admits, the geological finds are full of gaps, and even if we do not like to say so, we must realise that we are only speculating in this connection. (27)

Can the origin of intelligence be deduced from the evolution of some branch of the apes on the basis of so little verified knowledge?

I read: 'Primitive men lived in packs and so developed a form of social behaviour.' That is less than a theory, it's sheer nonsense. Many other species of animals live and lived in packs besides the apes, but apart from a social pecking order they have no developed intelligence.

'Man became intelligent, because he adapted himself better than other species.' What did *Homo sapiens* adapt himself to better? As palaeontology essentially elicits the history of descent from apes, the adaptation motivation is no more than an air balloon. And if our hirsute ancestors adapted, why didn't the primates, such as gorillas, chimpanzees and orang-utans? Following the laws of evolution, these droll creatures would 'inevitably' have had to become intelligent in the long run. Evolution cannot be made valid at will for one chosen (and chosen by whom) species. Moreover there are infinitely older forms of life than the primates. Scorpions and cockroaches date back 500 million years. Because they survived so gallantly these species must have adapted themselves much better than the very much younger *Homo sapiens*. Have scorpions and cockroaches become intelligent?

'Man has no fur, because he understood how to wear the fur of other animals.' That's a bit too much. Because man was not hairy, he had no fur, he wore the furs of others. But the hairs on his own body did not fall out because he wrapped himself in furs!

'Primitive man climbed down from the trees for climatic reasons.' Really? What a bright idea! As if one species of ape had realised that they would be needed in the theory of the evolution of man, it clambered down from the trees, but left its colleagues, who were exposed to the same climate, to go on hopping about in the branches of trees until the present day. The *social* behaviour of our ape ancestors was quite undeveloped.

Primitive man was forced to stand on his hind legs for fear of stronger animals and also because it was easier to feed that way. Very funny. Monkeys' imitativeness is proverbial. Why did not the other species of apes follow this intelligent behaviour? Were they less afraid of wild animals? Were they less hungry?

Primates in the line that led to *Homo sapiens* began to eat meat so that they could feed themselves more easily and better, indeed by eating meat 'our' apes had made a leap ahead of other species of apes to intelligence. First it does not strike me that it is 'easier' to kill a gazelle or a salamander than to pick fruit from the trees, secondly it is a physiologically and nutritionally crazy and out of date idea that meat-eating develops and preserves intelligence. There are great scholars who never eat meat – I mainly met them in India – and I know contemporaries who live on steak. Moreover wild cats and predatory fish ate only meat for millions of years. Have they become intelligent?

No, no. If one took this and a hundred other motivations from the same treasure-house to justify the theory of evolution, our planet would be teeming with countless forms of intelligent life including those who were much older than the millions of years in which the 'hour of our birth' is supposed to have struck.

Claims that the organs or abilities of organisms came into being *because* the organisms used them lead into the wilder realms of absurdity. The little word *because* can establish a causal connection when it deduces an accepted possibility from a proven fact. *Because* the amino acids needed a protective covering, they entered the protective unit of a cell. How on earth did the amino acids know that a cell offered them protection? *Because* a cell needed energy it produced chlorophyll. How did a cell 'surmise' that it needed energy? *Because* the cell wanted to survive and multiply it produced chlorophyll via its pigments. *Because, because, because* . . .

EFFECT – WITHOUT A CAUSE?

All these adaptations were chemical alterations of the genetic code. Brainless organisms did not mutate *because they needed something.* If we admit the many *becauses,* we must also admit that an order was given before the cause. *Because* every effect has a cause.

As we have all read reports of successful manipulations of the genetic code, we laymen can at least imagine how difficult it is to exchange a single nucleotide in order to alter a DNA programme. According to the prayerbook of the theoreticians of evolution, what our perfectly equipped scientists succeeded in doing in a single case after hundreds of thousands of experiments is supposed to have been going on non-stop during evolution owing to milliardfold coincidences. *Because* a nascent organism needed new information?

In order to alter something genetically, to place a single nucleotide in another place, a mutation is necessary. I have explained that mutations can also occur spontaneously, for example, under ionising radiation or specific chemicals which work on the cytoplast. *But the desire for a mutation is not enough to exchange individual nucleotides or sequences of bases.* Wishes can only proceed from a brain, and brains that *want* something have not long been in a position to realise their wishes. Will anyone contradict me if I state categorically that the most primitive organisms (I am thinking of microbes or the first multicellular organisms) had no brain, and they still have no brain? This removes the prerequisite for *wishers* or *orders* and also the possibility of converting them into fact.

The inconsistency of the many *becauses* in the textbooks is obvious. In a logical sequence the *becauses* would only have a place when, according to the law of cause and effect, an unknown *someone* stood behind every *because,* activating the wishes and causing their fulfilment. Brainless organisms cannot make wishes for *something* effective and hence cannot initiate any changes in the cytoplast.

Inasmuch as they took the non-existent cause into account, the most important factor has evaded the theoreticians of evolution: the executive organ, the creator, the gods or whatever one likes to call the unknown.

Although it is not the case with brainless organisms, the wish for change is quite understandable in intelligent creatures with brains – but is still not *explicable.* Here are some examples in support of that statement:

Because a tiny reptile needed protection, it developed armoured scales. Easier said than done. For this hairsplitting logic requires nothing more nor less than that the genetic code, the basic sequence of the DNA, must be altered so that protective armour develops around the soft-skinned creature. Perhaps someone would be kind enough to explain how the wish for protection can effect the regrouping of nucleotides in the cell! Not any old regrouping but one working towards a goal!

Because primitive man suddenly ate meat, he developed *(needed)* stronger teeth. Because he needed them, according to this distorted logic, they promptly grew. Did primitive man possess parapsychological or some other kind of transcendental faculties which told the DNA in the genes: As from the next generation we absolutely must have strong teeth? Did the DNA begin to restructure the correct cells so that, abracadabra! future generations would be equipped with perfect sets of teeth for eating meat?

Today of all times, when planned mutations are undertaken, especially now when the intricacy of genetic information with thousands and thousands of genes in a single chromosome has been understood, in the year 1977 of all years when man finally knows how incredibly difficult it is to effect a single *positive* mutation in the cell, people still cling to the senseless belief that mutations took place spontaneously from generation to generation, *because the organism needed them.*

The claim that organisms developed what they needed *by themselves* or rejected what was superfluous, during thousands of years of evolution, I find equally contradictory. I read that 'Nature' looks after our needs in a wonderful way. If so, I am very sorry to say that miraculous nature has failed dismally. In spite of her continuous chance interventions in the DNA with results that are always positive! She has provided man (by chance?) with a brain that is much too large for his needs. She gave her master product miserable eyes which can only look straight ahead. Yet she gave her less developed products, e.g. insects, a wide field of vision – she actually supplied snails with an apparatus with which they could make their eyes project so that they could see in every direction. Man seems to be a master-product with all kinds of deficiencies.

Has something essential escaped me, for all my intensive reading? I have never found it stated that the first ape-Adam suckled his baby. To the best of my knowledge it was always Eve who gave the child her breast. Is the ape-Adam an evolutionary mistake? Was he supposed to produce and suckle children? Did his voluptuous breasts shrink over millions of years, *because he did not need them?* Otherwise why was Adam left with the rudiments of dugs?

From time immemorial men have wanted more pleasure. There, too, nature left intelligent men in the lurch. Man's desire for more love, more understanding, more peace has always been powerful. *Because* he urgently needed those things, and even more. Here the cause on which a theory was constructed clearly failed. It would not only be useful as regards an untenable theory if the *becauses* were eliminated from its structure, it would also be fruitful for a new discussion if what has not yet been considered was finally included.

How could what Darwin himself described as a *theory* of evolution be turned into a *dogma* of evolution?

It *seems* to be logical because all the gaps in proving it can be filled by pointing out that milliards of years were available for evolution and during this virtually interminable period everything would have been possible. Including the impossible, obviously.

Anyone who is prepared to accept a dogma involving such

abnormal chances should be happy with it. But perhaps even the most diehard adherent will realise its improbability when he reflects that his own body has come into being from 50 billion cells. Darwin's proposed theory fell in no-man's land, so to speak. People were glad to have an ideological model on which they could work. It fitted many speculations too. From then on famous architects joined in the building and because they were so famous they quickly found 'fellow-travellers' who created an astonishing edifice: 'What a marvellous theory we've got! In with everything that fits.'

Critical scientists dare not open their mouths among this gigantic congregation that is so ready to bow down and worship. Who would climb into the ring against Nobel Prizewinners, who had in their pockets the power to destroy dissidents? Scientists who incurred the displeasure of professorial chairs could be dissolved into atoms. Yet such 'annihilation' of academic opponents is fairly humane compared with the perfidious art of making a laughing stock of them. So the theory stands that chemical and biological evolution are to be attributed not to a plan, but to the interplay of insanely improbable chances.

Life is chemistry; chemistry is matter; life is an out and out materialist business. In ideological terms, this view is the mirror-image of dialetical materialism, a philosophy, the essential tenets of which accept all phenomena in the world as material or as having proceeded from matter. '. . . the prevailing law separates man from his universal being, it turns him into an animal . . .' (25.)

Such a purely materialistic theory, in which the strongest always triumphs, obviously has no place for a concept like creation; it cannot tolerate the supernatural or include the undefined power known as God. 'Darwinism is the basis of its natural science and also the basis of its whole ideology, whether economic or political.' (12.)

Once, ecclesiastical institutions blocked progressive thinking and new knowledge. Today, it is ideologies that put the brakes on. In the past people believed in religions and their founders; today, according to the same formula, people believe in ideologies and their inventors. Belief still goes on.

I did not understand why critics in Communist countries called me anti-Marxist from the appearance of my very first

book. I had never said a word against the stylite Karl Marx.
The reason only became clear to me when I was dealing with
the theory of evolution. The collaboration of extra-terrestrials
is not allowed in dialetical materialism! The inconceivable
and supernatural is dangerous. Man might lose the halo of his
omnipotence and his central importance.

Professor Wilder-Smith explains this position:

> For men who have come to the conviction that higher
> development according to the Darwinian theory, must be
> 'good' because its 'fruits' are good, cannot object if scholars
> want to help this development along by ordering natural
> selection into the battle for existence. Accordingly, it must
> be a 'good' deed when we let certain inferior individuals or
> races die out or 'erase' them. After all, nature (or God) has
> made use of this practical method, so what objections can
> we put forward on moral or intellectual grounds? By using
> the same method we shall only speed up evolution to a
> superman. According to these principles, we ought to
> approve the destruction of inferior individuals and races for
> the good of the masses . . . The 'outstripped' capitalist
> world will turn into the Communist world, according to the
> principles of political Darwinism; this transformation, too,
> represents an 'evolution'.

With the courage of the conviction given me by my
preoccupation with the age-old concerns of mankind, I have
tried to demonstrate with precision that it cannot have been
the way we were and still are taught. Since neither animals,
nor plants, nor even man can have originated from a total
vacuum, and since a real event *must* have real originators, all
that remains is the hands of extraterrestrials, whom people
called gods in the oldest traditions. A planned creation can
only have come from thinking brains of intelligent beings with
a standard of knowledge far above our own. Undoubtedly
mankind by continuous research can also reach this stage in
the very very distant future. But we could be close to the goal
we seek for, if we finally included the unthinkable in our world
picture. For I consider that this much is certain: *we did not
originate by ourselves and by chance!*

Will the possible truth – formerly hindered by religions and
now by ideologies – be left by the wayside? I hope not and find

consolation in the poet Christian Morgenstern:

When the bright stars plunge into the dark sea of ether, and in mysterious exhalations, the spirit soars up to lively dreams in the vast sacred kingdom of the night, winging to boundless spaces . . . In the soft magic of such nights the Creation seems to unfold and we get a faint idea of the powers who control our lives.(26)

6: A Plea for the future

Supreme Court!
Ladies and gentlemen!
In spite of all the attacks on me in newspapers and periodicals, I still have enough sense of humour to accept the role of accused that I presumably have to play here. It is obvious to me that those publications which accept my theory wholly or partially are not included in the debate. But perhaps the very whirlwind I stirred up has made the Supreme Court suspicious? Perhaps it had asked itself whether there may not be something in my theory because otherwise the popular method of hushing me up would have been used.

I am delighted to hear how many exalted scientific journalists are not frightened of producing their own series of books, in my footprints, so to speak. Supreme Court, what an amount theory must be able to carry if its opponents can quarrel about sucking enough honey from out of the cornucopia while the controversy still rages!

I have kept my sense of fair play despite the heat of the controversy. So I can say that well-known colleagues have for years been patiently ploughing furrows in the same field that I have been tilling. I leave it to the Supreme Court to decide why the opponents of the 'Gods were astronauts' theory fired their guns at me in particular. Do they imagine that I'm wearing a bullet-proof vest – thanks to my circumstantial evidence! Or do they sense that I have more stamina? I was useless at sprints at school, but almost unbeatable over long distances. Let the gong sound for the next round.

I am told that because interstellar spaceflight is not possible extra-terrestrials could never have visited us. Through a competent expert I have supplied a counter-proof that interstellar space-flight *is* possible, and with a wealth of documentary evidence, I have supported this claim – the Court must forgive me ! – but I assure the Court that I can multiply these documents twelvefold at any time. The plaintiffs can put their wishes on record with the Clerk of the Court.

It is claimed that the origin of the first life and of human intelligence is attributable to a series of chances. Thanks to many conversations with biologists, physicists and mathematicians, but mainly through the instruction of an outstanding expert, I can *prove*, not merely claim, that the prevailing dogma is absolutely wrong. The plaintiffs cannot dispute the results of physical and biological-chemical research, unless they want to fall flat on their faces from the highly polished parquet flooring of purist science.

Supreme Court, what objective proof is required of me? Shall I bring the mummy of a space traveller into the Court? Shall I put parts of a crashed spaceship on the table? Shall I produce the mouldering bones of an extra-terrestrial preserved in alcohol? Do you want to see a time capsule with news for us and hear it ticking?

The plaintiffs must understand that: the land area of our planet comprises 148.8 km^2, but land area is not the same as habitable area! Take away the ice-caps at the North and South Poles, remove the uncultivable desert regions and the area shrinks. Subtract the mainly uninhabitable, impassable jungle regions in parts of Central and South America, Africa and India and the area gets smaller and smaller. The Alps and the Urals, the Rocky Mountains and the mountains of Alaska are not habitable, nor must we forget that the genuinely habitable parts of the earth float in a great pond. 70.8% of the earth's surface is covered by water. And who lives in the water? A bare 20% of the blue planet is inhabited and to date only 1% of this area has been archaeologically explored! It is reasonable, I ask the Supreme Court, to ask me for a tangible proof, a legacy of the 'gods'? Yet such proof

could be everywhere! It could be found just as easily under the
polar ice as under the sand and stones of the deserts; it could
be waiting for discovery in the steaming jungles or under a
neglected overgrown hill somewhere in the world. In any case
it seems absurd to expect the objective evidence to appear at
those archaeological points which in total only make up 1% of
the inhabited areas. It is easier to find a needle in a haystack
on a dark night than to stumble on a relic of the extraterrestrials by chance at some place or other. No, the gods I am
trying to lay are not the relics of the gods left behind and
found *by chance*.

I willingly admit that a proof that was deliberately left
behind is due! Extra-terrestrials mutated men 'in their own
image'. So they knew what to expect from their creatures!
They knew that sooner or later man would begin to play with
technology and that spaceflight would be the goal of the game.
It would be only logical for the 'producers' of human
intelligence in prehistoric times to have deposited evidence of
their aims and actions.

How should such proof be provided? I ask the Supreme
Court to ask the plaintiffs how they would like it. Would a
time capsule with microfilms and tapes, and technical plans
and diagrams be enough? Why not? If such evidence were
found one day, it would not surprise me in the least; a
prehistoric deposit for future generations. If we switch off the
light of the halo around man as supreme being and find the
courage to admit that there were cleverer people than
ourselves thousands of years ago, it will not be fantasy, but a
real possibility. Unfortunately we all think we are Mohammed Ali. We are the greatest!

Supreme Court! I beseech you to believe me. We are not.
My readers will ask where might we find a deliberately hidden
legacy? That's a question I ask myself, too. Easily visible on
the top of a mountain? That would be a crazy place. Anything
seen in such a prominent spot would have been taken away by
much earlier generations and they would not have realised
what they found or how precious their discovery was. Found
by the *wrong* generation at the *wrong* time? Nonsense. Knowing
their own historical development on their home planet, the
extra-terrestrials calculated on a long-term basis. They obviously dedicated their gift to those descendants who would at

some time travel in space and discover the connection with their genetic constructors. They did not leave any goods for immediate consumption. Consistency, packing and the contents of their legacy were intended for much later generations and the men who find it will be able to see a distant future that is worth striving for.

Where to place the gift? In a temple? Or in the new expensive soil of Manhattan which could have been had for nothing in those far off days?

The extra-terrestrials were not born yesterday! They knew that natural catastrophes and wars could destroy temples and similar sanctuaries over the millennia; they knew the effects of floods and the annihilating power of earthquakes. So where to put the proof they wanted to be quite safe? Hidden in a cave? It might still lie there without our knowing it.

The plaintiffs behave as if we were looking for an Easter egg our parents have hidden in a bush in the garden! I assure the Supreme Court that if it were so simple, I would have found that egg long ago.

What we are talking about here, is a hiding place that was meant to be left undiscovered for thousands of years.

Only logical and mathematical sites could be considered – places on the earth's surface such as the magnetic North Pole or points on the Equator where land and water counterbalance each other. That is more or less the direction in which to seek the terrestrial possibilities. I find it much more likely to postulate logical/mathematical points inside our solar system, for example at libration point $L = 5$ or in the centre of a field of gravity formed by the gravitation of three planets. May I put on record that a prominent scientist has already suggested such possibilities. (1).

Given one of these assumptions, the extra-terrestrial Easter egg would be hidden in a calculable, but unknown place. Would this match the great intelligence of our extra-terrestrial visitors? How should we find their legacy if there were no traces leading to it? It is my personal and unshakable conviction that traces are to be found in age-old myths; to be sought in the originally oral scriptures of ancient religions and now the signs and codes in rock and cave drawings must be interpreted. Naturally, so long as the plaintiffs are not prepared to check these suppositions, but simply mock at them, I shall keep up the attack with my theory that these traces exist.

It should be possible to find the factual records of the extra-terrestrial visitors somewhere. Many of the ones I introduced into the discussion as speculations have since been proved valid.

Perhaps we are looking for objective proof that is before our eyes all the time? Surely man himself as the only intelligent organism on this planet is *the* proof of extraterrestrial interven-tion in evolution on earth?

Parrots, who imitate our words, are living proofs that they have been in the company of man. If our genetic engineers make monkeys intelligent in the future by planned artificial mutations, surely the new species will be the visible product of human action. Monkeys would never become intelligent without our manipulative intervention.

Is not the existence of men evidence enough of the intervention of extra-terrestrial creators? How else can we convincingly prove that *homo sapiens* in particular, was cut off from the great monkey family and became intelligent? Man, as the sole intelligent being, may seek for his creator in vain. The fact that he has one is proved by his own existence. Is there anyone in court, may I ask, who believes that man was made of clay, then filled with his innards and finally given the 'kiss of life'?

Permit me to introduce a mental aid. If a trouser-button were found on Mars, we could state quite definitely that a being wearing clothes must have been on Mars at some time. There could be an endless wrangle about what race the trouser-wearer belonged to, but no question about the fact that he had existed.

The simple trouser-button enables us to make further assumptions; that there was a workshop or factory in which it was manufactured; that there was thread with which it was sown on the material. Material plus button make it a certainty that the beings who lived on Mars did not run around naked. If the fossil also enables us to show the material (wood, metal, man-made, etc.) from which the button was made, and whether it was hand or factory-made, certain assumptions could be made about the state of economic development of the country from which the man wearing the trousers came.

Please, Mr Prosecutor General! What has the Martian trouser-button to do with the proofs of my theory? The button doesn't prove anything? I beg to contradict you.

Early human history is one big 'trouser-button' shop! I use the 'buttons' that I find wholesale and retail, in myths, religions and popular legends to guess who the strangers were, what they looked like, what they did, what machines, weapons and know-how they had at their disposal and what methods they used to colonise our planet. They are not cheap 'buttons'. They are often decorated with gold and precious stones. If no one else bothers to pick them up, I do!

May I mention that the value of conclusions drawn by analogy for the discovery of new knowledge is undenied. I am only using a method prevalent in science.

I understand from the headings under which I am charged that the plaintiffs – represented by authorities such as Professors Fred Hoyle and Carl Sagan – claim that given the multiplicity of habitable planets in our galaxy it would have been impossible for extra-terrestrials to have reached our planet in particular and even more so, at a time when the first glimmerings of human intelligence were just beginning to stir. As I have already refuted this argument in detail*, I shall only pick the weak point in my opponents' logic. The extra-terrestrials did not visit earthmen who were already intelligent! *Homo sapiens* did not become intelligent until after the visit by the 'gods'! I have no desire to repeat myself here, so I respectfully ask the Court to put my previous deposition on the record.

Basing myself on the countless habitable planets assumed by Hoyle and Sagan, I foretell that the first extra-terrestrial visitors or their descendants will return! Our position in the galaxy is known to others; the intelligent forms of life visited *before us in time* know where we are. I have already said that it would be logical if the alien visitors had left an objective proof of their presence. This supposition applies equally to other solar systems visited by the extra-terrestrials *before* their visit to earth! I wish to emphasise that I am now only speculating: beings on other planets similar to man on earth could have found the objective proofs bequeathed to them long ago by the

Miracles of the Gods, pp.

extra-terrestrials! They have the advantage of being well ahead of us. So I suspect that these people know from the objective proof they have found where the fathers of intelligence, if I may so call the 'gods', went when they said goodbye. So, I conclude, bright as a button, that not only 'our' extra-terrestrials know our galactic position, but also all the other beings had an extra-terrestrial visit before us. Consequently we are likely to get further visits; not only from the discoverers of space-travel, but even from those who now have an advanced technology owing to their temporal advantage over us.

Mr Prosecutor General? No, I do not want this statement to be put on record as proof. I state firmly that it is a speculation. The fact that it seems logical to *me* does not raise it to the status of proof. The Court can be sure that I shall always say loudly and clearly when I am submitting hypotheses and not proofs. Hypotheses are preliminary drafts of a theory *per definitionem*. I operate within the bounds of the admissible. Only dictatorships can forbid us to develop theories. Thank you.

I am reproached for anthropomorphic thinking and crediting the extra-terrestrials with actions and reactions of the kind current among us. It would appear that my critics have overlooked the salient point of my theory – or refuse to look at it.

The gods created men in their own image. Consequently not only I, but all of us are thinking in 'divine' terms. We all think and act according to the genetic model after which we were created. Since men have been producing offsprings, they have been begetting 'children of the gods', i.e. descendants of their images.

Possibly, and this is a hypothesis, the 'gods' or their descendants are once more staying in our solar system and observing us. Of course I know that my critics think this supposition is absurd, but a sense of responsibility drives me to include it in the speech for my defence.

Ladies and gentlemen, I see that you smile when I talk about responsibility. All too often people are exposed to enormous psychological shocks without being prepared for the experience. Do you want that to happen to you? *I* think the return of the extra-terrestrials is possible, therefore I feel that

I am responsible to my fellow citizens for preparing them for the event. Millions of the inhabitants of this earth could be shattered by such an event, but since I find it conceivable I give it a place in my plea for the future.

I am no UFO fan. I have never seen a flying saucer, even in the distance.

After reading many serious works on the subject and after countless conversations with people who have all their wits about them, I know that inexplicable phenomena are piling up in alarming numbers. Pilots, radar operators, sober scientists and men like Barry Goldwater and Jimmy Carter assure us that they have seen UFO's. There is no reason to doubt the credibility of all these people. Or have the plaintiffs got the nerve to accuse these honourable men of lying?

So far – and that we are all agreed on – no one knows what the Unknown Flying Objects are. Let me make myself clear. I am not claiming that UFO's are always extra-terrestrial phenomena but I plead, in the name of all those who have seen them, for the fact that they exist.

My critics ask why they do not land officially if they exist and are possibly of cosmic origin. Why don't the Commanding Officers of the strange celestial carriages allow themselves to be greeted by the President of the United States, with a red carpet and all the trimmings?

Why don't UFO's *insofar as they are of extra-terrestrial origin,* make an *official* landing?

While studying myths it occurred to me that the 'gods' always had a complete mastery of the language of the earth-dwellers. This linguistic ability presupposed that prehistoric man on earth was 'observed' and 'studied' over lengthy periods. Otherwise there is no explanation of how the extra-terrestrials managed to arrive on earth as polyglots. They spoke in the current vernacular, in which there were obviously no technical concepts.

It will never be known how many languages there were in the catalogue 'at that time'. Today 2,986 languages are spoken on our planet. Among them there are the six universal languages which extra-terrestrials must know so that they can understand worldwide communications by radio, TV and teleprinter. Long periods of observation are necessary for their linguistic studies alone.

Bacteriological and virological conditions on the earth have changed considerably since the gods' last stay thousands of years ago. New dangerous diseases have originated, their carriers are unknown to the strangers. Before they plan an official landing – with shaking hands, fraternal kisses, the exchanging of gifts, etc. – they have to learn about the unknown diseases and possible infections. May I remind you that the first astronauts were put straight into quarantine on their return from the moon, for fear they might infect us with a dangerous unknown disease. Extra-terrestrials who are preparing for a visit will be at least as cautious. Medical patrols will observe us closely, frequently and in many different parts of the world before the landing.

Men, too, have changed radically since the gods' last visit. That is why the extra-terrestrials will want to know how far and in what direction the abilities of their descendants have developed. Are they already familiar with atom and hydrogen bombs? Do they use devastating poison gases and frightful bacteriological weapons? Are the men of the day powerful enough to constitute a potential threat to the 'gods'? How has the state of consciousness changed? Has the seed of the artificial mutations grown up according to plan? Or have new spontaneous mutations made quarrelsome creatures of the human-kind? What is the political line-up? Is power exercised dictatorially or democratically? Which religions are dominant? How great is the risk of a landing?

The number of questions would presumeably fill many pages and they would all have to be answered in advance. What I am saying here sounds fantastic. I have been able to take part in the disputes of serious research workers who are concerned with interstellar expeditions. It is incredible how much they have to think out in advance. We can assume empirically that the extra-terrestrials proceed with equal method and use similar strategies. After all we are their images.

That might be a reason why patrols using small space craft carry out research somewhere 'at the end of the world'. No one knows, but I think that we are on the right track if we foster such suppositions. And in line with modern research into behaviour it seems only right to me that we should be studied as we really are. As soon as we appear officially, as soon as we know that we are being observed, we shall stop acting 'naturally'.

In order to get all the UFO's sighted in this world out of my sight, I should like to say that we know nothing *for certain*, but *everything* is possible. We must wait and see. Two figures should make the Court thoughtful. Twenty years ago a representative sample of the population of the USA was asked: Do you believe in UFO's and do you think they are manned by extraterrestrial beings? Twenty years ago 3.4% answered 'yes'. In the autumn of 1975 the same sample was asked the same question. In 1975, 51.7% answered 'yes'.

If the extraterrestrials are trying to prepare people psychologically with their UFO's, one can say 'hats off' to them. The method is fulfilling its purpose.

Supreme Court, ladies and gentlemen!

Since I wrote about subterranean tunnels in Ecuador*, headlines like these have never ceased:

DÄNIKEN UNMASKED!

THE CHARLATAN MAKES A FOOL OF HIMSELF-DÄNIKEN'S CAVES ARE EMPTY!

What are they still on about? In 1972 I wrote that I had been in a cave by a side entrance. Down below there was a 'metal library' and a zoo with sculptures of many kinds of animals. The printers' ink was not dry when the first vehement attacks began. Apart from *Der Spiegel*, which asked me for an interview, was given it, but did not print it, none of my critics approached me for my opinion. In the summer of 1976, a Scottish expedition penetrated five kilometres into one of the Tayos caves, at the request of the Government of Ecuador. There was no trouble about publicity, for Neil Armstrong, the first man on the moon, was one of the party. This expedition found 'no trace of extraterrestrials', saw 'no gold', but did find 'various interesting cult objects'. Däniken was unmasked once again.

Neil Armstrong tracking down Däniken. That was, of course, a signal for this expedition to be given world-wide publicity. Picture articles ten pages long appeared in various places in the world! Armstrong exposes Däniken!

Did Armstrong know how he was being duped? He

* *The Gold of the Gods.*

obviously did not.

On 24 February 1977, Professor Neil A. Armstrong of the University of Cincinnati, Ohio, wrote this in a letter to me:

> The Los Tayos Expedition, a joint project of the British and Ecuadorean expedition was formed to conduct a scientific study of the *"caves de Los Tayos"*. It is my understanding that the British Army was involved in some 400 such expeditions in 1976.
>
> Because of my Scottish ancestry, and the fact that the U.K. side of this project was largely Scottish, I was invited to act as honorary chairman of the expedition, I accepted.
>
> I visited the exploration site in early August this past summer. I had not read your books and did not know of any connection that you might have had with the caves. I made no statements regarding any hypotheses you may have put forth.
>
> I understand that there have been magazine articles in Germany and Argentina which reported on the expedition and related it to your theories. Pictures were included which showed me at the site. I was not interviewed by representatives of either publication. I was asked in Ecuador whether I had observed any evidence of highly developed societies having been in the area, and I answered that I had not.
>
> I accept no responsibility for anything you may have read in the European press.
>
> I appreciate your kind invitation to join you in your forth-coming expedition, but am unable to accept.

I had not, of course, believed that Armstrong was responsible for this nonsense. He did not, after all, say it himself. It was simply invented, put into his mouth. If you want to finish Däniken off, no method is taboo.

Seventy-five members of the expedition lived for six weeks in the Tayos caves of Ecuador. So we must assume that Armstrong had it in mind, when the expedition set off, to expose Däniken! We must also assume that the members of the expedition did not know that they were to expose me — with the exception of the ink-slinging pamphleteers!

There are hundreds of caves in Ecuador. Armstrong himself knows of four hundred. I do not know exactly how many there are, but I think this number is realistic. How could anyone know, then, that he was on my tracks? In articles published all over the world – I got them all from my press-cutting agency – I read 'the greatest expert on life outside the earth has been included in the team', in other words, Neil Armstrong. But he knew nothing about his task of exposing Däniken.

Every expert knows that there are hundreds of different caves in Ecuador. I ask the Court to explain why the expedition crawled about in *any old* cave and not in *my* side entrance to a tunnel? They could not have known its position, because I promised its discoverer not to tell it to anyone. I am used to keeping my word.

I am taking the liberty of giving the Court a photograph for the record. It shows me with the discoverer of 'my' cave, Juan Moricz, and his lawyer, Dr Matheus Peña, outside a side entrance.

Fig. 102. Erich von Däniken with the discoverer of the caves Juan Moricz and his lawyer Dr Mattheus Peña at the side-entrance to a cave.

Why didn't the Scottish expedition take with them, if not myself, at least the discoverer of *the* cave, Juan Moricz? After all he confirmed the existence of a 'metal library', in an affidavit. Why did they not arrange to put the native cave expert on the trail that I followed?

It is both unfair and uncomfortable to try to squeeze the results of the 1976 expedition into my size shoe! I must say at once that I respect critical objective journalism, even when I have to suffer as a result. But I have no sympathy at all when only one party is heard and the other disregarded. Speleologists and journalists alike can be sure that they will find no one more interested in their researches than myself. Fairplay should not be a foreign word in any language.

There is another similar case which I should like to submit to the Court for judgment.

On two occasions I spent several days with Father Carlo Crespi in his pilgrimage church of Maria Auxiliadora in Cuenca, Ecuador. Today Crespi is well over eighty and slightly senile. He takes an impish delight in bamboozling his visitors and shows it with a broad grin. But when Crespi was younger – he has lived in Cuenca for fifty years – he was accepted as the acknowledged expert on Indian culture. He collected ancient Indian works of art and set up a museum with Vatican support. For reasons that were never explained his life's work was burnt to the ground. He was only able to save a few precious unique pieces. Since then he guards them like a hawk. Suspicious as he is, he never shows them to strangers. I did not come as a tourist or a pilgrim, who hurriedly takes a couple of snaps of the pastor and his church. I stayed for days and won the old man's confidence. I was that close to him! After much delay he showed me some gold plaques, Indian works, that he had saved. Altogether I took a couple of hundred photographs. Also of the everyday objects that lay in the courtyard of the church. I showed the artefacts I was interested in to a wide public*.

What happened?

Given urgent commissions by their editors, journalists flocked to Crespi. I was told that some of them stayed with him for a few hours, but most of them stayed less. This lightning troop only saw what Crespi shows all the tourists: cheap gimcrack stuff, mass-produced Indian culture for tourists!

'Däniken talked about gold plaques and steles – all we saw was tin-plate.' Bang! 'Once again we've given the storyteller the works.' To stick to the jargon: 'unmasked him'.

* In Search of Ancient Gods.

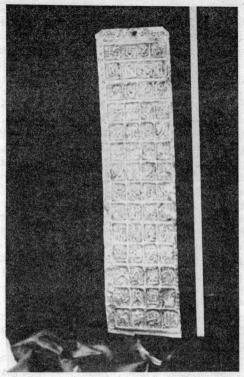

Fig. 103. Professor Kanyilal, a leading Sanskrit scholar, was able to identify the majority of the signs as Indian characters of Brahmanic origin.

I photographed and published a stele which had fifty-six different signs in fifty-six squares. I asked whether characters, letters of an unknown alphabet, had been hammered into the metal by the ancient Indians. I can still hear the scornful laughter at my question. Meanwhile Professor Kanyilal of Calcutta was able to verify the majority of the signs as ancient Indian characters of Brahmanic origin. It would be a fine job for the journalists to find out where the 'forgers' got their knowledge of Brahmanic characters from! But it's a job they won't tackle; it won't supply any ammunition to attack Däniken with.

hen Charles Berlitz published his book *Mysteries of Forgotten Worlds* and illustrated it with some of the *the same* objects from Crespi's collection, there was no protest, no calumny, no 'unmasking'. I am glad Berlitz was spared the unpleasant ordeal but I can't help asking the simple question: What kind of journalistic justice prevails here? Is there a special criterion for Däniken? Without wishing to influence the Court, I may mention what a famous American journalist said to me when I told him about the charming way in which many of his colleagues treated me. He said: 'Look, Erich, it's your hard luck that you've got to write to tell people about your theory. Writing is a journalist's job. But when someone else writes and is as successful as you are, we don't like it. So we yank you down from the top rung of the ladder until you're on our level. That seems to be the whole secret of the exceptionally charming treatment you're getting from some of my colleagues!'

It would be carrying coals to Newcastle if I now went into details about how the former NASA engineer J. Blumrich succeeded in reconstructing the spaceship described by the prophet Ezekiel, on the basis of the details in the Bible. What is *not* known is that Ezekiel was taken on various flights by the commanding Officer of the spaceship. After one of these flights the prophet was put down near a temple. This is his description:

In the twenty-fifth year of our exile, at the beginning of the year, on the tenth day of the month, in the fourteenth year after the city was conquered, on that very day, the hand of the Lord was upon me and brought me in the visions of God into the land of Israel, and set me down on a very high mountain upon which was a structure like a city opposite me. When he brought me there, behold, there was a man, whose appearance was like bronze, with a line of flax and a measuring reed in his hand. And the man said to me, 'Son of man, look with your eyes, and hear with your ears, and set you mind upon all that I shall show you, for you were brought here that I might show it to you . . .' (Ezekiel 40, 1-4).

Ezekiel also gives the exact measurements which were taken at the spot. He describes the four main gates of a temple, gives the points of the compass at which the gates lie and lastly mentions a small stream which rises at the side of the temple and becomes an enormous river in a large valley. The chronicler specifically says that he was taken to a very high mountain.

Blumrich had the questions ready: 'Where was Ezekiel? Where had he been taken to?' (3.)

The prophet did not know the name of the mountain. So he could not be in the vicinity of Jerusalem, for Ezekiel grew up there. There are very few hills in the neighbourhood of the city and they were undoubtedly known to him. The temple in question could not have been the Jewish temple, for Ezekiel served as High Priest in the temple at Jerusalem. The strange edifice seems to have been similar to the one he knew so well, yet he is very curious about it and gives detailed descriptions of it.

Where did the extra-terrestrials fly the prophet to? Which temple tallied with the exact description he gave? I kept on asking myself these basic questions. I dragged some ponderous archaeological tomes into my studio and looked for temples in them. It must have four doors and a forecourt, colonnades and a stream which rose just beside the temple and broadened out into a river in the valley. And there was a very high mountain in the vicinity of the temple.

Fig. 104. The Temple of the Jews (Temple of the Sun) near Marand lies in the biggest ruined site in Kashmir.

Could it have been an Inca temple somewhere in South America? No, those temples have neither four doors, nor columns nor a forecourt. Was the prophet thinking of a pyramid when he described his temple? Was he talking about a temple in Central America? I could not find a very high mountain near a pyramid. Was the temple to be sought in Babylon or Persia? There was no very high mountain to be

Fig. 105. The sanctuary mainly lies in the middle of the temple layout. Radioactive traces have been registered on the line that leads from the centre of the sanctuary through the main door and into the open.

found in those countries, either. Besides Ezekiel was familiar with the lay-out of the Babylonian temple. He had been in captivity there.

I began to search for temples in upland valleys. The post brought me a hot tip from a German reader, Karl Maier who wrote to me:

There are various temples at Shrinagar in the Vale of Kashmir. Strangely enough, one of them is called the 'Jewish Temple', and this temple has four doors, a forecourt and everything else a Jewish temple should have.

This kind reader enclosed with his letter the ground plan of this temple near Marand, thirty kilometres from Shrinagar.

Close study of the map gave the encouraging information that a stream rose right next to the temple; that it grew into a river in the Vale of Kashmir and that there really was a very high mountain range in the background, namely the Himalaya. Had Ezekiel been brought there?

In fact the 'Jewish Temple' at Shrinagar, also called 'Temple of the Sun', is the biggest ruined temple in Kashmir. Since religious Hindus rebuilt the temple for their own purposes only three doors exist today. But when I stood there in 1976, I saw the forecourt with the main door, the seven steps and the sanctuary inside. There was the stream next to the ruins and there gleamed the Himalaya, the high mountain range. If Ezekiel had been brought here, the ferry ship must have landed in the forecourt. I quote from the German Bible:

Afterward he brought me to the gate, the gate facing east. And behold the glory of the God of Israel came from the east; and the sound of his coming was like the sound of many waters; and the earth shone with his glory . . . And the mobile vessel that I saw was like the vision which I had seen by the river Chebar and I fell upon my face . . . The glory of the Lord entered the temple by the way *above the door,* whose front side was facing east . . .   Ezekiel 43, 1–4

It says clearly in the text that the space ship went into the temple. Were there measurable traces here? For two whole days we walked around with our measuring apparatuses. Nothing happened. We covered the terrain metre by metre. Suddenly, in a line projecting from the main door, the needles vibrated like mad. Unpleasantly loud crackling noises came over the earphones for a few seconds. I went back to the start with my apparatus. The phenomenon was repeated at exactly the same spot. The area of radioactive radiation was 1.50 m wide. How long was it? Slowly I left the right-hand corner, going left. The crackling in my earphones still continued, but became irregular and sometimes disappeared altogether. The instruments seemed to have gone haywire. I was using a portable electronic monitor, Type TMB2.1, made by the Munich firm Münchner Apparatebau. This apparatus is used to measure and control alpha, beta, gamma and neutron radiation.

I reduced the incoming amount of radiation per fiftieth of

a second. It made little difference. In certain places the needle stuck at the end of the scale.

What was going on? Were we walking over a deep-lying seam of uranium? Was there radioactive ore in the ground? Was the reflecting solar radiation laying us a trick at this height in the clear mountain air? All considerations that could not be dismissed out of hand.

In the sanctuary of the ruined temple lay a massive squared stone which externally looked uncannily like a block of concrete made in a mould. Its sides were 2.80 m long. I could not measure its height because the base sank deep into the ground. The needles of our detectors occillated more than ever above the block of stone. Presumably it had a core of metallic material

The next day companions, the archaeologists Professors Hassnain and Kohl, took us to the ruins at Parhaspur,

Fig. 106. The remains of three temples can be clearly recognised among the ruins at Parhaspur, Kashmir. A landscape that might have been heavily bombed. In fact attacks with unknown weapons of destruction are mentioned in myths.

which is also quite near Shrinagar. There they showed us in three different temples the same massive squared stones that we had examined at Marand. Did these stones conceal a mystery? Again it was the text of Ezekiel that surprised me. He claimed that the Lord had said to him:

Fig. 107. Three squared stones lie in the centre of the ruins at Parhaspur and there is a surprisingly similar one at Marand. They look like precast concrete from the same 'factory'. Measuring apparatuses suggest that some kind of metal shapes must be concealed inside the stones.

> And he said unto me, Son of man, hast thou seen the place of my throne, and the place of the soles of my feet, where I will dwell in the midst of the children of Israel for ever?
> Ezekiel 43, 7

Did the Lord leave a trace in the floor of the sanctuary that marked a deposit? Did the alien visitors put *something* in the stone blocks that could still announce its presence after centuries?

I do not know. Nor do I know whether the radioactivity in the temple of Marand and above the stones at Parhaspur has any connection with my gods. I do not want these observa-

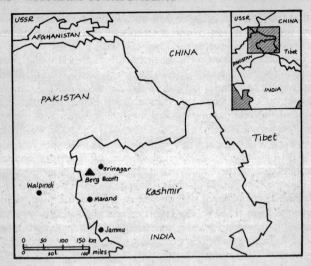

tions to be assessed as proofs. Nevertheless I mention these phenomena because I would dearly like to persuade Indian scholars to break open one of the stones and find out the reason for the radiation!

Nearly all the details given by Ezekiel about the temple to which he was taken can be verified in the ruins of the temple at Marand. I hand on the task to the competent scientists.

Ladies and gentlemen, it is a strange enterprise for the man who stands before you to have to point out curiosities which have been overlooked and forgotten in our busy age, and which always lead to puzzles the solution of which should be an important task for us and for every generation.

Everyone was told at school about manna, which nourished the Jews on their long journey through the desert. What has never been properly explained is what this inexhaustible source of nourishment really was. Perhaps a solution to *this* puzzle has been provided. Let me tell you about it:

George Sassoon is English. He is an electronics consultant by profession and a linguist as a hobby. Sassoon read my books. We corresponded and got to know each other. He told me that among the evidence on which I based my theory he found certain clues which made him suspect that there were tangible things to be 'revealed' in ancient scriptures which had solely been interpreted in mystical and religious terms until now.

Sassoon got hold of an English edition of the Cabbala*, but he soon found out that the translation was far too complicated and woolly to be any use to him. He began to learn Aramaic so that he could study the original. In it he came across the story of the biblical manna and it electrified him because he thought he could see the construction of a manna machine in the text.

With his accurate translation he sought out Rodney Dale, the biologist and technical writer. Like Sassoon, Dale deemed to find the description of a biochemical laboratory in the code-like language. When the two men had coordinated their concepts from the Cabbala text, they asked the technical and scientific draughtsman Martin Riches to prepare construction plans according to their specifications. A biochemical laboratory was put on paper. George Sassoon told me this preliminary history of a discovery.

As I have long been convinced that a lot of technical knowledge is hidden in old traditions, I was surprised by the find, but not staggered. I had almost forgotten the story when a copy of the *New Scientist* with an article by Sassoon and Dale entitled 'Deus est machina?' (Is God a machine?) reached me in the spring of 1976. When a periodical like the *New Scientist* devoted three pages to a subject, there must be something in it.

Deus est machina?

Was manna from heaven really single-cell protein manufactured in a special fermentation unit, long interpreted in Aramaic texts simply as a god called "Ancient of Days"? But if it was a single-cell protein plant, a light source akin to the laser would have been needed to operate it

"And the Children of Israel did eat Manna forty years until they come to a land inhabited" (Exodus 16:35)

George Sassoon is a linguist and electronics consultant, and **Rodney Dale** is a biologist and freelance engineering writer

There has long been speculation as to what the "manna" which fed the Children of Israel in the desert was. One tradition is that the biblical manna was from the secretion of *Coccidae* which parasites on tamarisk trees (*Tamarix mannifera*). The insects extract the sap (which is rich in carbohydrates) of the branches of the tree, and the excess which their bodies

the books of *Sepher-ha-Zohar* (*The Book of Splendours*), most of which was apparently written from oral traditions by a Spanish jew, Moses ben Shem Tov of Leon, in the 13th century.

Our earliest source is the Aramaic *Cremona Codex* (1558), from which was derived the Latin *Kabbalah Denudata* (1644) and the English *Kabbalah Unveiled* (1892). Our original work was carried out using the English translation, and we are currently verifying the uses of the various words involved by retranslating the early Aramaic

---

The Kabbalah Unveiled. Containing the Book of Concealed Mystery – The greater holy assembly and the lesser holy assembly. By S.L. MacGregor Mathers.

Sassoon allowed me to make a resumé of the very long and technically written article. Anyone who reads the results of their research will realise that manna did not fall from heaven, as we read in Exodus, 16, 4–25.

Was manna a single-cell protein that was prepared in a special fermentation unit?

Was manna identical with the God, who was long known in Aramaic texts as 'the Ancient of Days'? In other words, god as a synonym for a thing?

If this 'Ancient of Days' stood for a factory in which single-cell protein was produced, a light source (photosynthesis) with the strength of a laser beam must have been available at the time when manna was the basic food.

Centuries of efforts to clarify what manna really was produced no definitive result. Usually it is described as a secretion of *Coccidae* which parasitise on tamarisk trees *(Tamarix mannifera)*. The insects extract the sap (which is rich in carbohydrates) from the branches of the tree and the excess of which their bodies secrete in the form of transparent drops. These solidify into little white balls which contain grape-sugar and glucose, and small amounts of pectin (of the kind used for making jelly). Ants collect it and carry it off to their hills. Incidentally Bedouins still use manna as a substitute for honey; they call it *man*.

Although there is a similarity between this secretion and the biblical manna, it lacks the characteristic qualities of the fare praised by Moses. It contains no protein, whereas manna is described in the Pentateuch as 'bread' and a basic article of food. Besides *man* is only found for a few months and then in such small quantities that it could not satisfy a people wandering in the desert. Sometimes the biblical manna is also identified with lecanorales *(Aspicilia esculenta)*, the largest order of lichens, but it has not been proved that this species of plant has ever been found anywhere in the Middle East. Its home is in the tundra and alpine heaths.

So where did manna come from, because food for the people had to be available daily in sufficiently large quantities? Sassoon and Dale are convinced that they have found the answer in the Cabbala.

As is well known, the Cabbala has been used since the twelfth century as a collective concept for the esoteric teaching of Judaism. The concept is derived from the Hebrew QBLH 'That which is received'. A part of the compendium of traditional Jewish mysticism is to be found in three books of the *Sepher-ha-Zohar* (The Book of Splendours), which Simon Bar Jochai is supposed to have written down in the second century, but which was probably written by the Spanish Jew Moses Ben Shem Tov of Leon in the thirteenth century. Our earliest source is the Aramaic *Cremona Codex* (1558), from which was derived the Latin *Kabbala Denudata* (1677) and the English *Kabbalah Unveiled* (1887).

The Zohar text contains the exact physical description of a God, 'the Ancient of Days'. A remarkable ancient! He consists of a male and a female part. This strange method of taking a god to pieces and putting them together again puzzled Sassoon and Dale. They eliminated glosses from the text and realised that a machine, not a god, was described. Here, too, the writers of the Kabbala, who knew nothing about technology, used familiar human qualities to give an idea of an apparatus which was unknown to them. I may add that the

Fig. 109. Artist's impression of the manna machine which Martin Riches design after reading the Cabbala.

Apaches still use this method today. To make a car intelligible, they call the headlights *inda* = eye, electric cables *tsaws* = veins, the radiator *chih* = entrails.

Sassoon, the linguist, tried to translate the description of the 'Ancient of Days' using adequate technical language. It turned out that magicians had so mystified the ancient text down the centuries that literally hard facts disappeared behind an esoteric cloud. Only today is it possible to interpret old texts technologically.

I quote verses 51 to 73 of the book *Hadra Zuta Qdisha* (The Lesser Holy Assembly):

The Skull

The upper skull is white (1). In it is neither beginning nor end. The hollow thing of its juices is extensive and intended for flowing (2) . . . From this hollow thing for the juice of the white skull the dew falls every day into the Small-faced One (3) . . . And his head is filled and he falls from the Small-faced One on to a field of apples (or blowers). And the whole field of apples flows with that dew (4). The Ancient Holy One is mysterious and hidden. And the higher wisdom is hidden in the skull (5), which was found (is seen), and from this to that the Ancient is not opened (i.e. there is no visible opening) (6). And the head is not for itself (or: alone), as it is the uppermost part (or: head) of the whole head. The upper wisdom is in the head (7): it is hidden and is called the upper brain (8), the hidden brain (9), the brain that moderates and is calm (10). And there is no son (of man) who knows it (i.e. it is not intelligible to anybody). Three heads are hollowed out: this (11) into that (12) and this above the other (13). One head is wisdom (14); it is hidden from the one that is covered (15). This wisdom is hidden, it is the uppermost of all the heads of the other wisdoms. The upper head is the 'Ancient and Holy One', the most hidden of all the hidden. He is the upper part of the whole head, of the head which is not a (normal) head and is unknown. (The description reinforces what was said before: the head concerned is not a normal one, capable of thought. It is not known what goes on there, because the head is hidden.) And consequently the 'Ancient Holy One' is called NOTHING. And all those hairs (16) and all those cords (17) from the brain are hidden and in containers (18). And the throat cannot quite be seen

(19) . . . There is a path which flows in the division of the hairs from the brain (20) . . . And from this path flow all the remaining paths, which hang down in the Small-faced One (21) . . .

Out of the context of the Kabbala, this is the situation:

The 'Ancient of Days' had two skulls, one above the other. Both were surrounded by another skull. The upper skull contained the upper brain in which dew was distilled; the lower brain contained the heavenly oil. The Ancient had four eyes, one of which shone from inside outwards, three were not self-illuminating: from left to right they appear to have been black, yellow and red. As befitted an Ancient he had a luxuriant beard in thirteen different forms. The hairs appear to have grown out of the face and back into it. The hairs were soft and the holy oil ran through them.

The special characteristic of the Small-faced One was his hard skull, in which fire developed on one side and air on the other. In addition, he whirled fine air round from the one and fine fire from the other. The oil flowed from the upper to the lower skull and there changed colour from white to red. Around the hard skull lay the lower brain which distilled the dew, which filled it daily, over its outer form. What trickled from it was manna. It was collected below in Hosts (testicles) and sucked up through a penis.

The Cabbala gives only a few details about the female part of the 'Ancient of Days'. It had multi-coloured hair, which finally all ended in a golden colour and, joined into a cord, led back to the upper skull. Every Sabbath the 'Ancient' fell into a trance. Then his parts were cleaned and put together again.

The English investigators found out that the upper part was a distilling apparatus with an undulating cooled upper surface over which air was conducted and condensed by means of water. The water was led into a container in the middle of which there was a strong light source which irradiated a culture, possibly a green alga of the chlorella type. There are dozens of species of chlorella. The balances of protein, carbohydrates and fat could be varied by providing suitable conditions of growth.

Algae cultures which produced the product desired circulated in a system of pipes which effected an exchange of oxygen and carbon dioxide with the atmosphere and discharged excess heat. The chlorella slime was led off into another vessel where it was treated in such a way that the starch partly hydrolised into maltose, which when lightly toasted acquired a honey flavour. Exodus 16, 31, tells us that manna was as white as coriander seeds and tasted like honey cakes.

The dried product was put into two containers: one of them was emptied for the day's needs, the other filled up gradually so that there was two days' supply for the Sabbath, the weekly day of rest on which the machine was at a standstill. It was cleaned and serviced so that it started producing again the next day.

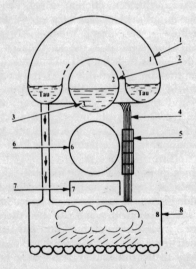

Fig. 110. Technical drawing of the manna machine made by Rodney Dale from the descriptions of the 'ancient of days' in the Cabbala: 1. Upper 'skull' with undulating, water-condensing surface – 2. Container with source of light that irradiates a culture of algae – 3. Container in which the dried product originates – 4. Filaments, cords, ducts which...5. lead into a system of pipes – 6. The invisible 'head' in which the malt sugar is hydrolised – 7. The product is led through the 'neck' into the collecting basin – 8. Basin in which the production is collected.

The machine had to supply one *omer** per day per person and as it had to supply 600 families, its daily output amounted to 1.5 cubic metres of manna.

What happened to the machine when the Israelites left the wilderness and it was no longer needed? (Joshua 5, 12, tells us that the manna ceased that very day.) After the capture of Jericho the machine was kept at Shiloh as a holy object (1 Samuel 4, 3). Later it was captured by the Philistines, but brought back very quickly, because it killed many of them. Naturally. The Philistines had never seen the manna machine working, nor had they obtained any instructions for use when they pinched the apparatus. It has always been thus. Technology with which people are unfamiliar is dangerous. Flavius Josephus, the Jewish-Roman historian of the first century A.D., noted that the Philistines all suffered from diarrhoea after enjoying the products of the machine. After it was returned King David put the apparatus in a tent in Jerusalem as a ritual artefact (1 Chronicles 15, 1). His son Solomon had a temple built for the mysterious machine (2 Chronicles 2, 5). During one sacking of the temple, the machine was destroyed as well.

Sassoon and Dale end their article in the *New Scientist* as follows:

Machines of this kind would be essential equipment in spaceships, as they fulfil a dual function. They provide oxygen for breathing *and* nourishment. Soviet scientists have built such a machine and use it for cleaning the air in an enclosed environment on board the Salyut laboratory, in which men lived for several months. The cultures were fertilised by the astronauts' excreta and so presumably not eaten. Our present-day fermentation technology is not nearly so advanced as that which was used in the manna machine. The component mainly lacking is a light source of high intensity and efficiency. Laser may meet these requirements.

The question remains: where did the Israelites' manna machine come from? People have speculated that the earth

---

*Omer: a Hebrew dry measure of about three litres.

was visited by beings from space about 3000 years ago and that these visitors brought the machine with them. This speculation creates as many problems as it solves. We should prefer not to put forward this hypothesis today. Perhaps we shall be able to answer this question one day when we have finished our researches

This article first appeared in the *New Scientist* (1 April 1976). Clever journalists – perhaps a bit too clever – tried to follow it up and fell into a trap. It was, they discovered, published on April fool's day! But the journalists did not do their research well enough, and they did not know that the authors, Sassoon and Dale, had on several occasions published the results of their research elsewhere, for example, in *Interface*, the house journal of Cambridge Consultants. The journalists had no idea that the authors published a report in the Chicago journal *Ancient Skies* (June 1976), describing the lectures that they gave about their research work. Above all, the April fools did not know that Sassoon and Dale were preparing for publication an exhaustive study entitled *The Manna-Machine*. Surely judgment has been passed on these journalists already? Why did they not ask the only people who could have known whether they were simply playing April fool's day jokes, or were involved in something more serious? Is any old trick permitted in this game of catch as catch can?

I do not claim to count the Englishmen's article as proof of my astronaut theory. But I think it is important that factual details are extracted from old traditions, that modern technological knowledge be used to interpret mistaken and antiquated words where it is legitimate, as Sassoon and Dale did with the Kabbala text. We must reconstruct the picture of our early past with the tiny pieces of a gigantic jigsaw puzzle.

I would like the Court to assess such remarks as a sign of my constant endeavour to draw the attention of scholars investigating our past to interesting phenomena.

A large question mark stands just outside our portals. India is far away and I am afraid the temples of Kashmir will guard their secrets for a long time yet, but Turkey is nearer, only one and a half hour's flight from us. There lies Nemrud Dag, the sacred mountain of Commagene. Far in the south-east of

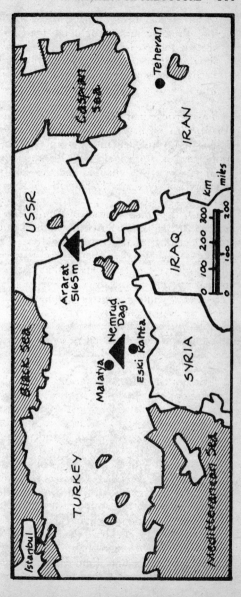

Fig. 112. Nemrud Dag, with its pyramids made of heaps of broken stone, rises to a height of 2150 m in south-east Turkey. Antiochos I had a sanctuary built here.

Fig. 113. A gallery of stone monuments rots away on the ground . . . gods and a monolithic eagle.

Turkey, 2.150 m high, it rises in the middle of the Taurus massif. Archaeology has little to say about the riddle of Nemrud Dag. Neatly carved inscriptions on the colossus tell us that Antiochos I (324-261 B.C.) had a tomb for himself and a sanctuary for the gods built there, buildings which were renovated and enlarged by his descendants, but no one really knows if these inscriptions are correct.

I consider one inscription especially worthy of notice. It says that Antiochos had these buildings erected in order 'to leave behind an unshakable law of time, in that he entrusted immortal messages to an inviolable monument'. What kind of unshakable law of time, what kind of immortal message did Antiochos entrust to the mountain?

The summit of Nemrud Dag is like a gigantic pyramid of piled up broken stones. We shall never know whether Antiochos's messages are hidden there or what form they took until a deep borehole is sunk into the interior of the mountain from the tip of the cone. I look on inscriptions over 2000 years old as important indications. They should not be overlooked.

There are two terraces facing each other on the flat ground at the foot of the pyramid. There heads which once stood on large square stone blocks are mouldering on the ground. From left to right there is an impressive gallery: a stone lion, a monolithic eagle, next to it the proud gods Apollo, Fortuna, Zeus, Herakles and Antiochos. Eagles and lions are represented twice in beautiful stonemason's work. Much further down the mountain an ox is carved on a rock face.

What did I read in Ezekiel?

As for the likeness of their faces, they four had the face of a man, and the face of a lion, on the right side: and they four had the face of an ox on the left side; they four also had the face of an eagle.

Ezekiel 1, 10

It has been established when Ezekiel is supposed to have written his account. It was dated to 592 B.C. Antiochos I is reputed to have begun the giant buildings on Nemrud Dag around 320 B.C. About 290 years lie between Ezekiel's description and the building of the tombs. Antiochos was the last in the sequence of the kings of Commagene; his forefathers were certainly ruling in the prophet's life time. The Kingdom of Commagene embraced the extensive area between the Upper Euphrates (the Roman province of Asia Minor) and present-day Persia. The capital of the kingdom was Samosata.

A look at the map makes it clear that the royal forebears of Antiochos I reigned in the immediate vicinity of the prophet. Ezekiel is supposed to have had his first contacts with the 'gods' during the period of his Babylonian captivity. It was only a stone's throw from Babylonia to Persia. Ezekiel speaks of four symbolic faces. Antiochos had such heads cut from the rock as nine-metre-high colossi and transported to Nemrud Dag, the highest mountain peak in his kingdom. Why? He wanted 'to be near the gods', the gods who came from heaven. Watched over by symbolic figures which lie prostrate on the ground today, Nemrud Dag guards a secret. Perhaps it is identical with the enigmatical message Ezekiel handed down? The monuments of Nemrud Dag combined with the prophet's text give an indication. Ought we not to follow it. 'I have entrusted an immortal message to this inviolable monument.'

If an expedition should make its way to Nemrud Dag as a result of this information, I recommend that at the same time they have a look at another puzzle which also raises a question mark over the skies of Turkey. These are the details: the subterranean cities of Kaymakli and Derinkuyu lie between the villages of Nevsehir and Nigde. You can't miss them because since access has been granted by the Turkish Government they have become a tourist attraction, under-standably enough, for what you can see there, even on superficial examination, is well worth the journey.

I should like to talk about Derinkuyu as an example of other underground cities that are in the process of excavation.

There was once an underground city here that housed 20,000 people in several storeys going deep into the ground. When the city was inhabited, it was no improvised refuge. The community had a most sophisticated infrastructure. There were enormous communal rooms, dwellings with bedrooms and livingrooms, stables and even an extensive winecellar, not to mention shops and other amenities. The rooms were on different storeys. So far thirteen storeys, going deep into the earth have been excavated at Derinkuyu. The separate storeys are connected with each other by shafts, the

Fig. 114. Colossi nine metres high guard the 'immortal message' of Nemrud Dag.

entrances closed by large round stones which were bolted from inside, but could not be opened from outside. In the deep storeys, wells, tombs, arsenals and escape routes were found. Their brilliant architects also knew something about airconditioning. 52 air-shafts have been excavated so far. Through them fresh air was brought to every corner of the city by a sophisticated circulation system. Derinkuyu and Kaymakli, which is very similar, are only two of the fourteen underground cities that Turkish archaeologists know about. The excavators already know the underground connecting routes which linked all the cities together. According to calculations, no less than 1.2 million people lived in these catacombs for long periods of time. 1.2 million people! That means that adequate supplies of foodstuffs must have been procured. How? And where from?

Archaeologists think that these cities were dug in the ground in the first century A.D. Christians dug themselves in here for fear of their persecutors. The worm of doubt gnaws at this explanation. The underground men had to live. For all their intelligence, they could not install fields that bore crops

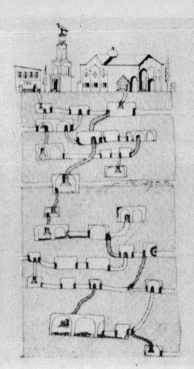

Fig. 115. Cross-section in depth of a dwelling complex at Derinkuyu.

underground. There was no light to stimulate growth. But if they had to till the soil and rear cattle above ground, their subterranean dwellings were no longer a safe refuge! Fields and stables would have betrayed the fact that men lived there. Besiegers could have sat down calmly at the entrances and waited until the hungry humans were forced into the light of day. They did not even have to fight their opponents; they could starve them out. Blockade!

Apart from this criticism, another objection to the theory is that the excavation of such gigantic underground settlements would mean mountains of sand and rubble rising on the surface. Anyone who has been in these cities realises that they were not temporary dwelling places. People had planned and built here for decades, perhaps for centuries. Where digging went on that scale, there must have been mountains of debris and any enemy would have been suspicious of them. I don't like the smell of the archaeological hypothesis.

Fig. 116. Entrances and connecting galleries were closed by large round stones which could be bolted from inside but not opened from outside.

I offer a logical explanation from the arsenal of my theory about the gods.

The inhabitants of this territory had received a visit from extraterrestrials in the distant past. When they started their return flight, they told the natives that they would come back in their flying machines to punish anyone who did not obey the orders they had given. So an attack from above might come at any given time. Fear of what might come down from heaven drove people both here and in South America into these incredible underground lay-outs. We must even ask ourselves whether the underground dwellings were built with technological aids left behind by the messengers from un-

Fig. 117. View of the enormous communal rooms at Derin-kuyu. The accommodation built here was obviously meant for long periods of time.

Fig. 118. This is how the landscape above Derinkuyu looks! There is not a hint of the underground city.

known stars. Burrowing thirteen storeys into the earth with primitive metal spades? That seems to be attributing far too much to our ancestors.

Ladies and gentlemen!

Objective proof of the former presence of extra-terrestrials is asked for! The gods reproached Ezekiel and told him that men had eyes to see, but did not see. We are still open to the same reproach.

Allow me to mention yet another curiosity in this birds-eye view of my theory. It can be found in the Bolivian jungle. The little village of Samaipata is 150 km from Santa Cruz. 30 km further away lies El Fuerte, a strange mountain in the middle of the jungle.

Archaeology knows very little about El Fuerte. All it can offer are theories ranging from the miserable to the ridiculous. There is no tradition worth using.

A mountain lies before us in the jungle. Two deep artificaly made grooves lead upwards and stop suddenly. Above, on the plateau, there are tanks of various size cut out of the rock, circles, drainage basins, raised triangles, miniature towers. All these shapes are connected with each other by a mysterious system of channels. Even if it was a utilitarian structure, art was not forgotten. Panthers and jaguars symbolise power at the foot of the deep grooves. Steps and washed out niches make

Fig. 119. The mountain El Fuerte with its mysterious scars of artificial origin towers up in the midst of the Bolivian jungle.

Fig. 120. The mountain has basins for collecting rainfall carved out of the rock, as well as accurate triangles and circles in relief which are connected by a puzzling system of channels.

one think of a pre-historic stadium. The deep symmetrical grooves are not unlike launching ramps. Neglected by the world, El Fuerte slumbers away in the Bolivian jungle. El Fuerte, the highest mountain at Samaipata, carried a secret on its age-old shoulders. Will it be revealed one day?

It need not always be mountains or vast underground cities on which we turn our curious gaze. We must also take into account the little scribbles on rock faces and cave walls in our search for *the* objective proof of extra-terrestrials. They have never been investigated and recorded on the assumption that they might be messages from the 'gods'. I have filed away thousands of such signs and I gladly put them at the disposal of those who are seriously interested.

In years past, tens of thousands of engraved stones were found in Peru. I would like to contribute a sample of them to the records.

Professor Dr Javier Cabrera has made the largest and most interesting collection of engraved stones. For generations his family has lived in the old town of Ica, in the south of Peru. I first heard about the engraved Ica stones in a book by my colleague Robert Charroux (4). When I saw the pictures I knew I would have to go there. But ladies and gentlemen, don't think that I dashed off blindly! First I asked the archaeologist Dr Henning Bischof of the Völkerkunde Museum in Mannheim if he knew of the engraved stones from Ica and what he thought of them. Dr Bischof wrote, saying that the Ica stones were forgeries which the Indians made to sell to tourists for a few soles (Peruvian coin).

Unlike my opponents, I am always ready to hear both sides. Now I knew that official archaeology looked on the engraved stones from Peru as forgeries.

I flew to Peru.

Fig. 121. Deep symmetrical grooves, which lead from the foot to the top of the mountain where they end suddenly, look not unlike well-built launching ramps. – There are some archaeologists who think they are draining channels for 'ritual beer'. No theory can be too ridiculous!

Fig. 122. Professor Dr Javier Cabrera, Ica, Peru.

The Cabrera family owns a large house in the Plaza de Armas in Ica and it needs it, for the Cabreras are very fertile. Three large rooms are fitted with shelves from top to bottom on which lie massive stones. One must imagine the room, in which the collector's desk stands among stones and shelves, as an egg-shop, except that the eggs are stones and decorated with the most fantastic engravings. You can make out Indians riding on birds, on others they are immortalised with strange tools in their hands. On one stone an Indian is using a magnifying glass so that he can see better, another is a pocket-size globe on which the outlines of strange countries, continents and oceans are carefully incised. One is startled by symbolic monstrosities the like of which one has never seen before. Dr Cabrera, who is a leading surgeon, showed me a series of stones which depict a heart transplant in process. The heart is taken out of the patient, who lies on a kind of operating table. Tubes feed him with infusions. A new heart is introduced. Two operators close the arteries. The opening in the chest is closed up. The pictures, which I ask to be put on record, show the whole process better than I can describe it.

Professor Cabrera is a self-willed man. He does not easily tolerate opinions that run counter to his own, but he is as passionately interested in his collection as I am in my theory. For two whole days he dragged me from stone to stone. 'Look,

Fig. 123. The desk in the eminent collector's 'egg-shop'. Over the years Cabrera, distinguished surgeon at the University, has made a collection of more than 14,000 stones.

Erich. Look here!' No sooner had I got one stone in my sights than he pulled me along to the next one. Collector's pride. Cabrera has about 14,000 stones in his collection. The Indians brought most of them to his home and he found some of them himself. The majority of the stones are the size of a fist and have subjects like birds, flowers, mythical trees and men. The larger stones are covered with such complicated intricate subjects that Picasso would not need to blush if the authorship were attributed to him.

I was constantly nagged by the question: are some of these stone engravings genuine (old) and some forged (modern)? And if there are forgeries, does Cabrera know about them? Is he a credulous, blind victim? Dr Cabrera replied:

In a village 26 km away there are forgers who copy the engravings and sell them to me, but I can tell straightaway

Fig. 124. An Indian rides on a fabulous creature.

by the subjects which stones are genuine, I mean old, and which were forged and perhaps only made yesterday. In doubtful cases I have geological analyses made.

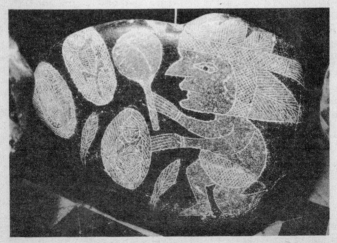

Fig. 125. An Indian looks through a magnifying glass.

Fig. 126. A 'globe' which shows unknown continents. Lemuria? The former bridge between India and Madagascar? Drowned Atlantis?

And I asked him to lend me a stone which he guaranteed was genuine. With this stone I drove to a tiny coastal hamlet to meet the forger Basilo Uchuya. I told him that I would buy some of his stones as long as I was allowed to see how he did the work. After a lot of haggling, he agreed. With his twelve children dancing around him, we went into the hut. The master fished a fist-sized stone out of a basket, drew pencil lines on it and began to engrave with what was left of the blade of a saw. Forty minutes later he pressed the stone into my hands with the outlines of a dove on it.

'Do you also make large-scale engravings here?' I asked. The stonemason smiled proudly: 'Everything!'

'The big stones in Dr Cabrera's collection have complicated historical patterns. Where do you get all your knowledge?'

'From illustrated papers.'

Had I met genius?

While we bumped back to Ica in the jeep, I began to calculate. Cabrera owns 14,000 stones, his neighbour another 11,000. That makes a round 25,000 stones. Basilo took forty minutes over the simple lines of the dove. It was primitive

Three of the many phases in which Indians depicted a heart transplant.

work which could not be compared with the majority of Cabrera's stone engravings. Moreover Cabrera's stones have an average diameter of 40 cm. So twenty engravings of the kind Basilo scratched on his fist-sized stone would fit on it. The stones in Cabrera's collection were executed much more artistically. More painstakingly, with lots of imagination. If twenty times forty-five minutes work was needed for a stone of the type collected by Cabrera, a forger would take fifteen hours on one stone. To make the 25,000 stones of both collections would take 375,000 working hours, providing the forger worked for twelve hours without a break every working day, 31,250 working days without interruption. The diligent forger of both collections would have to work twelve hours a day for 85 years. But if we assume that his kindred cooperated, the output could be reached.

In a bright light we compared the stone that Cabrera lent me with the freshly carved stone from Basilo's hut. Right-

Fig. 129. This rock is 1.41 m high and covered with engravings. The star-studded heavens, stars connected by lines, a comet with a tail...and, just as on Sumerian cylinder seals, a symbolic tree of life.

angled, clean scratches showed on the new stone under the microscope, whereas micro-organisms could be seen in the grooves of Cabrera's stones under a fine glaze. That was the tiny major difference between genuine and false stones!

There is a decisive argument in favour of the genuine stones. For his forgeries, Basilo claims to have taken his subjects from illustrated papers. Picture papers publish photographs of things that exist! There are no models to photograph for the complicated motifs on Cabrera's genuine stones. To pick the most daring subjects: When Dr Barnard and other colleagues of his started to perform heart transplants, there were exciting photographs of this surgical undertaking in the illustrated magazines. But the engravings on Cabrera's stones show no similarity to these documentary pictures. Modern surgeons, for example, tap veins and arteries in the arms. On the old stones the tubes end in the patient's mouth. Who ever snapped a bird that was steered with pedals and on which a creature is riding? When were fire-spitting dragons printed in our magazines? Where did a reporter meet a being with a halo round his head?

I admit that I was still gnawed by doubt when we met again in Cabrera's house. I told him so . 'Come here, my friend,' he said and led me to his desk. He laid before me the originals of the geological opinions which he later published in his book*. The first opinion dated from June 1976 and had been prepared by the Mauricio Hochschild Mining Company in Lima. Signed by Dr Eric Wolf, the laboratory report said:

This is definitely a natural stone which was rounded off

* *El Mensaje de las Piedras Grabadas de Ica*, Lima, 1976.

Figs. 130, 131. Microscopic photographs taken by Joseph Blumrich, Stone surfaces and incisions had become porous and granulated by long-time oxydation.

by being carried down a river. Petrologically it can be classified as andesite. The andesites are stones whose components were caused by mechanical movements and simultaneous high pressure. In this specific case the effects of an intensive transformation of feldspar into sericite are demonstrable. This process increased the compactness and specific gravity of the stones and brought about a surface quality which the old artists appreciated when carrying out their work. This opinion should now be confirmed by a more precise verdict by the Technical College.

I can state definitely that these stones are covered by a fine but natural oxidation film, *which also covers the grooves of the engraving*. This circumstance allows me to estimate the great age of the stones.

I cannot establish any notable irregularities in the execution of the actual engravings, from which one can deduce that the engravings must have been executed not far from the place where they were found. Lima, 8 June, 1967.

Ladies and gentlemen, I should like to draw your attention to three statements in this opinion:

1. The engraved stones have a higher specific gravity than

other stones of the same kind with rounded edges. Stones of this kind were found in indigenous rivers and lakes.

2. The engraved stones are very old, a fact that can be deduced from natural surface oxydation. The oxydation covers the whole surface.

3. Oxydation also covers the engravings, an irrefutable proof that the engravings were made on the stones before oxydation.

Dr Cabrera also got the expert opinion that the first assessor advised, from the National Technical College (Facultad de Minas). It is signed by the engineer Fernando de las Casas y Cesar Sotillo in the name of the Faculty. I quote:

All the stones are highly carbonised andesites. That can be unequivocally inferred from their colour and their external surface stratum. The stones come from strata which were formed by ejected volcanic material, corresponding to the typical Mesozoic of this zone. Various environmental influences have attacked the surfaces of the stones and turned the film of feldspar into arcilla. Thus the external degree of hardness was weakened and a softer shell

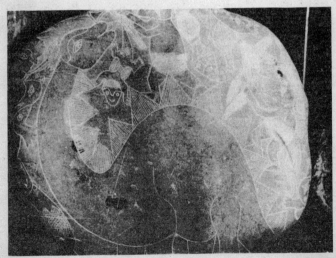

Fig. 132. Saurian and man on a friendly footing! An ancient stone from the Cabrera collection and...

Fig. 133. ...an artefact the Indians gave Father Crespi decades ago!

formed around the inner part of the stone. The mean external hardness corresponds to degree 3 on the Mohn scale, yet the interior of the same stone reaches 4.5 degrees on the same scale. The stones can be worked with any harder materials, such as bones, mussels, obsidian, as well as with any pre Spanish metal instrument.

These statements are enough to take one's breath away. The Mesozoic comprises the Jurassic and the Cretaceous eras of our planet, the time when saurians thrived, who ostensibly never cast eyes on a man, because – so the dogma has it – there were no men in the time of the saurians.

Qualified experts have attested that the engravings were scratched on the stones before the oxydation films formed. Here, ladies and gentlemen, I present genuine stones from the Cabrera collection. They clearly show man and dinosaur in cosy proximity!

Father Crespi showed me stone plaques which the Indians had presented him with. There too man and saurian were friendly neighbours!

Will it always be the case that what is said not to exist does not exist?

Dinosaur tracks and human footprints in the Paluxy River. Identical finds in South America. When excavating near El Boqueron in the State of Tolima, Colombia, in April 1971, Professor Henero Henao Marin found the 20-m-long skeleton of a dinosaur of the iguanadont family — and next to it a human skull! Millions of years had transformed the skull into a delicate fossil, grey in colour with fine ramifications. Those, ladies and gentlemen, are the kinds of finds that science accepts enthusiastically . . . provided they fit into the accepted world picture. Saurians and man on friendly terms? That does not fit into the codex of the theory of evolution. So scholars make the walls thick to keep out the light which draws their eyes to such awkward presents.

It is incumbent on me to tell the sceptical antics what the stone picture book from Ica has to do with my theory. At Cabrera's I saw one *genuine* ancient stone on which the heaven of fixed stars is engraved, with a comet, several larger stars, all linked together by lines . . . and between which ships sail. Between mountains and mythological trees, Indians squat and they are gazing at this heaven through *telescopes*! Those are tangible traditions for our remote past.

Taught by the experience I had with Father Crespi's treasure, I say clearly and write in the note books of the journalists who now undertake the journey to Ica: I know that they will find forgeries there, of the type mass-produced for tourists. This time I don't want anyone to come out with the platitude: 'Daniken unmasked – there are only forgeries at Ica!' They unpack their bags and take a quick snap of the tourist junk as they walk past. They make no effort to get the *genuine* stones in their lenses.

I am now coming to the end of my statement:

It is not my fault if the Brasilian Kayapo Indians still sing about visitors from space at their festivals and wear straw garments which are modelled on the clothing of the early astronauts their legends talk about . . .

It is not my fault if prehistoric men all over the globe painted 'gods' on cliffs and cave walls, with their heads wearing coverings like astronauts' helmets and with rods sprouting from their heads that look damned like short-wave antennae . . .

It is not my fault if Enoch and Elijah, like many others,

Fig. 134. Yesterday it was supposed to be a high priest at the altar. The most recent interpretation of this relief says it is 'a young maiden who falls victim to a mythical being' or a 'young ruler'! But supposing it is really 'my' astronaut in a space capsule?

disappeared into heaven in a fiery chariot.

I cannot help it if the Turkish Admiral Piri Reis in 1513 made maps of the world showing – before Columbus – the coasts of North and South America and even the outline of the Antarctic which were hidden under layers of ice; these are contours which *we* first discovered by echo-sounding during the Geophysical Year, 1957. I really do not know who put an observer-satellite and ultra modern observation apparatus at Piri Reis's disposal.

People can torture me and stand me on my head and I shall still not be able to answer the question how various accurately described flying machines got into 230 Sanskrit verses of the Samarangana Sutradhara. I assume that someone had seen them at the time.

I swear by everything that is holy that I am not the author of the *Book of Enoch*. Nor was I present when the prophet Ezekiel had his encounter with spaceships, which he described with such accuracy that a NASA engineer of our own day was able to reconstruct them.

Moreover I did not make the Sumerian cylinder-seals which show great numbers of machines flying in the sky, as matter-of-factly as if it were a daily occurrence.

You can safely credit me with a lot of imagination. Nevertheless the ancient sagas about flying dragons and heavenly snakes do not stem from my pen. I did not come into the world until 1935. Those tradition had a few thousand years behind them by then.

A stumbling block: the stone relief from the tomb at Palenque! I confess that I look on it as the brilliant technically successful depiction of an astronaut in a space capsule – as opposed to the archaelogical interpretation that it shows a high priest at an altar. Once again my opponents do not seem to be so sure about their version. *The National Geographic*, a famous scientific periodical, recently interpreted it as follows: No, it is not a high priest, but a young maiden falling into the jaws of a mythical being. Good heavens, the poor thing! Scholars also talk of a 'young ruler' alighting. Just wait. I am pretty sure that one day people will settle for my astronaut. But that needs courage and decision and a gigantic leap over one's own shadow.

Schadenfreude is alien to my nature, but it would be dishonourable if I did not admit that now and then satisfaction warms me up like a hot grog on a cold winter's night.

May I remind the Supreme Court of something I have already mentioned in other places. Ten years ago I saw for the first time the dead-straight kilometre-long lines drawn on the ground in the Plain of Nazca, Peru, in the foothills of the Andes. From an aircraft these lines look like a big landing-ground and because the network of lines was laid down in early times, I interpreted the lay-out as the landing-ground of the 'gods', as their operational base in South America.

After decades of research, scholars claimed that the lines were an astronomical calendar. Although I have many other doubts about that explanation, I should like to ask this question: What were the natives supposed to do with a calendar which was *only* recognisable from a very great height? (Science never bothers about that kind of practical question, when it can put something forward as knowledge, it is perfectly happy.) Anyway, the lines on the Plain of Nazca appear in all the scholarly books as an astronomical calendar.

Fig. 135. The airport of the gods at Nazca.

That was why I was so surprised when the archaeologist Professor Barthel of Tübingen told me after a TV discussion that we can forget about the interpretation of the Nazca lines as an astronomical calendar. All the data of the positions and courses of the stars as well as the coordinates of the lines had been fed into a computer and in not a single case had it been able to calculate a relation from below to above or from above to below that justified the calendar theory. That does not mean that my theory is right, but the view prevailing to date is no longer tenable. Meanwhile I read the book*, which Professor Barthel spoke about. It refutes the calendar theory once and for all.

Americans, who are curious and often have amusing ideas, knocked up a hot-air balloon out of materials the ancient Incas would have had at their disposal. In it they ascended from the plain. I think it is a wonderful experiment, but I do not understand the reports that went round the world after it: DÄNIKEN REFUTED! Have I ever claimed that Incas did not possess hot-air balloons? If I had made that claim, the

* Archaeo-Astronomy in Pre-Columbian America, London, 1976.

Americans' flight would have refuted it. But they do not even scratch the surface of my theory with their balloon ascent. Since when do hot-air balloons need landing strips? Did the Incas want to have a look at the calendar to see what day of the week it was? Excuse me, that cannot have been so, because it has been proved the geometrical lines did not form a calendar. So it *was* a landing-ground for the extra-terrestrials. Wait and see.

Supreme Court.

I consider it beneath the dignity of the plaintiffs to dismiss my circumstantial evidence as the shimmering soap bubbles of pure imagination. When will new theories be put forward, the evidence for which can be *photographed?* Do the plaintiffs realise that after my books two long documentary films were shot? Films that put the facts on celluloid on the spot and projected them on to the TV screen for everyone to see? None of my opponents can excuse himself by saying that he missed these documentations of my theory. Anyone can see them in the USA, the USSR and Red China, as well as in the twenty-nine other countries in which my books also appeared. Supreme Court, anyone who avoids filmable proofs, can only be fleeing from uncomfortable truths, like Mr Kimble.

Supreme Court,

Ladies and gentlemen,

During this trial, I have woven a thick chain of circumstantial evidence. I produced authentic sources. I exhibited illustrations supporting the theme of my proof. I gave first-class experts the floor.

I accepted the role of accused of my own free will!

Now I ask the Supreme Court for the burden of proof to be reversed:

LET THE PLAINTIFFS MAKE *THEIR* CIR-CIRCUMSTANTIAL EVIDENCE THAT EXTRA-TERRESTRIALS DID *NOT* STAY ON EARTH EQUALLY CONVINCING!

REFERENCES

CHAPTER 1

Quoted:
  (1) NAVIA, LUIS E., *Unsers Weige steht im Kosmos*, Dusseldorf, 1976.
General:
Buchers Illustrierte Geschichte der Erfindungen, Lucerne, 1974.

BRUGG, ELMAR, *Tragik und schopferischer Mensch*, Baden/Switzerland, 1965.

FELDHAUS, F. M., *Die Technik*, Wiesbaden, 1970.

HIEBERT, RAY AND ROSELYN, *Atomic Pioneers*, USAEC, 1974.

KEMMERICH, MAX, *Kultur-Kuriosa* I, Munich, 1910.

KEMMERICH, MAX, *Kultur-Kuriosa* II, Munich, 1910.

LARSEN, EGON, *Zwolf, die die Welt veranderten*, Munich, 1960.

NAGEL, HEINRICH, *Die Grundzuge des Beweisrechts im europaischen Zivilprozess*, Baden-Baden, 1967.

POZNIAK, HEINRICH VON, *Lexikon der Erfindungen*, Frankfurt-/Vienna, 1954.

RODIG, *Die Theorie des gerichtlichen Erkenntnisverfahrens*, Berlin, 1973.

ROSENBERG-SCHWAB, LEO, *Lehrbuch des Zivilprozessrechts*, Munich, 1974, 11th Edition.

SZABABDVARY, FERENC, *Lavoisier*, Stuttgart, 1975.

CHAPTER 2

  (1) HARRISON, LEE, 'Intelligent Life exists in outer space.' *National Enquirer*, Lantana, USA, 9 March, 1976.
  (2) HEUSELER, HOLGER, *Der Zweiten Erde auf der Spur*, Zurich, 1976.
  (3) SAGAN, C. AND DRAKE, F., *Scientific American*, No. 232, 80/1975.

(4) FREUDENTHAL, HANS, *Lincos – Design of a language for cosmical intercourse,* Amsterdam, 1960.

(5) DRAKE, FRANK, *Probleme eines Funkkontaktes.* From: 11 contributions to *Sind wir allein im Kosmos?,* Munich, 1970.

(6) PAUL, GUNTER, *Unsers Nachbarn im Weltall,* Dusseldorf, 1976.

(7) *Der Spiegel,* Hamburg, 1.9.1975, 'Weltraumkolonie im Jahre 2000?' *National Enquirer,* Lantana, USA, November, 1975, 'City could be built in space – A paradise for 10,000 people.' *Die Weltwoche,* Zurich, 28.1.1976, 'Bahn frei für Weltraum-Kolonisten. *Bild der Wissenschaft,* Stuttgart, 19.5.1976, 'Umzug ins All von Gerard O'Neill.'

(8) *Die Welt,* Hamburg, 15.6.1975, 'Spionagefotos aus dem Weltraum.'

(9) *Der Spiegel,* Hamburg, No. 40, 1974, 'Panzer mit Todes-strahlen.'

(10) *Daily Express,* London, 22.5.1973, 'Death Ray – Britain's most secret weapon.'

(11) *Der Spiegel,* Hamburg, No. 31, 1973, 'Wellen gestört.'

(12) *Die Welt,* Hamburg, 16.6.1975, 'Sieben neue schrekliche Waffen.'

(13) *Basler Nachrichten,* Basle, 22.3.1975, 'Das Wetter als Waffe?'

(14) *National Zeitung,* Basle, 11.11.1973, 'Das Wetter als Geheimwaffe?'

(15) *Umschau in Wissenschaft und Technik,* Stuttgart, Vol. 21, 1975, 'Hat der Energiesatellit eine Chance?'

(16) MEADOWS AND OTHERS, *Die Grenzen des Wachstums – Bericht des Club of Rome,* Stuttgart, 1972.

(17) *Neue Zürcher Zeitung,* 8.7.1974, 'Die Wasserstoff-wirtschaft.'

(18) *Umschau in Wissenschaft und Technik,* Stuttgart, Vol. 13, 1976, H. W. Köhler, 'Raumfähre, 'Planeten-Sonden und Anwendungs-Satelliten.'

(19) *Die Welt,* Bonn, 4.10.1976, Fred de la Trobe, 'An Japans Auto-Fliessbändern arbeitet Kollege Roboter.'

(20) *Westdeutsche Zeitung,* 4.3.1975, 'Das Wissen der Welt in 16 Supergehirnen.'

(21) *Neue Zürcher Zeitung,* 13.8.1973, 'Tiergehirne als Lenkwaffen-Computer.'

(22) *Die Welt,* 25.3.1976, 'Ingenieure sehen Chancen für

Erzbergabu im Weltraum.'
(23) *Bremer Nachrichten*, 12.11.1974, 'Anti – Schwerkraft-Motor soll einmal den Flug zu den Sternen ermoglichen.'

Explanations for experts:

1

Fraction a of the fuel mass m is converted into energy. Optimistically $a = 3 \cdot 10^3$ for fusion. All this energy recurs as motive energy of the exhaust jet – with the mass $m(1 - a)$, which shoots out with the speed v.

Then we have:

$v = c\ 2a - a^2$ c – the speed of light.

The relativistic rocket formula is as follows:

$$\frac{M_o}{M} = \frac{1 + u/c}{1 - u/c} \quad \frac{c/2v \quad \text{and with} \quad M_o = Y:}{Y\ 2u/c + 1} \quad u/c = Y\ 2u/c - 1$$

u = Maximum speed of vehicle
With $= 3 \cdot 10^3$ we get v/c = 0.0774

If we choose $= M_o/M = 10$, we get u/c = 0.176:
the speed of the vehicle comes to 17.6 of the speed of light.
Possible fusion reactions (selection depending on not too high ignition temperatures, faster reaction etc.) are:

given		v(real-istic)	$= (2-)$
D + D T + p + 4.0r MeV	a = $1.05 \cdot 10^{-3}$		
D + D He^3 + n+ 3.27 MeV	0.85 $\cdot 10^{-3}$	8000	13070 kmg/s
D + T He^4 + n+ 17.59 MeV	3.7 $\cdot 10^{-3}$	5000	25780
D + He^3 He^4 + p + 18.35 MeV	3.9 $\cdot 10^{-3}$	9000	26460

(Cf: fission in nuclear reactor: $= 0.7 \cdot 10^{-3}$
             chemical: max $= 2 \cdot 10^{-10}x$)
Tritium T is radioactive with a disintegration value of
years, so we cannot use it because it is not storable. He

choose the last reaction – it has the addition advantage of producing none of the neutrons thare hard to absorb. (Because $D + D$ and with the T produced finally $D + T$ occurs, the neutron production is not exactly nil!)

2

Type of drive	v^{km}/s	Thrust acceleration
Fixed nuclear reactor/	7.5–10	$\sim/g_0/g_0 =$
	acceleration	of earth's
hydrogen as discharge		gravity
of mass		
reactor/10-11		0.1-1
as above		
Fluid nuclear reactor/		
11-12		
10^{-4}-10^{-5}		
as above		
Gas nuclear reactor/17-25$\sim$/		
as above		

Pulse drive		
Fission	25-50	~ 1
Fusion	50-100	~ 1
Controlled fusion	100-1000	10^{-4}–10^{-3}
Ion drive/	50-300	10^{-4}
Fixed nuclear reactor		
(fission)		

3

Degrees of effective reaction ($D + He^3 \longrightarrow He^4 + p + 18.35$ MeV) of over 40% seem difficult to attain and the exhaust jet will scarcely be concentrated in to an angle of less than 60° – thus an effective jet speed of 10^7 m/s is produced. If we tauake $v/c = \eta \, \xi\alpha(2 - \xi\alpha)$, then $\xi = 0.4$, $\eta = 0.6$ is chosen, with $\alpha = 0.0038$.

Magnetic fields as jets and electrical MHD by currents in supraconductors (which must be kept at 10K) and induction (for producing energy for igniting the fusion) play an important role in Daedalus.

Helium 3 is difficult to obtain. It is assumed that it would either be bred on the moon by nuclear methods or obtained from Jupiter's atmosphere. (It is probably very rare in nature.) The craft will be assembled in the inner solar system, depending on where suitable works are at the time. Then it will refuelled, either in orbit round the moon or Jupiter. The journey proper starts from this parking orbit.

CHAPTER 3
Quoted:

(1) TEMPLE, ROBERT K. G., *The Sirius Mystery*, London, 1976.

(2) *Journal de la Société des Africanistes,* Tome XXI, Fascicule 1, Paris, 1951, 'Un systeme soudanais de Sirius.'

(3) GRIAULE, MARCEL, *Schwarze Genesis,* Freiburg, 1970.

(4) *Nature,* Vol. 261, June 17, 1976, 'Mustard seeds of mystery.'

(5) BAUMANN, HERMANN, *Schopfung und Urzeit des Menschen im Mythos der Afrikanischen Völker,* Berlin, 1936.

(6) FROBENIUS, LEO, *Volksmärchen und Volksdichtungen Afrikas,* Jena, 1921/1928.

(7) TESSMANN, G., *Die Pangwe,* Vol. II, Berlin, 1913.

(8) TORDAY, E and JOYCE, *Notes éthnographiques sur les Peuples communement appelees Bakuba, ainsi que sur les Peuplades apparentées les Bushongo,* Brussels, 1910.

(9) CORJU, P., *Entre le Victoria, l'Albert et l'Eduard,* Marseilles, 1920.

(10) MÜLLER, PROF. MAX, *Beiträge zu einer wissenschaftlichen Mythologie,* Vol. 2, Leipzig, 1899.

(11) STUCKEN, EDUARD, *Astralmythen der Hebräer, Babylonier und Ägypter,* Part I.

(12) EBERMANN, PROF. OSKAR, *Sagen der Technik,* Leipzig, 1930.

(13) WENDLAND, PROF. JOH., *Die Schöpfung der Welt,* Halle, 1905.

(14) MÜLLER, PROF. MAX, *Einleitung in der vergleichende Religionswissenschaft,* Leipzig, undated.

(15) FLORENZ, KARL, *Japanische Mythologie,* Tokyo, 1901.

(16) GUNDERT, WILHELM, *Japanische Religionsgeschichte,* Stuttgart, 1936.

(17) FLORENZ, KARL *Die historischen Quellen der Shinto-Religion,* Göttingen, 1919.

(18) ROY, POTRAP CHANDRA, *The Mahabharata,* Calcutta, 1891.

(19) FLORENZ, KARL, *Japanische Mythologie,* Tokyo, 1901.

(20) FREUCHEN, PETER, *Book of the Eskimos*, London, 1962.

(21) BRUGGER, KARL, Die Chronik von Akakor, Düsseldorf, 1976.

(22) CAMPBELL, H. J., *Der Irrtum mit der Seele*, Berne, 1973.

(23) FEER, LEON, *Annales du Musee Guimet, Extraits du Kandjour*, Paris, 1883.

(24) LAUFER, BERTHOLD, *Dokumente der Indischen Kunst, Vol 1, Das Citralakshana*, Leipzig, 1913.

(25) OLSCHAK, BLANCHE, *Tibet – Erde der Götter*, Zurich, 1960.

(26) CHRISTIE, ANTHONY, *Chinese Mythology*, London, 1968.

(27) DEUSSEN, PAUL, *Die Geheimlehre des Veda*, Leipzig, 1921.

(28) LUDWIG, ALFRED, *Der Rigveda oder die heiligen Hymnen der Brahmana* Vol. 1, Prague, 1876.

(29) SIMON, PEDRO, *Noticias Historiales de las Conquistas de Tierra en las Indias Occidentales*, Bogota, 1890.

(30) GRÜNWEDEL, ALBERT, *Mythologie des Buddhismus in Tibet und in der Mongolei*, Leipzig, 1900.

(31) BOPP, FRANZ, *Ardschunas Reise zu Indras Himmel*, Berlin, 1824.

General:

BEHR, H. G., *Nepal, Geschenk der Götter*, Düsseldor f, 1976.

BIEZAIS, HARALD, *Die himmlische Götterfamile der alten Letten*, Uppsala, 1972.

DÄNIKEN, ERICH VON, *Return to the Stars*, Souvenir Press, 1970.

DÄNIKEN, ERICH VON, *The Gold of the Gods*, Souvenir Press, 1973.

DÄNIKEN, ERICH VON, *In Search of Ancient Gods*, Souvenir Press, 1974.

DIETERLEN, G., *Les ames des Dogons*, Paris, 1941.

GUERRIER, ERIC, *Essai sur la cosmogenie des Dogon*, Paris, 1975.

GRAY, JOHN, *Near Eastern Mythology*, London, 1969.

GRIAULE-DIETERLEN, *Le renard pâle. Le mythe cosmogonic, Travaux et mémoires de l'Institut d'Ethnologie*, Paris, 1965.

KHUON, ERNST VON, *Waren die Götter Astronauten?*, Düsseldorf, 1970.

KRASSA, PETER, *Als die Gelbern Götter kamen*, Munich, 1973.

LEIRIS, M., *La langue secrete des Dogons*, Paris, 1948.

MÜLLER, PROF. MAX, *Vorlesungen über den Ursprung und die Entwicklung der Religion*, Strasbourg, 1880.

MÜLLER, PROF. M AX, *Die Wissenschaft der Sparche*, Vol. II,

Leipzig, 1893.

MÜLLER, PROF. MAX, *The Upanishads, Part II,* Oxford, 1884.

MÜLLER, PROF. MAX, *The Dhammapada,* Leipzig, 1906.

NICHOLSON, IRENE, *Mexican and Central American Mythology,* London, 1967.

OSBORNE, HAROLD, *South American Mythology,* London, 1968.

PARRINDER, GEOFFREY, *African Mythology,* London, 1967.

PAULINE, D., *Organisation sociale des Dogons,* Paris, 1940.

Fipa-Ugalla, the primitive mother Ekao fell from heaven.

Itawa, the first couple came from heaven to earth with seeds in their hair.

Bena-Mitumba, the God Kamana sent his first children from heaven to earth.

Chokwe, God sent the first men from heaven.

Nyanja-Yao, the first men fell down from heaven.

Vili-Flote, five or ten men burst through the god Nsambi and reached the earth on a cobweb (or a rainbow).

Dkoi, The man Etim-Ne and his wife Eyaw, both dwelling in heaven, were the first couple to come to this planet.

Ibo, their first two kings settled on a termites' nest after their arrival from heaven and founded their kingdom.

Yukun, the 'founder' Afuma climbed down out of the clouds to earth on one thread of a spider's web.

Edo, heaven was originally the home of all mankind.

Ewe-Ho, celestial men with tails who had climbed down on a rope were taken prisoner and had to stay on earth.

Lobi, the first men let themselves down from heaven on chains.

Zulu, the word 'Zulu' means 'Heaven'. All pure Zulu tribes trace their origin back to heavenly beings. They call their traditional tribal territory on the Indian Ocean in South Africa the 'Land of the Heavenly People'.

Jagga, the ancestor of a tribe came down to earth from heaven on a thread from a cobweb. He was called 'the tailed one'.

Kamba, the first couple were thrown on to the earth from the clouds by Mulungu.

Ndorobo, one Ndorobo and one Masai used a rope to climb down from heaven where they had previously lived together.

God made a great rain come down that destroyed the hunting grounds of the Ndorobo. Ndorobo cut the rope and it stopped raining. From then on the connection between heaven and earth was destroyed. Bantu-Kavirondo, the first couple appeared from heaven. Nuong-Nuer, once in the past the inhabitants of heaven came down to earth on a cord to fetch food. Men also managed to reach heaven on a cord. During their two months' absence they were considered dead, but they returned to earth safe and sound. Once the young Rill fell from heaven with a fish in his hand; a Mandari found the young man and brought him up. When Rill later fell in love with a 'celestial maiden', the inhabitants of heaven cut the cord.

Kumbi, the first men that God created had tails.

Tusi of Ruanda, all mankind once lived in heaven. The first man and woman fell to earth from heaven.

CHAPTER 4
Quoted:

(1) SPIEGEL, FRIEDERICH, *Avesta, The Religious Book of the Parsees,* London, 1864.

(2) DALBERG, F. VON, *Scheik Mohammed Fani's Dabistan oder Von der Religion der ältesten Parsen,* Aschaffenburg, 1809.

(3) LUDWIG, A., *Abhandlung über das Ramayana unde die Beziehungen desselben zum Mahabharata,* Prague, 1894.

(4) JACOBI, HERMANN, *Das Ramayana,* Bonn, 1893.

(5) ROY POTRAP CHANDRA, *The Mahabharata,* Calcutta, 1896.

(6) DUTT, NATH. M., *The Râmâyana,* Calcutta, 1891.

(7) PROF. DR. DILEEP KUMAR KANJILAL, Communication of 17.3.1973.

(8) BERLITZ, CHARLES, *Mysteries from Forgotton Worlds,* London, 1972.

(9) DITFURTH, HOIMAR VON, *Der Geist fiel nicht von Himmel,* Hamburg, 1976.

(10) BIREN, ROY, *Das Mahabharata,* Düsseldorf-Cologne, 1961.

(11) GRASSMAN, HERMANN, *Rig-Veda,* Leipzig, 1876.

(12) DEUSSEN, PAUL, *Sechzig Upanishad's des Veda,* Leipzig, 1905.

(13) BURROWS, MILLAR, *More Light on the Dead Sea Scrolls,* London, 1958.

(14) RIESSLER, PAUL, *Altjüdisches Schrifttum ausserhalb der Bibel,* Augsburg, 1928.

(15) KAUTZSCH, EMIL, *Die Apokcyphen und Pseudepigraphen des*

Alten Testaments, Vols 1 and 2, Tübingen, 1900.

(16) LUNAN, DUNCAN, *Man and the Stars,* London, 1974.

General:

ALFRED, LUDWIG, *Die Nachrichten des Rig- und Atharvaveda über Geographie, Geschichte und Verfassung des Alten Indien,* Prague, 1875.

DUPONT, A., *Les ecrits esseniens decouverts pres de la mer morte,* Paris, 1959.

DUTT, ROMESH C., *The Ramayana & the Mahabharata,* London, 1910.

GELDNER, K., and KÄGI, A., *Siebenzig Lieder des Rigveda,* Tubingen, 1875.

IONS, VERONICA, *Indian Mythology,* New York, 1967.

KRASSA, PETER, *Als die gelben Götter kamen,* Munich, 1973.

KRASSA, PETER, *Gottkam von den Sternen,* Freiburg, 1974.

LOHSE, EDUARD, *Die Texte aus Qumran,* Munich, 1964.

MEYER, EDUARD, *Der Papyrusfund von Elephantine,* Leipzig, 1912.

MÜLLER, PROF. MAX, *A History of Ancient Sanskrit Literature,* London, 1859.

MÜLLER, PROF. MAX, *Rig-Veda oder Die Heiligen Lieder der Brahmanen,* Leipzig, 1856.

RAJAGOPALACHARI, C., *Râmayâna,* Bombay, 1975.

SÄNGER-BREDT, IRENE, *Ungeloste Rätsel der Schöpfung – Die kosmoschen Gesetze,* Düsseldorf, 1971.

SCHLISSKE, WERNER, *Gottessöhne und Gottessohn im Alten Testament,* Berlin, 1973.

SEN UMPADA, *The Rig Vedic Era,* Calcutta, 1974.

Die Heilige Schrift des Alten und des Neuen Testaments, Verlag der Zürcher Bibel, Zurich, 1942.

CHAPTER 5

Quoted:

(1) WILDER-SMITH, A. E., *Die Erschaffung des Lebens,* Stuttgart, 1972.

(2) COPPEDGE, JAMES F., *Evolution: Possible or Impossible?* Grand Rapids, 1973.

(3) MACDONALD, M. R., *Woher kommt der Mensch?* Zurich, 1976.

(4) ADLER, IRVING, *Probability and Statistics for Everyman,* New York, 1963.

(5) MONOD, JACQUES, *Zufall und Notwendigkeit,* Munich,

1975.

(6) EIGEN, MANFRED, *Das Spiel – Naturgesetze steuern den Zufall*, Munich, 1975.

(7) KUHN, HANS, 'Zur Evolution eines sich selbst organisierenden präbiotischen Systems', off-print of *Nova Acta Leopoldina*, No 218, Vol 42.

(8) CRICK, F. H. and ORGEL, L. E., 'Directed Panspermia', *Icarus*, No 19, 1973, London.

(9) MILTON, S. and LEWIN, ROGER, 'Is anyone out here?' *New Scientist*, August, 1973.

(10) 'Leben – älter als die Erde?', *Umschau in Wissenschaft und Technik*, Stuttgart, 1972, No 17.

(11) DARWIN, CHARLES, *Die Entstehung der Arten*, Stuttgart, 1974.

(12) WILDER-SMITH, A. E., *Herkunft und Zukunft des Menschen*, Stuttgart, 1975.

(13) 'Die Welt in der wir leben – Die Naturgeschichte unserer Erde.' No number, Munich, 1956.

(14) HALSTEAD, L. B., *Die Welt der Dinosaurier*, Hamburg, 1975.

(15) DOUGHERTY, C. N., *Valley of Giants, The latest Discoveries in Palaeontology*, Cleburne, Texas, 1971.

(16) JACK BOWMAN JR., *Ancient Astronauts*, Vol I, No 4, 1976, 'The Footprints of the Gods.'

(17) STEIGER, BRAD, *Mysteries of Time and Space*, New York, 1974.

(18) TOMAS, ANDREW, *We Are Not the First*, G. P Putnam's Sons, 1971.

(19) WEIDENREICH, F., *Apes, Giants and Man*, Chicago, 1946.

(20) SAURAT, DENIS, *Atlantis und die Herrschaft der Riesen*, Stuttgart, 1955.

(21) FREUCHEN, P., *Book of the Eskimos*, London, 1962.

(22) UPI, Honolulu, 17 June, 1976.

(23) KOESTLER, A., *Die Wurzeln des Zufalls*, Berne, 1972.

(24) *Die Welt*, Bonn, 30.8.1976, p. 1.

(25) MARX ENGELS, *Staatstheorie*, Berlin, 1974.

(26) MORGENSTERN, CHR., *Gesammelte Werke*, Munich, 1965.

(27) NAVIA, LUIS E., *Unsere Wiege steht im Kosmos*, Düsseldorf, 1976.

General:

BENDER, H., *Biologie und Biochemie der Mikroorganismen*,

Weinheim, 1970.

BERNAL, J. D., *Der Ursprung des Lebens,* Lausanne, 1971.

BLÜHEL, K., *Projekt Übermensch,* Berne, 1971.

BOSCHKE, F. L., *Erde von anderen Sternen,* Düsseldorf, 1965.

BOSCHKE, F. L., *Die Herkunft des Lebens,* Düsseldorf, 1970.

CALDER, N., *Das Lebensspiel,* Berne, 1973.

CORLISS, W. R., The Unexplained: a Scourcebook of strange Phenomena, New York, 1976.

EIBL-EIBESFELDT, I., *Der vorprogrammierte Mensch,* Vienna, 1973.

EINSTEIN-INFELD, *Die Evolution der Physik,* Hamburg, 1956.

EISELEY, L., *Von der Enstehung des Lebens und der Naturgeschichte des Menschen,* Munich, 1959.

FLINDT, M. and BINDER, O., *Mankind – Child of the Stars,* Greenwich, Conn., 1974.

FREESE, W., *Die Sachte mit der Schöpfung,* Munich, 1973.

FUCHS, W. R., *Leben unter fernen Sonnen?,* Munich, 1973.

HABER, H., *Der Stoff der Schöpfung,* Stuttgart, 1966.

HEBERER, G., *Homo-unsere Ab- und Zukunft,* Stuttgart, 1968.

HEISENBERG, W., *Schritte über Grenzen,* Munich, 1971.

(1) HEUSELER, H., *Der zweiten Erde auf der Spur,* Stuttgart, 1974.

(2) HÜBNER, P., *Vom ersten Menschen wird erzählt,* Düsseldorf, 1969.

KOESTLER, A., *Die Wurzeln des Zufalls,* Berne, 1972.

KNAURS TIERREICH, *Niedere Tiere,* Munich 1960.

Amphibien, Munich 1957.

Reptilien, Munich 1957.

Insekten, Munich 1959.

HEMLEBEN, JOH. DARWIN, Hanbury, 1968.

OSTEN-SACKEN, P. V. DER., *Die neue Kosmologie,* Düsseldorf, 1974.

PAUL, G., *Die dritte Entdeckung der Erde,* Dusseldorf, 1974.

POPP, G. and PLETICHA, H., *Wir leben erst seit fünf Sekunden,* Wüzburg, 1958.

SÄNGER-BREDT, I., *Spuren der Vorzeit,* Düsseldorf, 1972.

SCHRADER, H. L., *Der achte Tag der Schöpfung,* Berlin, 1964.

SULLIVAN, M., *Die Betschaft der Gene,* Frankfurt, 1969.

TAYLER, G. R., *The Biological Time-Bomb,* Thames & Hudson, 1968.

VOGT, H. H., *Das programmierte Leben,* Zurich, 1969.

WATSON, J. D., *The Double Helix,* Weidenfeld & Nicholson,

1968.
WILDER-SMITH, A. E., *Die Demission des wissenschaftlichen Materialismus,* Heerbrugg, 1976.
WILDER-SMITH, A. E., *Grundlage zu einer neuen Biologie,* Neuhausen-Stuttgart, 1974.

CHAPTER 6
Quoted:
(1) DUNCAN, LUNAN, *Men and the Stars,* London, 1974.
(2) BERLITZ, CHARLES, *Mysteries from Forgotten Worlds,* London, 1972.
(3) BLUMRICH, JOSEPH, *The spaceships of Ezekiel,* Bantam Books, 1974.
(4) CHARROUX, ROBERT, *L'enigme des andes,* Paris, 1974.
(5) CABRERA, JAVIER, *El mensaje de las piedras grabadas de Ica,* Lima, 1976.

CHARIOTS OF THE GODS?
By ERICH VON DÄNIKEN

What possible explanation accounts for a huge block of stone in Peru the size of a four-storey house, weighing 20,000 tons, complete with steps, ramps and decorations—and then turned upside down?

'In CHARIOTS OF THE GODS? Erich von Däniken takes a fresh look at ancient mysteries of the world in today's knowledge of space travel.' *Aberdeen Evening Express*

'The author's theory is that in the earth's remote past the planet was visited by beings from space who perhaps fathered humanity as we know it. A challenging contribution to discussion about our past—and future.' *Sunday Mirror*

'Powerful stuff which, no matter how one tries, cannot be discarded as crackpot theories.' *Daily Mail*

0 552 08800 5—**85p**

RETURN TO THE STARS
By ERICH VON DÄNIKEN

Not long ago the world witnessed the drama of a crippled American space-craft being nursed back to earth. Supposing it had landed on another planet at the same stage of development as the earth was 50,000 years ago—what would the astronauts have taught the inhabitants? What remnants of their efforts to return to earth would they have left behind? How would the inhabitants remember them in myths and in art? The answers we would give fit exactly the vast number of unexplained mysteries which have been found all round the world. RETURN TO THE STARS is another fascinating examination of a part of our history which has been, until now, neglected.

0 552 09083 2—**85p**

'They came to Earth in 3003 B.C. . . . and even now they continue to observe us. On December 24, in the year 2011, they will return!'

This daring prediction gives the exact date that travellers from a distant galaxy will return to Earth. It is the result of many years' investigation and research into the origins of mankind . . .

THE OUTER SPACE CONNECTION
By ALAN *and* SALLY LANDSBURG

Why were the Ancient Egyptians so eager to preserve the bodies of their dead? Was it merely superstitious nonsense —or did they have a solid scientific reason for their belief in reincarnation?

Among the archaeological remains of the Mayan pyramids were found skulls showing evidence of advanced surgery, and even brain transplant. What happened to that ancient medical knowledge? And how does it compare to the progress of surgery today?

'Cloning'—the process of duplicating an entire being from one cell of an original is not just a theory, but a proven scientific operation. But it may also be the vital link between our Earth and visitors from outer space . . . THE OUTER SPACE CONNECTION . . .

0 552 09911 2—**75p**

THE GOLD OF THE GODS
By ERICH VON DÄNIKEN

On a journey covering 76,000 miles, von Däniken traced the clues to the birth of mankind and to the history of the planet Earth.

He found incredible treasures of ages past, undeciphered writings and drawings in solid gold—relics of civilisations long-dead. But he also found startling evidence to suggest that way back, before the dawn of recorded history, the Earth was host to extraterrestrial visitors who colonised our planet . . .

'Fantastic? Certainly. But very, very convincing . . .'
—*Sunday Mirror*

0 552 09689 X—**85p**

IN SEARCH OF ANCIENT MYSTERIES
By ALAN *and* SALLY LANDSBURG

In the middle of the Atlantic Ocean is an area known as the Bermuda Triangle which covers approximately three-hundred thousand square miles of open sea. Within this comparatively small patch of ocean more than a hundred ships and aircraft have been permanently listed as missing during the last two centuries . . .

What really happened to these fated vehicles? Could they somehow have wandered into an ancient force-field, left by an alien technology who once tried to colonise Earth?

Alan and Sally Landsburg found themselves on the trail of this and other enigmas of history—colossal temples and monoliths built by the Incas, parts from a digital computer dating from 50 B.C. and the brilliant architecture of the ancient Egyptians—when they began their journey—In Search of Ancient Mysteries.

0 552 09588 5—**50p**

UFO'S FROM BEHIND THE IRON CURTAIN
By ION HOBANA *and* JULIEN WEVERBERGH

Are UFO's extraterrestrial in origin? Are they connected with attempts to communicate from civilisations far beyond ours, in other galaxies? Are they connected with other psychic phenomena such as thought-transference?

Despite the sensational nature of their material, the authors' approach is coolly objective. Their conclusion is that reports of UFO sightings in the East reveal a pattern of similarity and repetition exactly parallel to experiences in the West, that 'conventional' scientists have been much too quick to dismiss. The authors have no theory to explain the mystery, but they believe that there is a mystery to be solved, and that the present research should record all the detail possible, in the hope of finding a method of studying the phenomenon.

0 552 68898 3—**65p**

THE U.F.O. EXPERIENCE—A Scientific Enquiry
By J. ALLEN HYNEK
(Technical adviser to the film 'Close Encounters of the Third Kind')

For centuries man has sought an explanation of strange unknown objects seen in the sky, which we now term Unidentified Flying Objects (UFO's). Official enquiries have been opened and closed with no results, other than a feeble insistence that UFO's do not exist.

But do they?

Can we afford to blatantly disregard the hundreds of reports made by apparently sane, responsible people who insist, despite all ridicule, that they saw and experienced something completely alien to this world? In THE U.F.O. EXPERIENCE Dr. J. Allen Hynek describes individual cases from the files of Project Blue Book, the U.S.A.'s official investigation committee, and explains the process of scientific verification which he believes should be employed if UFO's are ever to lose their mystique and become Identified Flying Objects . . .

0 552 09430 7—**85p**

MIRACLES OF THE GODS
By ERICH VON DÄNIKEN

Today's most original investigator of the unexplained takes a penetrating look at miracles, visions and all the supernatural wonders that Churches throughout the centuries have recognised as 'holy'. What are visions? Are they supernatural phenomena, or the product of mass auto-suggestion? Can they be divine revelations, or extra-terrestrial communications? Erich von Däniken's theories are far more fascinating than any one of these . . . In this latest book, the best-selling author of CHARIOTS OF THE GODS?, RETURN TO THE STARS, THE GOLD OF THE GODS and IN SEARCH OF ANCIENT GODS turns his ever-questing mind to Christianity—and the religions that reach back far beyond Christ . . .

0 552 10371 3—**85p**

A SELECTED LIST OF BOOKS
ABOUT UFO's AND OTHER STRANGE PHENOMENA

WHILE EVERY EFFORT IS MADE TO KEEP PRICES LOW, IT IS SOMETIMES NECESSARY TO INCREASE PRICES AT SHORT NOTICE, CORGI BOOKS RESERVE THE RIGHT TO SHOW AND CHARGE NEW RETAIL PRICES ON COVERS WHICH MAY DIFFER FROM THOSE ADVERTISED IN THE TEXT OR ELSEWHERE.

THE PRICES SHOWN BELOW WERE CORRECT AT THE TIME OF GOING TO PRESS (MAY 78)

All these books are available at your bookshop or newsagent, or can be ordered direct from the publisher. Just tick the titles you want and fill in the form below.

CORGI BOOKS. Cash Sales Department, P.O. Box 11, Falmouth, Cornwall. Please send cheque or postal order, no currency.

U.K. send 22p for first book plus 10p per copy for each additional book ordered to a maximum charge of 22p to cover the cost of postage and packing.

B.F.P.O. and Eire allow 22p for the first book plus 10p per copy for the next 6 books thereafter 4p per book.

Name (block letters)..

ADDRESS...

(MAY 78)..